The Consolidation of Dictatorship in Russia

THE CONSOLIDATION OF DICTATORSHIP IN RUSSIA

AN INSIDE VIEW OF THE DEMISE OF DEMOCRACY

Joel M. Ostrow, Georgiy A. Satarov, and Irina M. Khakamada

Foreword by Garry Kasparov

PRAEGER SECURITY INTERNATIONAL
Westport, Connecticut · London

Library of Congress Cataloging-in-Publication Data

Ostrow, Joel M.
    The consolidation of dictatorship in Russia: an inside view of the demise of democracy /
    Joel M. Ostrow, Georgiy A. Satarov, and Irina M. Khakamada; foreword by
    Garry Kasparov.
        p. cm.
    Includes bibliographical references and index.
    ISBN 978–0–313–34594–4 (alk. paper)
1. Russia (Federation)—Politics and government—1991– 2. Democracy—Russia
(Federation) 3. Democratization—Russia (Federation) 4. Political leadership—Russia
(Federation) I. Satarov, G. (Georgii) II. Khakamada, Irina. III. Title.
JN6695.O87 2007
320.947—dc22   2007027878

British Library Cataloguing in Publication Data is available.

Library of Congress Catalog Card Number: 2007027878
ISBN: 978–0–313–34594–4

First published in 2007

Praeger Security International, 88 Post Road West, Westport, CT 06881
An imprint of Greenwood Publishing Group, Inc.
www.praeger.com

Printed in the United States of America

The paper used in this book complies with the
Permanent Paper Standard issued by the National
Information Standards Organization (Z39.48-1984).

10 9 8 7 6 5 4 3 2 1

Contents

Foreword

Any observer of world history knows that political crises are rarely sudden or unexpected. And yet again and again, the politicians, and the journalists, are surprised by a coup, a collapse, a public uprising, or even a genocide. Closer analysis inevitably shows that the signs were all there, often in big red letters.

The Russian regime of Vladimir Putin is headed toward a crisis as it reaches its final months. The shape of that crisis has yet to take form. One possibility is that Putin and his puppet parliament will eviscerate our constitution to extend his rule. Another is that the current mafia structure of the administration will attempt to keep up business as usual behind a weak appointed successor. Or they will name someone they hope is strong enough to keep the lid down tight on the media and the populace while protecting his predecessors.

Each of those possibilities contains contradictions, and each presents a danger to what matters most to Putin and his gang: protecting the flow of money and concealing the rampant corruption that produces it. If Putin stays, his government will lose its little remaining credibility as a democracy, which would lead to uncomfortable scrutiny. A weak successor will be unable to prevent factional infighting and eventual chaos. A strong replacement cannot be controlled, and the members of the current regime will not be safe for long as the country continues to slide into economic and political ruin.

This impending crisis should not come as a surprise to anyone by this point. The signs of its approach have been in the news on an almost daily basis since the middle of 2006. Not coincidentally, July 2006 marked the launch of a true opposition movement in Russia. The inaugural "Other Russia Conference" united disparate political and human rights groups into a nonideological coalition against the antidemocratic rule of the Putin regime.

Two coauthors of this book, Irina M. Khakamada and Georgiy A. Satarov, played an active role in this unique moment in contemporary Russian history. At that conference, together with our compatriots, we launched a campaign to shine light on the shadows enveloping Russian democracy.

Other Russia continues to battle for the right to free and fair elections and the rule of law in our country. We have repeatedly taken to the streets in energetic protests despite frequently brutal crackdowns by the Kremlin security forces. With the media under state control this is the only way we have of alerting our countrymen, and the world, to the growth of a real democratic alternative.

This is essential, as Putin is still passing off his authoritarian regime as a democracy and many of the world's leaders are still participating in the charade. As the authors state so poignantly in the pages that follow, "Calling a state a democracy does not make it so. Politicians labeling themselves pro-democratic or dedicated to building democracy does not make them so. Observers wishing a country were democratic do not make it so."

Anyone wishing to understand how this Russian beast was born and raised could find no better field guides than Georgy A. Satarov and Irina M. Khakamada. These fighters have watched the rise and fall of Russian democracy up close and hands on. Their personal experiences and penetrating analyses make it crystal clear that the Russian plunge into KGB dictatorship was well underway long before Putin was placed in office.

I very much hope that the facts and arguments presented in this book receive the broad audience and attention they deserve. Not only should the looming Russian crisis not then surprise anyone, but we will all be better prepared to deal with events as they unfold instead of scrambling to manage the aftermath, as was the case with the fall of the Soviet Union.

The authors' systematic investigation goes well beyond the mandate of recognizing the symptoms and diagnosing the disease. They also look into the cloudy future of Russia, a future that will also have a great impact on Russia's neighbors, Europe, and the world. It is not a message of good news, but it is a message of vital importance.

Garry Kasparov

Preface

This book arose out of a shared disappointment with the realities of Russia's postcommunist political development among the three coauthors. Unfulfilled hopes of democratization have yielded to the reality of a new dictatorship. Georgy Satarov and Irina Khakamada were participants in the critical decisions detailed in this book, decisions upon which the potential for creation of a democratic political system hung in the balance. They have consistently both advocated and fought for democratization in Russia. But Russia is not a democracy, and it has made little sense to use the word in conjunction with Russia at least since the late 1990s. We decided to write this book to explain why and how democratization in Russia failed, in particular to explain why and how the decisions critical to that failure were made and the alternatives that were available in each case. In these respects, this book fills a void. We also lay out the case for categorizing Russia's political system as a dictatorship, and present our expectation of its future development.

At the time of publication of this book, the regime is taking an ever-increasing hard line, violent approach to any who dare attempt to exercise their rights to speak or organize. Garry Kasparov, the former world chess champion who contributed the foreword to this book, has recently seen his offices ransacked, and has been roughed up and arrested in Moscow for taking part in a small, peaceful political rally. Kasparov is the latest to attempt to unify the long-fragmented liberal, pro-democratic political elite in Russia. Even this small effort is enough to rouse a violent response by Russia's new dictator. Journalists have been fired for covering Kasparov and his organization, The Other Russia. Riot police have bludgeoned and arrested hundreds of people at small demonstrations in Moscow and St. Petersburg. Kasparov and the others were beaten and imprisoned in Spring 2007 for daring to publicly criticize the Russian President at peaceful demonstrations.[1] The reality in Russia today is that one takes a real physical risk when criticizing the current regime. Politics in Russia are closed, not open.

We share a conclusion and an understanding of how this dictatorship that President Vladimir Putin has consolidated came about. Virtually every book published about Russian politics in the last two decades has either assumed or argued that Russia is or was on an inevitable path to becoming a democracy. We do not present such perspectives as an alternative to our own. Nor will the reader find a general historical sweep of events or an encyclopedic compendium of documents. Such works already exist and appear in the notes and the bibliography.

The idea that Russia is some sort of a democracy is abundantly available in the literature. But sheer abundance does not make it so, just as ignoring the signals that something other than democracy was being created did not prevent dictatorship from arising. Our book serves as an alternate and, we are convinced, more accurate explanation of the decisions of the 1990s that propelled Russia's political development toward a new form of authoritarian rule, one that leads to a more accurate understanding of the consequences of those prior decisions.

We wish to explain what happened at select moments that, we argue, proved decisive for the development of Russia's political system toward dictatorship rather than toward democracy. Some may quibble with that conclusion, or critique the argument as too extreme or the conclusion as premature. But earlier works on what took place in the 1990s proclaimed Russia a "normal" democracy. Our analysis of the decisions of the 1990s serves as an explanation for the current reality, gradually finding acceptance in general accounts of Russia, that the country is at a minimum authoritarian. We provide evidence and an argument that dictatorship better describes Russia's political system.

Satarov and Khakamada bring their unique inside perspective on why Russia's leaders made those decisions, rather the alternatives available that would have promoted rather than prevented democratization. Their experiences in public service during the 1990s serve as the foundation for the analysis in this book. Ostrow and Satarov have known each other as colleagues and as friends for nearly two decades. Satarov and Khakamada have been political allies for nearly as long. And Ostrow first interviewed Khakamada during the first week of the Russian State Duma's existence in early 1996. In broad terms, this book is the product of more than a decade of conversation and commiseration about the direction of Russia's political life. We share a perspective on what happened and why, and what might have happened had different decisions been taken.

More narrowly, we agreed on the specific contours of the book in the summer of 2004. The critical junctures approach, and agreement about which events truly constitute the critical junctures, we arrived at then. As we wanted to write a book that could both explain what happened in Russia and still be generally relevant to the broader conversation about democratization, we identified tasks common to any democratizing state as critical junctures. What this meant was that Russia-specific factors, such as the war in Chechnya, must be understood and discussed in the context of these general tasks. This, we believe, is a strength of our work. Our framework can be used to anticipate challenges and suggest approaches in other states where democracy is a desired outcome.

The production of the book was far from typical. Ostrow compiled the initial manuscript from transcripts of lengthy discussions between the coauthors, held over a period of several weeks in Moscow. Added to these were the longer history of interviews and conversations recorded. A back and forth on the chapters over the course of a year resulted in agreement on the final manuscript. Wherever possible, that is, where the analysis is based on Satarov's and/or Khakamada's firsthand accounts rather than on the supplementary cited material, the voices of the coauthors are preserved, the words are their own words. Where their memories were incomplete or uncertain, we turned to secondary source material for confirmation, or to point the reader to sources for broader background discussion of particular events. We hope the reader will find a fresh and unique insight into the events and decisions that steered Russia on a nondemocratic path.

This project could never have gone forward without a generous faculty development research grant and sabbatical leave granted to Ostrow by Benedictine University's Faculty Development Committee, to whom the authors are most grateful. In Russia, Yuriy Baturin, Sergei Filatov, Lyudmilla Pikhoya, Ivan Rodin, Sergei Shakhrai, Viktor Sheynis, Paul Shirov, Ivan Trefilov, and Mikhail Zadornov all contributed generously of their time and considerable knowledge to this project. Elena Kushnir was simply tireless and always gracious in serving as an intermediary facilitating communications between the authors, and deserves a special thanks. Additionally, J.L. Black, Director of the Center for Research on Canadian-Russian Studies, The Council of Europe's Commission for Democracy Through Law, Julie Dugger, Richard Ellis, Eugene Huskey, Bob Sharlet, and Brian Taylor all contributed valuable insights and materials. These individuals all provided information, in many cases entirely irreplaceable, without which we could not have completed this book. Jack Fritts and Arlene Stefanik in the Benedictine University Library hunted down some quite difficult-to-find materials necessary for this book. Two anonymous referees provided useful corrections and suggestions that substantially strengthened the final manuscript, as did many fellow panelists and readers at the International Studies Association conferences in 2005, 2006, and 2007. We also are grateful to our wonderful editor, Hilary Claggett, for her attentive and always useful assistance, and V. Sivakumar, BeaconPMG Project Manager, for his copyediting expertise. The authors alone are, of course, responsible for the final content.

1

Critical Junctures and the Demise of Democracy in Russia

Journalists and politicians critical of the government are murdered, and no arrests are made, nobody is brought to justice. Businessmen who take an interest in politics are arrested, exiled or sentenced to hard labor, and have their assets seized by the state. The Kremlin controls the media, which operates under conditions of direct and indirect censorship. Political officials are appointed, or, where elections are held, the outcomes are predetermined. The parliament is a mechanical rubber stamp filled with secret security agents. Corruption and bribery are institutionalized throughout government, at all levels. In the one-party regime, all substantial decision-making is centralized in the hands of the leader in the Kremlin. Serious, organized opposition has been eliminated. The old Soviet Union? No, this is the "new Russia."[1]

It is not just that it is inappropriate today to describe Russia's political system as a "democracy." It may never have been appropriate and certainly has not been since the late-1990s. While Western analysts trumpeted democracy, Russia's leaders at each critical moment made decisions that were either explicitly antidemocratic or gravely impeded the development of a democratic system. Even after the undemocratic hand over of the presidency to KGB officer Vladimir V. Putin, academics and journalists alike have continued to use the term; authors who should know better have misled their readers. A normative bias encouraged many in the West, particularly in the United States, to cling to the term democracy, modified with myriad adjectives that do more to confuse than clarify. Whether "electoral"[2] "limited" or "partial"[3], "managed,"[4] or the ever-popular "transitional," analysts employing these modifiers always begin with the assumption that Russia *is* a democracy.[5] The "democracy" part of the compound label is rarely if ever explained or justified, much less questioned or challenged. Even many who have seemed to question whether Russia under Putin can be called a democracy with any sort of modifier at all conclude, as if out of nowhere, that there is something "hybrid" about the regime.[6] Whether or not any of these modifiers or the assumption ever offered accurate descriptions of Russia, today any use of the word democracy applied to Russia requires grotesque concept stretching.

How and why did this happen, when there was so much promise for and so many promises of a democratic outcome? Boris N. Yeltsin left a lasting image of a triumphant, wildly popular leader when he climbed down from that T-72 tank in August 1991. He had turned the military to the side of the demonstrators opposing the hard-line communist coup against hapless Soviet leader Mikhail S. Gorbachev, and led the defeat of the coup plotters. That victory marked the end of Communism and, shortly thereafter, of the Soviet Union itself. Three people died, crushed by tanks during the resistance, but Yeltsin's efforts were critical in persuading the military not to fire on the demonstrators, avoiding massive bloodshed, defeating the coup leaders, and bringing an end to the communist regime. He had won, decisively so, and was clearly ascendant over Gorbachev in appearances before parliament and other meetings over the next several weeks. In that capacity, he promised to lead Russia to a new, democratic and market-oriented future.

The August 1991 coup was traumatic, if brief. It was traumatic for the world, as it brought to an end the division between the liberal, democratic West and communist East that had defined international relations since the end of the Second World War. It triggered a reconfiguration of world politics, of alliances, and of internal state politics across the globe that continues as this book was being written. The hope was that a unified world of free, market-oriented democracies, with the United States and Russia in partnership, would emerge.

Boris Yeltsin was the unquestioned leader of Russia, and he had a team of reform-minded leaders who proclaimed democracy as their goal. They had the world open to them, and Yeltsin's popular legitimacy to rule was overwhelming. Indeed, it appeared that Russia had emerged as a new state and could chart a new course, for its transcendent leader had made a number of booming proclamations to the world of his and his country's democratic intentions, and that he would not repeat the indecisiveness and half-measures that marked Gorbachev's tenure and spelled his political doom.[7] Although the difficulties of such a project were obvious to everyone, there was also hope that a democratic outcome would be a reality. After all, Russia had many examples and lessons to learn from. The varied experiences across Eastern Europe since the domino collapse of communism in 1989 provided clear evidence of the importance of this brief window of opportunity for demolishing the old political system and creating a new one, and of seizing this opportunity if democracy was the objective. They set the example by demonstrating the obstacles that a democratizing state emerging from communism must overcome, and the steps needed in overcoming them that would move the country in a democratic direction. And the United States and its allies in the West stood ready to help their former enemy transform into a political and economic ally and partner. The year 1992, in short, opened with optimism for a democratic future for Russia.

None of these hopes were realized. This book seeks to explain why. Russia is once again a one-party dictatorship, and an increasingly violent one at that. The roots of this reality lay in decisions made when communism collapsed and in decisions made at each critical moment for the future of Russia's political system after that collapse.

Putin's Authoritarianism

Within ten years those dreams were thoroughly squashed. The final blow to hopes for democracy came when Yeltsin handed the presidency to a virtually unknown former KGB agent, Vladimir Putin, by resigning at the end of 1999. Since that day, Putin has systematically closed the political space in Russia. He has recentralized power in a steep vertical authoritarian structure. Controlling the top of that vertical are individuals drawn heavily from the security services, or *siloviki,* from where Putin hails. By the most reliable estimate, 70 percent of Russia's top government officials are drawn from the security services and the KGB.[8] They have brought their brutal methods with them.

Putin has overseen a relentless and often violent crackdown on independent media and has eliminated all independent national television media, restoring control to the Kremlin. As in the days of General Secretaries during Communist rule, Putin can and does remove and appoint broadcasters, editors, and directors of programs, and his office dictates content.[9] He has had the owners of critical independent newspapers arrested and exiled, and had independent voices removed from television stations across the country. Dozens of journalists, who have covered issues of corruption, ineptitude and failure of government, have been killed in Russia under mysterious circumstances in the last five years, and not one of the murders has been solved.[10] To suggest that Russia today has anything even approaching a free press requires gross exaggeration or self-deception. Any remaining independent media not controlled directly by the Kremlin are cowered indirectly into soft, uncritical reporting. Censorship has returned to the Russian media.

Many independent, liberal-minded politicians and even more political organizations have met the same cruel fate under Putin. Dozens have been killed, while a multitude of others have been prevented from seeking office on trumped-up criminal charges or imagined election law violations.[11] Parties are arbitrarily banned, and administrative rules prevent any serious challenge to Putin's United Russia organization. Russian authorities actively rig elections at all levels; citizens are denied hospital care if they are not able to produce absentee ballots, ballots are cast for voters who never appear at the polls. Massive vote fraud characterizes every election since Putin took office.[12] More troubling, a string of apartment building explosions before elections in 1999 and 2000, and another wave of deadly explosions prior to Putin's reelection in 2004, combined with the war in Chechnya, have generated widespread suspicion supported by strong evidence of government involvement, suggesting Putin has intentionally generated fear to secure support.[13] As with the murders of independent-minded journalists and politicians, the culprits behind the explosions have never been found.

Putin has systematically eliminated political competition and opposition. After gaining the power to remove governors, he in 2004 removed the power of the population to elect them in the first place. One of his first acts in 2000 was to decree into existence a series of "super-governors," appointed by and accountable only to the president, to oversee affairs around the country which the unprecedented decree segmented into seven large districts. Regional political actors are now subordinate to the Kremlin, unable to form an independent political base. Putin's selective attacks against high-profile business leaders, such as Vladimir Gusinsky and Mikhail Khodorkovsky, are limited to those who support the activities of independent politicians, political organizations, and interest groups. He has made it impossible for any aspiring liberal political organization to gain support for organizing and campaigning. He has intervened to ban candidates and parties from election ballots, and vote fraud is widespread, making elections once again a farce. By telling entrepreneurs that they may not use their resources to advance or protect their legitimate policy or ideological interests, he is encroaching on economic freedom. These are not liberal economic policies.[14] He has pushed legislation through his puppet-Duma, making the hurdle for competing in national elections so high as to prevent even major politicians from attempting to create political organizations for the purpose of contesting elections, and has eliminated elections altogether for regional and local offices.[15]

Putin has remade the Duma, the national legislature, into a collection of officials neither interested in nor adept at politics. Indeed, one description of the legislators indicates many "[forget] entirely that the parliament is not a ministry, let alone a special service. ...The word 'politics' is the most shocking obscenity." Asking the members "to evaluate any of the president's actions is futile; it's clear in advance that they'll be full of praise and admiration. Among the obligations of United Russia faction members, as set down in faction regulations, is the following: 'Avoid making any public statements, including statements to the media, which are not in line with the decisions of the faction.'"[16] He has created a "Civic Chamber"—appointed by the Kremlin—to substitute for and duplicate the national legislature, a seeming redundancy as he effectively appoints the upper house of the national legislature and controls over 75 percent of the lower house, most of whom are either former security officials or head state-run enterprises.

Putin has, as a result of these and other actions, effectively destroyed organized political opposition on both the left and the right. Far from the hopes of a competitive, democratic, multiparty system, Russia instead has returned to being a one-party administrative regime. All of this amounts to a coordinated attack on civil society which was only beginning to become institutionalized when he became president. While constantly trumpeting in speeches that Russia needs to "create" civil society, in fact the idea of the Kremlin trying to create civil society indicates a clear anti-civil society orientation of the Putin administration.

Perhaps most disturbing for the future is that Putin has brought with him a coterie of KGB and security service personnel that now dominates every branch of the Russian government, with over 6,000 of these *siloviki* occupying top positions in the apparatus of the presidency, government ministries, and both chambers of the legislature.[17] There is a real danger of the institutionalization of these services as the country's rulers. Each of these officials has brought others from the security forces as staff and aides, and to head regional offices around the country.[18] Putin has overseen changes to laws restricting the creation of political parties and interest groups, infringing on the rights of religious organizations, eliminating direct election of regional leaders, encroaching on economic freedom, and restricting freedom of expression and overt political activity. He has encouraged the arrest of those critical of his moves, along with the seizure of their assets and redistribution of property back to state control, and the imprisonment or exile of the individuals themselves.

Putin's most important acts since becoming president have aimed to recreate the "single center" form of administration that described Soviet rule.[19] He has eliminated the potential for organized political competition, closed curtailing opportunities for independent political activity, and silenced independent sources of information on or investigation into his regime. He has restored a closed political system dominated by a single party controlled by a single individual.

A Brief Word About Words

A long school of thought from Schumpeter to Dahl to Huntington defines "democracy" as a set of institutions, governmental and societal, that ensure open, competitive elections to select leaders who will make political decisions and protect basic rights and freedoms.[20] The theoretical literature on democracy is as voluminous as it is interesting. Some authors adopt a minimalist definition that equates elections with democracy. We prefer a more comprehensive definition, agreeing with Fish, who in his recent review of this literature in the Russian context adopts a broad definition of democracy as a system that ensures popular control over the state. This subsumes such aspects critical to a functioning democratic political system as transparency, accountability, and open competition that includes but goes beyond formal elections, to encompass a continuing role for the polity.[21] We embrace this definition of democracy as a system ensuring popular control over the state. Elections are formal events, and democracy certainly requires free, competitive elections, but democracy also requires more to ensure popular control over the state and protections from the state. Even by this minimalist definition, however, Russia falls far short of democracy.

It is inconceivable that one would apply the term to today's Russia, yet many Western academics have continued to insist that Russia has "a limited form of democracy."[22] Even recent studies bemoaning the failure of democratization in Russia fall short in their analysis of the reality of the current regime. Russia is again an autocracy, even if not in the pure sense of a single individual ruling. No modern state meets or can meet that ideal type, by the very nature of ideal types. Russia is what is commonly called an authoritarian regime, and more accurately a dictatorship, and it serves no useful purpose to shy away from the term.[23]

What Russia has consolidated since Communism's demise is dictatorship, not democracy. There are surprisingly few clear definitions of "dictatorship" or "authoritarianism" in the political science literature, with most authors using the terms in contradistinction to "democracy." One sourcebook defines authoritarianism as a system in which values and decisions are imposed on those who lack the right to respond or react freely, and dictatorship as rule by one person.[24] The former is plausible though incomplete, the latter is not even plausible.

When one can say of a country that how politics are conducted is determined by a single individual, where that individual makes decisions and imposes them on a populace that is denied the political freedom to organize, compete, and hold leaders accountable electorally or otherwise, that country is a dictatorship. The word democracy has no place. This certainly describes Russia under Putin, and is the definition we embrace for dictatorship. Putin has used the virtually unlimited powers of his office and the precedents set by Yeltsin to wipe out hopes for a democratic Russia for the foreseeable future. Politics are closed in dictatorships; political freedoms are minimal; political activity is severely circumscribed for individuals and groups alike. The nature of the system, whether it is benevolent or malign, depends exclusively upon the personal predilections of the leader.

Such is the case in Russia today. Of course, there are dictators, and there are dictators. Putin's is not rule by state terror, he is no Caligula, no Stalin, no Pol Pot. Russia is not again a totalitarian state. Yet there have been hundreds of unsolved murders of political figures critical of, investigating, or in opposition to Putin, his government and his policies. Putin is a dictator reared in and intensely loyal to the KGB, now the FSB, one of the most secretive and brutal government organizations the world has ever known.[25] He has promoted fellow officers to an extent far surpassing that which existed in the Soviet period. He has systematically eliminated all significant sources of political competition or opposition, while consolidating immense powers into his own hands. His is rule through consistent harassment of and often violent crackdown against organized political opposition, against individual opponents or critics, and against the media. Putin has effected the elimination or extreme isolation of alternative political parties at all levels, national, regional and local, and the return of one-party rule. He has systematically worked to constrain the rights of citizens, including economic rights, to eliminate elections as meaningful events and to abolish them altogether at many levels, and to hypercentralize all significant policy decision making in the Kremlin. He has presided over the return of rampant human rights abuses, rule by fear, and domination by the security services in positions of political rule across the country. He rode to prominence by launching and overseeing a war against Chechnya, one he has continued to pursue with massive human rights abuses of the most egregious sort, including a rampage of murder, rape, and terror unleashed by the Russian military and security services. The precedents Putin has set and the system he has solidified make real the prospect of a more malign dictatorship in the future, perhaps in the near future. The gap between the hopes of 1991 and the reality in 2006 is startling and saddening for those who worked for democratic political development in Russia after the fall of communism.

Critical Junctures

This book tells the story of why and how those hopes for a democratic Russia turned out to be merely dreams. It does so with the benefit of the inside perspective of two of the coauthors and the many other voices who contributed their firsthand memories of what transpired. Russia has been, is, and will continue to be a vital player in European and global security and stability. What happens there matters, and because it matters it needs to be understood. That means knowing both the "what" and the "why". Calling Russia a democracy simply because we want it to be one is not just wrong, it is potentially dangerous. So this book serves at least two important functions. First, it explains why Russia's leaders made decisions that undermined the prospects for democracy, and describes the parameters of the authoritarian regime that has emerged and the prospects for the future. Second, because the key points in the story of Russia's postcommunist political development have commonalities across the postcommunist environment, we offer a framework for explaining the keys to successful democratization. The framework, the authors believe, can be used to explain successes or failures elsewhere, and to offer guidance to other countries. Russia's leaders made choices at important moments and on important decisions that held real consequences for future political developments. The lessons of those choices are not just lessons for Russia. They are lessons for any country attempting to make a transformation from authoritarian rule to democracy.

We identify several "critical junctures" through which, we argue, all post-communist states pursuing democratic political development must pass. Indeed, any democratizing regime, it seems to the authors, must confront each of these junctures and resolve the inherent problems in a pro-democratic direction if a democratic outcome is to be likely. The choices leaders make at each of those junctures will either enhance or impede the establishment of a stable democracy. Put differently, each juncture has different potential paths that result from various possible decisions available to leaders. Only some decisions, or resultant paths, will be beneficial to the creation of a stable democracy, whereas some will directly impair the development of a democratic political system. One can, therefore, trace a state's path through these critical junctures, or major decision points, identifying each as one in which the prospects for a democratic outcome hangs in the balance, explaining the factors that led to one or another decision, and analyzing the consequences of each outcome for the future.

Our use of the term "critical junctures" adopts but also adapts somewhat the most well-known and cited application of the concept by David Collier and Ruth Collier.[26] We embrace the basic premise that decisions made in response to a problem at one point in time "establish distinct trajectories within which [quoting Paul David], 'one damn thing follows another.'"[27] Anyone familiar with any of the stories of postcommunist democratic reform can appreciate this observation. By their definition, however, historians, a century and more, hence would define the decade or two following Communism's demise in 1989, or in Russia's case in 1991, as a single critical juncture, with the problem or outcome explained being the creation (or not) of a liberal democratic regime. Whether or not a country developed a stable, liberal democratic regime as an outcome of this juncture would determine other outcomes over the following several decades. Indeed, the critical juncture the Colliers analyze, the rise of labor movements in Latin America, and the effects on regime dynamics, in some cases spanned several decades. While the Colliers offer that critical junctures may be brief or stretch over long periods of time, the demands of their schematic make it a bit difficult to conceive of how one could be brief.[28] Be that as it may, their framework has certainly proved valuable and has inspired insightful research in a number of different directions.

We are similarly inspired by their research. However, we find it not only unreasonably limiting but also unreasonable logically to consider the attempt to create a democratic political system as a single event. It is not particularly useful to conceive it as such, because doing so robs us of the ability to explain the success or failure of the project. We seek to "reach inside" and consider the critical decisions made that, in Russia's case, set it on a nondemocratic path. Democratic transformation is a project involving multiple processes with varying requirements that depend upon, among other things, the political, social, and economic preconditions. If we want to explain comparatively the relative success or failure of democratization, we need to identify the most important common aspects of that project, and an analytic basis for explaining varying outcomes. Despite its tendency toward gross misapplication and wildly unrealistic assumptions and predictions, the voluminous literature on "transitions" has identified some important legacies of Communism and tasks of democratization with which postcommunist elites attempting democratic political reconstruction have had to grapple. The list is familiar and lengthy: drafting new constitutions, defining the polity, establishing borders, instituting political competition, creating the rule of law, creating market economies, creating and protecting the institution of private property, and establishing basic freedoms are just a few of the tasks that have faced states embarking on democratization in the wake of the communist collapse. A postcommunist state attempting to create a new democratic political system may encounter a range of problems, and each state's political leaders and the political elite more generally must make decisions about how to solve these problems.

While the particular problems of democratization will vary from state to state, there are at least a few issues that every postcommunist state attempting democratic change will encounter. How it navigates those issues will affect the prospects for democracy either positively or negatively. When these issues pop up, the regime is faced, if not with a crisis, then with a series of difficult decisions. They become a dominant concern. Whether they realize it or not, and often they do not, the choices leaders make at these critical junctures will shape both the immediate and the long-term prospects for the creation of a stable democracy. In other words, leaders frequently have no idea that the problem they are confronting is in fact critical in this sense. This, it seems to the authors, is the essence of the phrase "critical juncture," for some decisions taken may unintentionally undermine entirely the prospects for democracy. The appearance of each of these problems represents a critical juncture for that state, for its leaders, and for the people, for some decisions and actions make democracy a more likely outcome, while others may impede or completely derail a democratic future. It is not necessarily the case that the leadership recognizes a situation as critical in this sense. It is also not necessarily the case that they see alternative solutions either, indeed, in some instances the characteristic seems to be ignorance of or even conscious denial of the existence of alternatives.

We identify four critical junctures that, we believe, are common to all postcommunist states, and likely to all states embarking on democratic transformation. We address them as they appeared chronologically in Russia, though this order may not be fixed. First is the question of what to do with the legacy institutions of the communist (or prior) political system. In short, the issue becomes when and how to eliminate them. Second is the issue of when and how to adopt a new constitution. Third, how will the state approach the new problem of political competition, including the rise of new political actors and interests. Fourth, how will the system handle the problem of leadership change. How the new leaders handle each of these problems as they present themselves will influence the options available for addressing the subsequent tasks when they arise. Indeed, particular decisions at point A will impede the ability to make certain types of decisions at point B in ways that may narrow the likelihood of creating a stable democratic regime. Although they may not recognize the fact, decision makers do have alternatives available to them for addressing these tasks. It is precisely the importance of each task for all subsequent tasks on the list, and the availability of distinct alternatives, that makes the process of resolving the issue a critical juncture in the country's development, and absolutely critical to the success of creating a democratic political system.

At each critical juncture, Russia's postcommunist leaders have consistently made choices that have undermined rather than furthered the prospects for democracy, and in some cases those choices have been unambiguously antidemocratic in nature. Agency, that is individual decisions of individual leaders, matters. So do institutions and structures, for individuals make decisions in the context of the institutional settings in which they act. While individuals are constrained by their institutional environment, their decisions also can serve to shape that environment at critical junctures. Russia's postcommunist leaders made antidemocratic choices at each critical juncture, choices that paved the way to the consolidation of dictatorship under Putin. This reality in 2007 is a consequence that can be traced to decisions made over how to demolish the communist political system, when and how to adopt a new constitution, how to respond to political competition, how to respond to new political actors and interests, and how to handle leadership change.

Overview of the Study

Russia is not destined, doomed, or otherwise fated to have an authoritarian political system. Alternative paths were available, alternate outcomes possible, but Russia's key decision makers either did not choose them and did not see them, or chose not to see them. The reasons for and consequences of their actions at each juncture explain Russia's divergence from a democratic path.

Ours is not an impartial analysis. The three coauthors shared a hope for democracy and share a disappointment with the political path Russia has instead taken. Two of the coauthors, Georgiy A. Satarov and Irina M. Khakamada, were firsthand observers and participants in the decisions and processes analyzed in this work. From 1993 through late 1998, Satarov served in a variety of positions under President Boris Yeltsin, including as a member of the President's Council, as chief political advisor, as legislative liaison, and as liaison to political parties and interest groups. Khakamada, a former Deputy Speaker in the Russian State Duma, was and remains a leader of the liberal, democratic wing of the Russian political elite, having founded and organized several factions in the Duma and election coalitions. She stood against Putin as his main democratic challenger in the 2004 presidential elections. From the beginning of our discussions about this project, we shared a common identification of what the critical junctures were, an understanding of what made them critical, and a general picture of what a pro-democratic outcome at each would have looked like. At the same time, our viewpoints are complementary, for we bring to this book different lenses through which we view the events that transpired. Combined, we have a multifaceted inside view of events from a Western academic who directly observed much of these events while living in Moscow, a Cabinet-level official in the Yeltsin administration who is also founder and president of one of the most prestigious think tanks committed to democratic principles in Russia, and an active and leading politician throughout the period who has served as party leader and organizer, legislator and legislative leader, member of government and presidential candidate.

The direct knowledge and experiences of the coauthors, who participated in the events covered, provides the bulk of the source material in the chapters that follow. Their memories, notes, and understanding of what took place, why, and what it all meant form the vast majority of the informational basis for this book. They conveyed their experiences and interpretations to Ostrow over many conversations spanning several years, with several intensive daylong conversations conducted during the preparation of this book. Their memories and analyses serve as the first and primary source for all of the analysis. Where those analyses were unsure or conflicting, or where information was simply lacking, we turned to additional or corroborating source materials and cited these in the footnotes accordingly.

The subsequent chapters of this book explain the nature of each of the critical junctures in Russia, and what happened in each instance. Together, they show how the choices at the early decision points narrowed the options at later junctures and made democracy a less likely outcome. Chapter 2 discusses the now difficult to comprehend decision of Russia's new political leadership to ignore political reform. In other words, on the question of when and how to destroy the ancien regime, they simply ignored the question altogether. Most important was what to do with the existing legislature, the

Supreme Soviet. Yeltsin and his advisors thought that the Supreme Soviet, having supported them before, would continue to serve Yeltsin into the future. It was a tragically flawed assumption that guided them, that democracy would develop on its own and they could focus exclusively on economic reform. However, attempting market reform in the absence of any of the institutions of democracy or Capitalism brought rampant corruption and a system that used conflict rather than compromise to resolve disputes. The chapter discusses the wide range of options that were clearly available and tells the story of just how and why none of these options were never even seriously discussed in the Kremlin. It also tells the story of something rare in the political affairs of a state: a second chance. In May 1993, Yeltsin had another chance to deal with the matter of existing institutions. A national referendum on the question of the locus of political power and trust in the leaders that gave the president wide authority provided an opportunity to resolve the deepening standoff with the Supreme Soviet. Although the questions put to the public were entirely vague, after the referendum Yeltsin again had the opportunity to use the results in his favor to take decisive action regarding the political system. He again squandered this chance, and blood in the streets was the ultimate result. Why did the Kremlin, which still claimed to have democratization as a highest goal, fail to seize the opportunity to create democratic institutions and use a democratic process in doing so? The failure cast a deepening cloud over democracy's hopes in Russia. This first critical decision seems incredible in retrospect. It seriously undermined democratic hopes going forward.

Chapter 3 explains how Russia arrived at the constitution it now has, one that enables dictatorial rule. After the second coup, in which the president bombed the Supreme Soviet out of existence, Russia's leaders made a conscious decision to hedge against democracy, and they did so in the most important aspects of the new constitution. After eliminating the Supreme Soviet and prior to election of a new legislature, Yeltsin ruled unchallenged and unchecked. The test was and the future of democracy in part hinged upon what he did with the unlimited power he held. Yeltsin's team had the potential and promised to create a democratic political system from above. Their actions, however, betrayed the hollowness of their promises.

It is generally forgotten and has not been explained why the constitution that was adopted in December 1993 deviated from the one published in the summer. Hundreds of people from all walks of life, civil servants, academics, politicians, and businesspeople, had convened to draft a new constitution. They reached agreement, and the president approved it for presentation to the public. That draft envisioned a presidential system balanced by real legislative and judicial powers. However, after the armed confrontation, a small group of advisors, with the president's approval, introduced several subtle amendments to the version brought to referendum for adoption. Those changes opened the door to dictatorship by stripping the legislature of most of its authority and autonomy, and vesting in the presidency wide-ranging power over virtually all policy and personnel matters. This opened the way for an individual so inclined to seize virtually unlimited power into the presidency. A more balanced draft constitution was available and had been approved by the president. Why did that draft not go forward? This chapter tells the story of the intrigue and machinations around the constitution, a story critical to understanding Russia's path toward authoritarianism.

Chapter 4 examines how Yeltsin and his team could not resist the urge to squelch real political opposition and competitive elections. The decisions made in 1996 set terrible precedents that accelerated the demise of basic democratic principles. As Boris Yeltsin's first term neared its end, his approval rating plummeted. The new superrich elite, whose wealth was without exception possible only through shady, often murderous practices, feared a return to power by the communists would endanger their wealth and, possibly, more basic interests. A group of these "oligarchs", led by two who owned independent media outlets, approached Yeltsin's top advisors with a proposal to guarantee his reelection in return for privileges, access, and protection after the victory. The cost of not allowing a real political competition and a truly free campaign proved to be the very demise of democracy itself. The welcoming of the oligarchs into the closest circles of power and the gross violations of election and campaign laws brought corruption and criminality directly into the presidency, and presaged the crackdown on independent media and political opposition that was to come.

Chapter 5 examines the final blow, the decision to abandon democracy altogether. Rather than allowing for electoral competition to decide the direction of leadership change when Yeltsin's second term came to a close, the sitting president decided to hand power to a chosen successor. There were some in the West who praised the coronation of former KGB spy Vladimir Putin as president as constitutional democracy in action. While it is true that the Russian Constitution has procedures for succession following the resignation, death, or incapacitation of a president, Boris Yeltsin was the first Russian president. Precedent matters. Yeltsin was the first Russian president to face the question of how to handle his exit from power. Yeltsin studied George Washington; he liked to refer to him. His speechwriter and close political advisors knew this. He had to have known his purported role model's example. Imagine if Washington, rather than staying on the sidelines while a spirited and at times brutal campaign raged for his successor, had intervened, chosen a successor, and resigned to hand the office over to that successor.

Yeltsin did just that, and more. He chose to invoke the extraordinary measures in the constitution before the normal procedures had ever been given a chance to work. He handed the presidency to a man virtually unknown, with no political base, and with no history of political activity or stated political program, a man whose career flourished in the most hated and feared agency of communist power, the KGB. The resignation reduced the campaign from 6 months to 90 days, a reality that compelled all of the leading contenders to drop out or to wage symbolic campaigns with no hope of success. Moreover, Putin used Yeltsin's example from 1996 to control media access and coverage of that truncated, farcical campaign—he and he alone dominated the airwaves.

Why resign? Why Putin? Why not allow an electoral system in place determine leadership change at the top? The requirement of leadership change as Yeltsin's second term came to an end offered a chance to resurrect some hope for democratic politics in Russia, and set a precedent that the constitution could promote democracy. A freewheeling campaign was just what Russian democracy needed, and it was just beginning to develop as Yeltsin announced his resignation. Why Russia's first president decided on one of the most nondemocratic methods of leadership change begs explanation, as does his choice of the shady KGB operative Vladimir Putin to assume the post of president.

Explaining why and how Russia's leaders made these choices is the focus of this book. In the concluding chapters, we explain what Russia has become by elaborating the nature of the dictatorship Putin has consolidated, and we speculate on what these past precedents portend for Russia's future. President Putin has ended open politics in Russia, restored a hypercentralized political vertical, eliminated competitive politics, made a farce of elections, restored censorship, and emasculated economic rights. Chapter 6 demonstrates how any many high profile figures who dare criticize his regime, such as Boris Berezovsky, Vladimir Gusinsky, Mikhail Khodorkovsky, Anna Politkovskaya, and Sergei Yushenkov to name just a few, face personal ruin, including arrest, seizure of assets, and exile, imprisonment, or worse. In short, the regime has all the signature trademarks of a dictatorship, and the arrests and political intolerance show every sign of increasing, rather than declining.

The seeds of this system were sown in the prior decade, when the opportunity to create democratic institutions was lost, and then squandered again after an unlikely second chance. The door was opened with the creation of a severely unbalanced constitution that vested supreme powers in an unchecked presidency. An example was set with executive branch meddling in elections and undermining the principle of political competition. The fate of democracy was sealed with a noncompetitive hand over of power to an individual schooled in the harshest institution ever created for the suppression of freedom of political expression, the KGB. We should not be surprised that this individual has used this constitution to create a strong authoritarian system. What this book seeks to do is to raise the blinders over peoples' eyes to the current realities of Russian politics, and to explain how this reality came about.

2

After the Fall: The Decision to Ignore Politics

The August 1991 coup against Soviet leader Mikhail Gorbachev was a traumatic shock, despite the fact that for months Moscow had been swirling with warnings and rumors. Indeed, Gorbachev's closest ally, Foreign Minister Eduard Shevardnadze, warned in a dramatic resignation speech before the Congress of Peoples' Deputies the prior December that "dictatorship is coming," complete with witch hunts and show trials.[1] Given that communist regimes had tumbled like dominos across Eastern Europe in 1989, one might have expected the Soviet Communist Party and KGB to fight to prevent a similar fate. When the coup failed, it marked the end of that system, and of the Party itself. The nature and depth of the shock was publicly evident in the final months of 1991.

The Soviet Union's final death throes were almost painful to watch. Gorbachev was still President of the Soviet Union, but he was severely weakened, visibly shaken, and disoriented. Here was the leader of the Soviet Union, a nuclear superpower, who had nearly been removed from power in a palace coup. How could he have allowed into and retained in his Cabinet people who would plot such a takeover? The contrast between Gorbachev and the new and ascendent source of power—Boris Yeltsin, President of the Russian Federation—could not have been more stark. During the country's final months, live broadcasts of the national legislature in session showed Gorbachev officially presiding, but Yeltsin fixed at his side, questioning, correcting, and generally controlling the proceedings.

Yeltsin clearly had the upper hand. As one analysis put it, "Yeltsin and his allies, having vanquished the Old Guard, now realized they could push Gorbachev, and the Union, aside as well."[2] During five years of struggle and tension between the two, it had been Gorbachev who dictated outcomes. Now, Yeltsin positively reveled in his dominance over Gorbachev, whose struggles to preserve the Union seemed almost pitiful and ultimately proved futile.[3] By December, all of the Soviet republics had declared independence, and Yeltsin signed an accord with the leaders of Ukraine, Belarus and Kazakhstan forming the Commonwealth of Independent States. On Christmas Day of 1991, Gorbachev, acknowledging the *fait accompli,* resigned, and the Soviet Union was no more.

Russia, now independent, faced a pivotal period. The first months after the final liquidation of the Soviet state proved to be a critical moment for the future of democracy in Russia. Yeltsin had a golden opportunity to annihilate the vestiges of totalitarian rule, to act decisively and rapidly to institute a democratic system of government. He could have announced a process for writing a new constitution and creating new political institutions based on freedom, political openness and competition, and checks and balances to prevent official abuse of power. However, the window of opportunity was short, the pressures were enormous, and the "honeymoon" with the public could not last long given the dire economic crisis. Yeltsin had to act fast if decisive political change was to take happen.

He blinked. Instead, he and his team chose to ignore political reform, leaving in place the communist-era institutions. They decided instead to concentrate all of their efforts, intellectual, creative, and administrative, on economic transformation. The decision to forego political transformation while embarking on rapid economic reform had a direct, nondemocratic influence at each successive juncture. Obviously, there is no guarantee that a democratic system would have emerged had Yeltsin declared an end to the legislature and the constitution in January 1992. However, the decision to retain the communist-era institutions placed a barrier across the path to democracy around which Russia has been unable since to navigate. It spawned a constitutional crisis that turned violent in October 1993, in which Boris Yeltsin ordered the physical destruction of the Russian Supreme Soviet. That trauma was a central reason for subtle changes made to the new constitution prior to its approval in a referendum, changes that created significantly unbalanced power and an unchecked super-presidency. This unchecked power brought corruption and abuse to the apex of power in Russia, and paved the way for presidential interference into the election system and restrictions on free political competition. It enabled a steady reduction in media autonomy and the steady restriction of democratic rights and freedoms that continues today. It fueled a suspicion of political opposition that led to a hand over of power rather than free and competitive elections to decide who would lead Russia after Yeltsin. The result has been restoration of dictatorship, not only in the personal leadership but also in the political system, under Vladimir Putin.

Russia's new leadership made that decision to leave the communist-era institutions and political rules in place while trumpeting democracy, proclaiming a democratic future, and professing a staunch commitment to democratic principles. Why and how did they arrive at this decision, in retrospect so unfortunate, to leave in place the old constitution and political institutions? What were the options they considered for political reform, how were they considered, and why did Yeltsin and his team reject them in favor of an exclusive focus on economics? Did they realize that the actions taken immediately after Russia became the successor to the Soviet Union would have long-lasting effects on the political system of the country? As important as this story is, certainly for Russia but also for all of Europe and for the world, to date it has not yet been told in full from the perspective of those involved in making those decisions. It is the focus of this chapter.

Opportunity

Boris Yeltsin was wildly popular in the wake of the collapse of Communism. Here was a leader with a booming voice, tall and confident, who had emerged victorious after years of struggle with the indecisive Gorbachev. He seemed single-handedly to have brought down the communist regime, all the while trumpeting the need for bold, decisive leadership in contrast to Gorbachev's incessant backtracking and indecisiveness. Yeltsin proclaimed a new direction for Russia, democratic politically and market-oriented economically, and promised to be decisive and swift.[4] The oppression, recession, and depression of Communism were over; he would bring real political and economic freedom, real political and economic competition, and real political and economic development for all of Russian citizens. The promise was realistic, as it had been realized already with decisive leadership in Poland, Hungary, and the Czech Republic, and would be in the former-Soviet republics Estonia, Latvia and Lithuania. Russia seemed to have a committed leadership, and had positive role models for achieving the desired results.

Although Yeltsin's authority was unparalleled and his popular legitimacy to rule overwhelming, the window of opportunity for democratic reform was brief. It was brief because the pain of rebuilding the ruined economy would quickly erode the popular support for the new regime. This was also the experience elsewhere, and those states that did move quickly are the ones that emerged with stronger democratic systems. Given the experiences of states such as Poland and Hungary on the one hand compared with those such as Romania and Bulgaria on the other, one might have expected Yeltsin and his team immediately to declare the Soviet-era constitution null and void and the legislature dissolved, and to convene a roundtable or assembly to decide how to create a new set of rules and institutions; in short, to eliminate the Soviet-era political institutions to compel focus on crafting a new political system.

But Yeltsin did nothing of the kind. If ever there was a critical juncture for Russia's political institutions and for the design of the political system, this was it. But Yeltsin decided to ignore politics altogether, leaving the existing political institutions intact rather than bringing about immediate political change. All efforts and all focus on institutions and rules, all energy regarding systemic change was focused entirely on the economy. Given Yeltsin's authority, he had the nearest thing to a blank slate to use if he so desired. His decision to do nothing—in terms of political change—demands explanation. Why did that triumphant new Russian leadership decide to leave the existing political institutions intact? Why did they decide not to engage in political reform and instead to focus entirely on economic reform? Why, at this critical moment for Russia's political development, did the new leaders ignore politics?

Four primary factors combined to steer Russia away from rapid political transformation immediately after the fall of the Soviet Union. First, while in retrospect it is somewhat difficult to fathom, it is nevertheless the case that the new leaders saw no particular need for rapid political change at the time. Second, there were no clear ideas for what to do, a symptom of an inertia in thought, in which the conflict over the future of the Union occupied such primary space that it was difficult to think on the matter of a separate, independent Russian state prior to January 1992, much less what form such a state would take. Even those who may have advocated radical steps lacked any plans or blueprints. Nothing of the sort had been seriously discussed. Third, President Yeltsin's personality and predilections militated against radical options that may otherwise have been considered. Finally, the economic disaster that was so deep and patently apparent, and the Marxist notion that politics follows from economics was so unquestioned and even unrecognized among virtually all Russian politicians, that a policy focus on economics rather than on rapid and radical political change was a convenient and attractive alternative. These factors combined to make economic reform not merely the lead focus, but the exclusive focus of the new Russian regime. How each militated against radical political reform is the focus of this chapter. The final section will discuss the short-term and long-term consequences that derived from this neglect of political reform, and how this narrowed options into the future.

"We Had All the Political Levers We Needed"

Virtually everyone who participated in or was privy to the decisions made in December 1991—January 1992 argues that nobody saw any particular need for immediate and radical political change in Russia. Although in retrospect this is hard to fathom, considering the circumstances surrounding the Soviet Union's demise, there was no sense of urgency to make as a first priority writing and adopting a new constitution, replacing the communist-era political institutions such as the legislatures both national and regional, or creating new rules for the functions of and relations between the various branches and levels of power. In fact, nobody really saw this as a critical decision. Nobody appreciated at the time the urgent importance of the political project. This retrospective consensus is shared by former cabinet-level political advisors to the president, experienced political analysts and politicians, in other words, virtually the entire Moscow political elite. Nearly fifteen years later, with hopes for democracy so seriously compromised, few exhibit any sense of regret for their earlier notions or would amend these decisions were they able to turn back the hands of time and do it all over again. Most of them are now former officials with, one would expect, a different perspective being out of public service. But that consensus against the idea of rapid political change remains largely intact, with the notable exception of the one coauthor of this book who was party to those early decisions.[5]

What makes the lack of urgency puzzling is that Russia's Constitution in late 1991 mimicked in almost every substantial way the Soviet Constitution, whose internal contradictions regarding the locus of power and the nature of the state produced the conditions that triggered the coup that had unraveled the country. The contradictions had emerged largely as a result of Gorbachev's start-and-stop approach to political reform, his hesitancy and lack of commitment generally to the concept of political change. It was that indecisiveness that fueled the collapse of the country.[6] Yeltsin was not merely aware of this, he and his advisors worried that Russia would experience the same fate, that it could dissolve into dozens of smaller states; he actively feared the "yugoslavization" of Russia.

One might think that this would have propelled him toward, rather than away from, rapid political change. In fact, he promised in interviews and speeches throughout the period that he would not repeat Gorbachev's mistakes, that he would be decisive. Paradoxically, though, this fear of disintegration steered conversation away from radical political change. The focus was on preserving Russia, by avoiding potentially explosive discussions on the nature of the federation and on the institutions.

The existing constitution could have been seen as a glaring obstacle to democratization. It dated to the Brezhnev era and was riddled with internal contradictions stemming from the reforms of the Gorbachev era. Those reforms brought confusion to politics by establishing contested authority between the communist-controlled legislative bodies and the newly created institution of the presidency, both of which claimed ultimate decision-making authority. Moreover, Russia's communist-dominated national legislature, divided into the unwieldy Congress of People's Deputies that met sporadically but held ultimate authority and the standing Supreme Soviet, mimicked the same structure of the Soviet Union's legislative bodies. It was from those bodies that much of the leadership of and inspiration for the coup emerged. It was from those bodies that much of the opposition that prevented decisive change in any sphere, political or economic, emerged.

But Yeltsin could rationalize that Russia's Congress and Supreme Soviet were different, that they had been elected in contests more competitive, more free, and more fair than the Union Congress and Supreme Soviet, and as such would avoid their problems. Russia's process had not reserved one-third of the seats for the communists, for example. Indeed, those elections were probably the freest, fairest elections Russia has had, as subsequent chapters will show. It seemed that Russia already had a democratically elected national legislature, and it was a supportive legislature. The commitment to democratic politics was, rhetorically at least, widespread. Furthermore, the legislature and its leaders had stood so firmly and resolutely with Yeltsin against the hard-line coup, and had stood with Yeltsin in favor of the creation of the Commonwealth of Independent States. There seemed to be no urgency for political reform, much less for demolishing the legislature, and this attitude offered a powerful disincentive to embark on a risky, controversial political gambit.

Most important, however, the prevailing attitude regarding the political system among Yeltsin and his advisors was of a victory won, not of a monumental challenge before them. There was good reason for this attitude. Gorbachev was gone. Communism was finished. Russia was on its own, and Yeltsin and his team held power. Why rush? Why panic? Russia had held free elections; there obviously existed political competition and opposition; free speech was evident; and the newspapers, radio, and television were all dynamic and uninhibited. There it is! Russia was now a democracy! All of the former subjects of the Soviet Union, all of the former communist republics, now had independence, and that meant they, too, had democracy. While the idea of radical steps, beginning with the dissolution of all communist-era political institutions including the legislature and the constitution, did exist in society, in some activist circles, and among some foreign observers, it simply was not voiced in the circles of power around the president as none of his advisors saw the need.

The attitude blinded the leaders to the strong warning signs that foretold a repeat of a dual power conflict with the Supreme Soviet. For example, the first pronouncements from the Supreme Soviet and its leader on Russia's first day as an independent state included the sharpest possible criticism of Yeltsin and his government, and of their very legitimacy to rule.[7] Supreme Soviet Chairman Ruslan Khasbulatov trumpeted the constitutional principle that the Supreme Soviet held supreme power, a foreshadowing of the irreconcilable conflict to come. Yeltsin himself had almost been impeached by that same legislature, in March 1991. It was only Gorbachev's political incompetence that saved Yeltsin. Gorbachev clearly wanted Yeltsin out. But he apparently did not understand the political situation or the motivations of either the political elite or the society. He sent military personnel to seal off the center of Moscow on the day impeachment was to be discussed, and the Russian legislators immediately changed their focus from impeachment to a vigorous defense of Russian sovereignty, and of Yeltsin.[8] Moreover, the Supreme Soviet failed in numerous votes to support Yeltsin's choice for his replacement as Chair.[9] The Supreme Soviet had never been particularly close to or supportive of Yeltsin and would certainly not become more so under Khasbulatov.

Given these signs and the continuation of the institutional framework from the Soviet period, it is surprising that Russia's new leaders paid no heed. Despite the warning signs that the legislature would follow the same obstructionist path as the former Union legislature, blocking market economic and democratic political transformation, there was no sense of a looming political danger. When Yeltsin climbed on top of the tank to declare the defeat of the coup plotters, right next to him was Supreme Soviet Chairman Khasbulatov, whom Yeltsin had handpicked as his successor to lead the legislature. They were allies; Yeltsin had worked hard through a lengthy ordeal spanning five separate votes to get the legislature to finally approve Khasbulatov as Chair. Indeed, Yeltsin had insisted upon Khasbulatov for that leadership post.[10] They stood together to win a joint victory against the coup. As one Cabinet member at the time recalled, "Yeltsin thought the Supreme Soviet would be his. Khasbulatov was his friend and owed his position to Yeltsin. So he said, 'let's go!' We had all the political levers we needed.... Maybe it was [Yeltsin's] mistake, but he led that very same deputy hall. He was elected by them. Yeltsin thought they would continue to support him."[11] Russia's leaders believed they had a winning team in place. Why shake the landscape and risk new elections? They had won together, they had stood together, they supported each other, and they could now govern together.

One source has suggested that Yeltsin did hedge when it came to the larger Congress of People's Deputies. Yeltsin's longtime speech writer, Lyudmilla Pikhoya, recalls that the president carried in the inside pocket of his suit coat, to every session when the Congress met, a speech declaring the dissolution of the Congress. She remembers frequently rewriting the speech to keep it current.[12] If this was in fact the case at the time, it may have been more in the vein of wariness rather than intent; there is no evidence that anybody around the president advocated dissolving the Congress at that time; nobody proposed such radical political measures.[13] It seems far more likely, however, that this individual's memories of the period from mid-1993 have been transposed onto the earlier period of concern here.

It also cannot be dismissed that a palpable fatigue with anything having to do with political reform blinded some to any need for such reform.

Halfhearted tinkering with legislative, executive, electoral, and other political institutions and rules had muddled and bogged down Gorbachev's rule for years, and people were tired of all of the talk without results. "You can't eat *glasnost*" was a popular refrain in Russian society, referring to the slogan, loosely translated as "openness," that stood for Gorbachev's political liberalization policies. The newspapers were thriving with criticism, but the quality of life continued to plummet. People were tired of political talk, and that fatigue extended into the very political elite that suddenly found itself in power. Paradoxically, at the same time this elite was so energized by the communist collapse and the new frontier ahead, they were also tired of discussion and debate about political reform. On some level, they did not see a need because they did not want to.

"Nothing Was Prepared"

Reinforcing perceived absence of need was the practical absence of a plan for rapid and radical political change. The two go hand in hand. The lack of a plan or even of ongoing discussions contributed to the lack of a sense of urgency, while complacency prevented attention to or inspiration for pursuing such discussions. One reason nothing was prepared was because nobody foresaw the sudden dissolution of the Union. It just had not occurred to any of Yeltsin's advisors that a new government of a new state on the territory of Russia was a possibility, much less an imminent possibility in 1991. Their efforts were not toward separating Russia from the Union, but rather on improving the Soviet system, on transforming the terms on which the Union was formed. The greatest intellectual legal and political energy at the time was invested in the Novo-Ogarevo negotiations for a "New Union Treaty."[14] Even after the failed coup in August 1991, triggered by the anticipated signing of that treaty, that process continued to occupy the time and effort of the Russia's political leadership. That a single state would not occupy the territory of the Soviet Union (with the possible exception of the Baltic States) came as a surprise even at the end of 1991 to most people inside Russia and abroad. That in retrospect the warning signs were there, and that the August coup seemed obviously to mark the end of the USSR, does not deny the fact that, in late 1991, the disintegration of the country caught most people, including Russia's political elite, off guard. It was a shock.

Several of Yeltsin's closest advisors in those first months confirm this as the central reason for the exclusive focus on economics. "We had no plan for democratic political reform. Nothing was prepared. We had no draft constitution."[15] The focus was on completing a new Union agreement and holding elections for the new President of the USSR. It was for that election that Yeltsin was preparing. He and his team had their sights on defeating Gorbachev for the leadership of the Union, not just of Russia.[16] When that process imploded and the Soviet Union disappeared, they were disoriented and unprepared for how to proceed. If anything, they fought the last war, worrying that the disintegration process would spread to Russia itself. And not without reason, given the fate of the Union and of Yugoslavia, another federated system.[17] Nobody can seriously argue that Russia enjoyed the sort of internal consensus regarding the political future that Poland, the Czech Republic, and the Baltic States, for example, enjoyed. There were legitimate worries that divisions in society and among the political elite could provoke Russia's own collapse.

On the other hand, none of these negates the fact that different responses to the situation, alternative courses of action, were possible. When communism suddenly collapsed in Czechoslovakia in November 1989, there was no draft democratic constitution to submit for adoption; there had been no ongoing intensive negotiations that had produced consensus about the shape of a new political system. Nor were plans in place elsewhere in Eastern Europe when communism collapsed. The collapse in those states was equally rapid, equally disorienting, and equally unexpected. Russia also could look at those states and draw lessons. The lessons learned in the two years between communism's collapse in those states and in Russia suggested that rapid political change, as occurred in the Czech, Polish, and Hungarian cases, was beneficial to democracy while delay, as in Romania, Bulgaria, and Yugoslavia, would put barriers in democracy's path. Such lessons were available on one level though not on another, which proved to be decisive. Russia's decision-makers were not used to taking their former client states seriously in terms of offering models for their own country's political development.

While it is true that Russia lacked a general national consensus in favor of democratic or capitalist transformation, the question remains whether it existed in the other postcommunist states or whether new leaders such as Vaclav Havel and Lech Walesa helped to forge and cajole a consensus. They certainly did push through democratic change. Russia's leaders blinked. Yeltsin could on January 1, 1992, have declared the end of the Soviet-era, suspended the constitutions and dissolved the political institutions, and convened all active groups to deliberate on Russia's political future. Had he done so, perhaps as happened elsewhere he could have forged some consensus in a roundtable process.[18] Without such steps, no consensus could emerge, no plan for a democratic future could develop. It was a monumental choice, and one that none of the central players even seems conscious of having made.

There is another important way in which the new team was unprepared to immediately introduce radical political change. Although Yeltsin enjoyed wide popular support, neither he nor his advisors had any faith in the loyalty of the military and in particular of the officer corps. As Yeltsin's former National Security Advisor, Yuri Baturin, put it, "A drastic action like shutting down the Congress of People's Deputies would have required that people take to the streets, and he did not want to do that. He could not rely on the security forces to support him because this was a period of transfer to a new state and Russia had no control of security forces before the coup."[19] That Russia was the legal inheritor of the Soviet military may have been logically clear and accepted abroad, but within the Russian military itself the issue was far from resolved. The military was as shocked as everyone else by the disappearance of the country it was sworn to protect. New allegiances, new lines of political subordination, had not even begun to be resolved internally. This was something that, for example, the new Polish leaders did not have to confront. Poland's military was Poland's military. There was no question that Poland was still Poland, although everything else may have changed. But Russia was not the Soviet Union. Indeed, even two years later the relationship with the military remained highly tenuous. It was only after lengthy negotiations in which Yeltsin personally intervened with the military leadership that units were found to implement the president's order to physically disband the Supreme Soviet.[20] In those first months of independence, as the President's Chief of Staff, Sergei Filatov, put it, "There were always doubts about the Army and security forces because their relationship with Yeltsin was very difficult. We worried about this."[21]

Finally, much of this new leadership was grossly inexperienced and unprepared for power. The most important individuals in the new Cabinet, Yegor Gaidar, Anatoliy Chubais, Gennadiy Burbulis, and Filatov, had little or no executive experience and less political training. Those who did have experience came from the Communist Party bureaucracy, in second- and third-tier positions. Yeltsin's inner circle, if not a group of dilettantes in power, was not a group of professional politicians either, and was most certainly not a group of experts on democracy. However, this should not be taken too far as an explanatory variable. It was precisely the lack of investment in the old regime that enabled the new leaders in Poland, in the Czech Republic, and in the Baltic States to move swiftly to demolish those old structures. As in those states, this could have worked in democracy's favor in Russia had the choice been made actively to pursue democratic political development. That choice, however, was not made.

"Yeltsin Always Preferred Compromise, To Work with Others"

Individuals matter in politics; leaders matter, so it is not trivial that Boris Yeltsin was Russia's president. Yeltsin assumed power proclaiming himself a liberal democrat, but he came to power after a thirty-year career in the Communist Party of the Soviet Union, including top leadership positions and a seat on the ruling Politburo in Moscow. It was not only Yeltsin's upbringing, however, that contributed to the aversion to rapid democratic political transformation. Other aspects of Yeltsin's personality mitigated against radical political moves in the winter of 1991–1992. Yeltsin has earned a public reputation as a radical, impulsive politician. Perhaps this was linked to his imposing physique, his booming voice, and his sometimes flamboyant behavior, penchant for the bottle not least among them.[22] Certainly his decisions often defied predictions and surprised even his advisors. He frequently shuffled Cabinet members, prime ministers, and advisors without warning or explanation, those demoted or removed learning of their fate in his public announcements.

While his decisions may have been unpredictable, they rarely were impulsive or rash. Particularly when dealing with political adversaries, Yeltsin was exceedingly cautious. Those who worked with Yeltsin consistently describe him as one who above all sought to avoid danger, indeed in times of danger he would gather himself and focus, seeking a compromise way out, rather than lash out and act rashly. He avoided radical steps, and "avoided confrontation until backed into a corner. He always sought compromise, to work with others, and only lashed out when given absolutely no choice."[23] The preponderance of the evidence supports this image of Yeltsin.

Until September 1993, he remained convinced that he could work with the legislature to find a common ground. He also closed his eyes to any evidence undermining his belief that the legislature and its leadership had no choice but to work with him. Another close advisor to Yeltsin offered a powerful example of this desire to seek compromise and negotiated solutions rather than imposing positions. In the days leading to the final clash with the Supreme Soviet, indeed up to the very moment when he ordered the tanks to fire on the parliament and after his opponents had begun armed violence in the capital, Yeltsin was still prepared to accept simultaneous legislative and presidential elections as a compromise way out of the crisis.[24] He offered and continued to offer this compromise.

This confirms another interpretation of Yeltsin by a longtime advisor that he "hated drawn-out fights, was always prepared to take risks in the name of victory, provided that victory was close at hand, but he often lost positional maneuvering."[25] Yeltsin understood after the dissolution of the Soviet Union that a painful period was coming, and focused his energy on forcing passage through that period as fast as possible. But he did not see the problems as political. They were economic. Political matters could be smoothed over and negotiated. Indeed, it was this orientation that set the tone among Yeltsin's team—they had reason to believe there was a unified approach in the country, that the legislature stood with them and that the constitutional structures in place were not a problem.

Such a view blocked consideration of radical steps such as elimination of Soviet-era political institutions, in particular the legislature, and suspending the Soviet-era constitution and convening a special assembly to write a new constitution. Despite the precedent elsewhere and the opportunity available to him to do so in Russia, this was simply not part of Yeltsin's reality. The consequence was that democracy would not become part of Russia's reality.

Objective Realities

It is difficult to fault anyone in Russia in 1992 for deciding to make economic reform a priority. On the contrary, it would have been scandalous and unforgivable not to. The objective realities of the time predisposed the new leadership to concentrate on the urgent problems in the economy. Economic collapse defined the basic condition of life in Russia at the time of the communism's demise. A massive economic crisis, a depression, stared the country's new leaders in the face. Gorbachev's half-reforms led to catastrophic budget deficits of nearly 20 percent of GDP covered by short-term borrowing and depletion of foreign currency reserves, official inflation that spiraled to over 200 percent with a real rate much higher, and a drop in national income in by over 20 percent. When prices were liberalized, Russia immediately experienced hyperinflation with rates as high as 1800 percent.[26] Industrial decline had brought domestic production nearly to a standstill. The ruble's black market rate fell more than a hundredfold. Money had lost meaning to the point where toilet paper was more valuable than the ruble.

Perhaps the most significant was the total absence of goods available to consumers. Store shelves were empty, and it did not matter what the store was. One afternoon in May 1991, a block-long, two-story bakery on Novy Arbat, in the center of Moscow, had thirty-six young female employees working back-to-back standing at empty candy counters. There was not a single piece of candy, not a single baked good, to be had on the second floor. On the first floor, a few scraps of hard, day-old brown bread littered a few of the bread bins. The other dozen or so bins intended to stock a wide array of fresh-baked bread were all empty. The sad sight was repeated across the city, and across Russia, in almost every type of shop. This was a full-blown economic disaster. Many goods were available only with ration coupons, and often not even then.

Among Yeltsin's most earnest proclamations upon assuming power in Russia was that he would not "repeat the mistakes made by Gorbachev."[27] When tweaking his former boss, however, he was mostly referring to economic, not political reform. Several detailed plans for economic reform, ranging from moderate reform to radical transformation of the entire economic system, had been developed, published, and widely discussed and were available for implementation. Gorbachev could never decide what he wanted, other than to remain in power. Although myriad economic reform plans existed, he never embraced one. Instead, he constantly shifted back and forth, seeming one day to embrace market reforms and the next acting contradictory to such a goal. This indecision and lack of commitment were maddening to Yeltsin and ultimately destructive to the Party and to the state.[28]

Yeltsin promised immediately to implement the most ambitious plan for radical economic reform in Russia at the time, which promised to create a market economy in 500 days.[29] His closest advisors were primarily economists, and they latched onto solving the economic crisis as the exclusive task. It was not the focus on economics was the problem. It was the exclusivity of the project, banishing political transformation from discussion, that was the problem for the future. It was not clear that there was ever a discussion or a conscious decision, either among Yeltsin's advisors or with the president, to pursue economic reform and ignore political reform. Rather, this decision was a result of a nondecision and lack of attention to the political question.

Several factors converged to direct the attention of Russia's leaders to the economic problems and neglect the political ones. First, the severity of the economic crisis was obvious, and there was a plan crafted and ready to implement, albeit a plan wildly optimistic in its claims.[30] Second, the Supreme Soviet and Congress had readily given over control of the economic sphere to Yeltsin in the form of temporary extraordinary powers. This was simultaneously a confirmation of the urgency of the economic problem and the absence of a political one, in the eyes of the president and his team. That the legislature's leadership foresaw the backlash to come, and positioned themselves to disassociate themselves from those policies, went seemingly unnoticed. The Kremlin, by ignoring political reform, allowed the situation to be set up precisely to divide those who they thought had been united. Third, there was at the same time a wariness of politics among those pushing the rapid economic reform. Not all lessons from the East European postcommunist experience were lost. It was well known that the first steps of liberalizing economic reforms would bring pain and hardship to many. It was also well understood that Russia retained a strong pro-communist presence. Elections would be risky, risky if not for the long-term possibility of market economic reform then for their own longevity in power, based on the experience across East-Central Europe. They deemed it better to hang on to power any way possible, in the name of advancing economic reform, than to risk elections in which a people upset over the course of economic policy would vote Yeltsin and those reforms.

If this sounds Bolshevik in its approach, the extant view of the relationship between economics and politics among the new Russian elite was Marxist. The prevailing attitude was that economic reform would be so effective, would bring such dramatic improvements to society, that politics would take care of itself. Put differently for these decision makers, economic reform *was* political reform, it would solve everything. Although the neoconservative Chicago school policies were hardly Marxist, the approach certainly was. One would be hard-pressed even today to find one of the architects of the reform, certainly not Yegor Gaidar, Anatoliy Chubais, or Alexei Kudrin, who would see any problem with this administrative approach to reform. They remain economic determinists to this day, believing that economic development will solve all other problems.[31]

This belief that Russia could enjoy successful liberal economic reform without simultaneously implementing democratic political reform was pie-in-the-sky thinking. But exactly such conviction was held by the highest decision makers in the Russian leadership, and was shared and advocated by foreign consultants and advisors, such as Jeffrey Sachs, who played a central role in designing the reform policies for the government, and by international organizations such as the International Monetary Fund and the World Bank, which were also involved in the creation of and mandated the adoption of those policies as the condition for financial and political backing.[32] The lack of attention to the importance of political institutions and rules for a functioning market economy was for the foreign advisors both inexcusable and inexplicably limited entirely to their advice to Russia. The blind eye turned to the attendant problem of corruption with economic reform carried out under these conditions was incredible. Nowhere else in the postcommunist world did those international advisors or institutions condone, much less advise, such neglect of political questions. The results were terrible for the vast majority of Russia's population, and in the end for open politics as well.

Traumatic Consequences

On October 3, 1993, armed violence erupted on the streets of Moscow. The Supreme Soviet had organized and armed thousands of communist and nationalist loyalists. These "Red-Browns" streamed from the Supreme Soviet headquarters on the Moscow River to take over targets in the center of Moscow, among them Ostankino, the main television broadcasting facility for the entire country. It was an attempted coup, and President Yeltsin took the only step he could. He struck back, ordering the physical destruction of the legislature, and the arrest of its leadership and the leaders of the armed groups. Army units in T-72 tanks carried out his orders, shelling primarily the top floors of the legislature, destroying the offices of the leadership and the document and communications centers. Later, special forces units entered the building, arresting the Vice President, the Speaker, and dozens of other prominent figures. Hundreds perished across the city.[33] The White House, the home of the legislature and the emblematic site of the dramatic resistance to the 1991 hard line communist coup against Gorbachev, was left a smoldering ruin.

President Yeltsin's Decree No. 1400 was the proximate trigger for the events. Issued on September 21, 1993, the decree dissolved Russia's legislature, suspended the constitution, and set elections for a new legislature and a referendum on the new constitution in less than three months.[34] This uni-lateral action was his long-awaited move to end the prolonged standoff with the intransigent legislature. In the year and a half since the Soviet collapse, the Russian legislature had become the center of an irreconcilable opposition to the president and his government, and found its *raison d'etre* in acting as a barrier to the adoption of a new constitution, as a block to fundamental change in the country. To enforce this role, its leaders had begun amassing arms and recruiting and training people to use them, housing militant leaders within its halls.

Decree No. 1400, however, cannot reasonably be called the cause of the conflict. The violent end to the constitutional standoff, and the standoff itself, was the consequence of the failure to introduce rapid political change immediately after the collapse. Had the same decree been issued twenty months earlier, and a constitutional assembly created to determine the country's political future, scant opposition would have been heard. Allowing the Soviet-era constitution and institutions to remain intact, however, propelled the Supreme Soviet into an oppositionist position, and its Speaker toward a strategy of ruling that legislature with an increasingly iron fist. The logic lay in the structure of that constitution and the rules of that legislature.[35] Guided by the incentives created by those rules, the Supreme Soviet developed into an uncompromising opposition to the president and his government, while claiming supreme powers for itself. Khasbulatov had steadily worked to elevate himself to a position of supreme authority in the country. Inside the legislature, he was virtually unchecked in pursuing political confrontation with the executive branch. He used Soviet-era consti-tutional provisions to pursue top authority in the country, issuing directives to and attempting to control regional legislative bodies, and issuing executive orders citing his authority under that constitution. He proclaimed himself equal to the president, and his acts created a situation of dual power in the country. He blocked any movement toward a new constitution, both inside the legislature he directly controlled and through instructives to the regional legislatures who were uncertain about the proper chain of command. He issued a stream of orders and resolutions on issues of national concern that were not directly legislative issues, and, ominously, created a Parliamentary Guard.[36] He led multiple attempts to impeach the president and increasingly used his power to call sessions of the broader Congress that effectively froze political activity in the country while challenging the authority of the president and his government. Dual power emerged in Russia, a dangerous situation that proved explosive. Left to fester for as long as it did, confrontation was inevitable, as it had been in the Union institutions two years earlier.

The window of opportunity in early 1992 was not the only one Yeltsin had to address the question of fundamental political change prior to the confrontation. Yeltsin and his team squandered an unusual second chance to bring about nonviolent political change in the months immediately preceding the "October events," as they have become known in Russia. In April 1993, Russia held a national referendum that registered a strong public expression of support for the president and his government's policies. This successful referendum offered an environment and a legitimacy to Yeltsin to take radical political action. The window of opportunity for change was exceedingly short after the referendum, and the president's advisors understood this too. All of the elements for rapid change were again in place. But for a second time, Yeltsin blinked. There is no guarantee that violence could have been avoided had he moved swiftly after the referendum to abolish the legislature, but it is certain that by not doing so he ensured a violent and more traumatic outcome later. Why the repeat of the paralysis on the matter of radical political change?

The president, exasperated over the mounting deadlock, issued a decree in December 1992 to hold a referendum on confidence in the president and to ratify the draft constitution he supported, which had been drafted by a team he had selected.[37] This plan never came about. The legislature went berserk, and the Constitutional Court ruled the president had violated the constitution as only the Congress had the power to call for a referendum. The Congress of People's Deputies, the larger assembly that elected the Supreme Soviet, in emergency session approved a different set of questions for the referendum: on trust in the President Yeltsin, on support for the government's economic reform policies, on the need for early presidential elections, and on the need for early legislative elections.

One wonders what may have happened had Yeltsin insisted on his two questions and gone ahead with them. The Central Election Commission is an executive body, in the sense that it implements decisions. Funding is released by the government. If the Kremlin had issued orders that the referendum contain the two questions initially announced, in trust in the president and ratification of the draft constitution he had endorsed, what would have transpired? There is no evidence, however, that anyone close to the president ever considered such an option. They instead accepted without question that the legislature controlled the right to write and submit questions for referenda. "Congress controlled the questions," which, while a fact, ignores the potential that existed to contest the reality.[38] It was probably a wise decision, however, as the legitimacy of such a move would have been hard to demonstrate. It would have been explicitly anticonstitutional and a direct violation of the Court ruling.

Khasbulatov, for his part, was not going to allow any questions about the dissolution of the legislature or any other question that would pose a threat to the legislature's existence or his leadership role. That meant no questions relating to a new constitution. Khasbulatov was steadfastly opposed to movement on a new constitution because the existing framework that endowed his legislature with supreme legal authority, or at least equal authority to the president, suited him perfectly well.[39] Although a Supreme Soviet commission had worked for nearly two years developing one, Khasbulatov and the leadership of the legislature had no interest in it, as adoption would have meant their departure from the stage. Khasbulatov had ultimate control over the legislature's agenda and consistently impeded any effort to move the discussion out of the commission. He had become an active barrier to the adoption of a new constitution. As a result, he successfully kept the question of the constitution off the referendum, and the legislature claimed for itself the right to interpret the results of the poll.

That claim was feeble however, as the results were clear for everyone to see. On all four questions, Yeltsin won. The Kremlin had aggressively campaigned for and the voters expressed trust in Yeltsin by a margin of 59–39 percent. Moreover, against almost everyone's expectations, the public supported Yeltsin's economic reform policies by 53–45 percent, despite the real difficulties the market reforms were causing for the majority of the population. There could hardly have been a clearer message of support for the president and opposition to the legislature than this, with the latter having staked its existence on opposition to further economic liberalization. On the other matters, the electorate rejected the idea of early presidential elections in a vote of 32–30 percent, while supporting early legislative elections, though without an absolute majority, by 43–19 percent.

President Yeltsin claimed a mandate based on these results, and not without reason. He had a strong basis for moving for bold political change. For one, the need was impossible for anyone to deny; the defects of the existing system were critical and obvious. The opposition was on the defensive, not having expected such strong support for the economic reforms and reeling from the clear expression of distaste for the legislature. Moreover, Yeltsin had encouraged a campaign leading up to the referendum that focused squarely on the need for a new constitution. A plan existed and had been brought to Yeltsin. The president's message in advance of the referendum was clear: a vote of support for the president meant a vote in support of rapid adoption of a new constitution for a new political system.[40]

If the window of opportunity was short immediately after the collapse, everyone knew it would be short after the referendum. The urgency was clear in the President's Council, where his closest advisors "expected a dramatic break, comparable to when Gaidar and his team of reformers first came to the government" and introduced radical economic change in January 1992.[41] They expected announcement of the dissolution of the legislature and a timetable and process for adoption of a new constitution. His speech writer acknowledged, "[Yeltsin] immediately understood that the Supreme Soviet needed to be dissolved."[42] A trusted political and legal advisor said, "he needed to name early elections."[43] Everyone expected Yeltsin quickly to end the standoff with the legislature and believed the referendum provided a firm basis for doing so.

The public once again was squarely behind the president and ready for radical political reform, and this time the political elite in Yeltsin's circle were advocating such change, had plans for how to carry it out, and had brought the ideas to the president. Yeltsin carried with him at all times a decree announcing the dissolution of the Supreme Soviet. The President's Council had given him a detailed plan for just such steps. He would use the expression of support for the economic policies to submit a new wave of economic laws on land ownership or privatization. These would be introduced with full expectation that the Supreme Soviet would immediately reject them. Yeltsin would then proclaim this as concrete evidence that the legislature ignored the will of the people and the referendum, and on this basis dissolve the body and call for ratification of a new constitution. Decrees had been drafted on these steps as well as on the formation of temporary legislative and administrative organs of power to function in the interim period. All of this could have been done in the first weeks immediately after the referendum, with a greater chance of avoiding violence. The legislature at that time had not organized such capability to cause violence and was still disoriented by the referendum results with many deputies who could have been expected to split with the legislature's leaders. Moreover, according to the military representatives on the President's Council, "the results of the referendum demonstrated the Army's support for the President."[44]

But Yeltsin took no such action. "The warnings issued by his closest democratic advisors, by many members of the President's Council, who called for using the results of the successful referendum to carry out more dynamic reforms and thereby limit the influence of the Communist Party, came to pass," as one authoritative account put it. "The President adopted virtually no measures to counter the preservation and in some regions increase in influence of the communists."[45] This time, we can squarely point to the president as responsible for inaction. The inaction is odd in retrospect given what he claims to have written in his diary:

> The people voted not just for Yeltsin. Yeltsin perhaps is not so important in and of himself. The people wanted something to happen. I consider this the main lesson of the referendum. Perhaps tomorrow they will reconsider, and support another authority. But today this craving for concrete action—which can be debated and argued about but in the end action—has not abated among the people even in this second year of reform.[46]

Spring of 1993 was not like January 1992. This time, the need for political change in Russia was obvious to almost everyone. Yeltsin's staff had placed such action squarely on the agenda. Not only was the need clear, the possibility had opened and plans had been crafted for radical political change. Economic reform was well under way, and the public had expressed support for continuing those reforms despite the widespread suffering. The people had also expressed confidence in and support for the president and his policies, while demonstrating opposition to the legislature and the political line being pursued by its leadership.

Former advisors offer myriad explanations for why he did not take such steps: he was sick; he was tired; work still needed to be done on the constitution before it could be adopted; one needed to prepare for the reaction of the legislature before announcing its dissolution; and the referendum results were ambiguous. These all have the air of grasping at straws, or befuddlement. Yeltsin was no more sick or tired the day after than he was the day before the referendum. One can announce a date for ratification of a constitution while leaving time for final revisions to the draft that existed. Dissolution of the legislature had been discussed, and now a basis for executing the decision existed. And while the referendum questions were not as clear as initially hoped, in particular on the ratification of a constitution, they did clearly signal public support for Yeltsin and for reform. The president and his advisors all understood it that way, as did their opponents who were shocked by the results.

It was the president who refused to act. He was a lifelong communist who seized opportunity to recast his image and propel himself to the apex of power. But that rise was not based on a deep commitment to the principles of liberal democracy or of limited government and sovereignty based on the will of the people. Yeltsin remained to the end naturally suspicious of and hesitant toward the implementation and the implications of a democratic political system. And so he wavered. His rationale followed a simple logic: "We won the referendum, we control the situation, and that means we get to choose the path." The Supreme Soviet would have "no choice" but to "heed the will of the people and work with him."[47] Rather than feeling backed into a corner, the type of situation that propelled him to decisive, unilateral action, Yeltsin saw himself as having been handed a clear victory. With this victory in hand, he followed his natural inclination to pursue a cooperative, compromise-seeking path. Reinforcing this was quite a bit of wishful thinking, namely, that the members of the Supreme Soviet, if not the leadership, would see the results of the referendum as he did and be guided by them.

As the subsequent and tragic events demonstrated, the wishful thinking was unfounded. Yeltsin decided to form a new deliberative body, the Constitutional Assembly to draft a new founding law for the country, including on that body members of the legislature, the business community, academics, and politicians. They spent two months working to take several draft constitutions, including those from the legislative commission and the president's advisors, and produce a single consensual document. They succeeded in reaching a compromise, published widely on July 12, 1993. But months had gone by and the people "less and less understood what was happening: what is this—reform or a revision of reform plans?"[48] The public was lost, and so was the opportunity for peaceful change. Within 100 days, public support for Yeltsin had plummeted and if the referendum were held again, he would have lost on every question.[49] It had been a short window, indeed. Yeltsin promised immediate action but did nothing concrete. The public became disillusioned.

Khasbulatov, meanwhile, was forming armed units within the legislature and reaching out to military units around the country.[50] As Yeltsin's window narrowed, he saw his opening. He began issuing orders to executive and legislative branch officials around the country in attempts to impede implementation of government decisions, citing the Supreme Soviet's role under the existing constitution. He issued confusing instructions to regional leaders regarding the Constitutional Assembly's draft constitution, which caused them to suspend analysis of the document, preferring to let the dispute in Moscow sort itself out before engaging in the labor-intensive effort of reading and proposing amendments to a draft constitution that may never see the light of day. The Russian Supreme Soviet did exactly what another legislature under an almost identical constitutional framework did at the Union level—became an intransigent opposition that claimed under the constitution supreme authority.[51] A dual-power situation arose, making implementation of government decisions increasingly difficult. Having ignored the question of radical political reform in January 1992, Yeltsin repeated the mistake after the referendum in 1993, the last chance to seize the initiative for nonviolent political reform. As it had at the Union level in 1991, the conflict between the Kremlin and the legislature turned violent in October 1993, this time with thousands of organized armed units attacking strategic locations around the capital, while army tanks countered by shelling the seat of the national legislature.[52]

It is no exaggeration to say that the demise of democratization itself was the long-term consequence of defaulting on the opportunity to shape a new political system at the start. The hesitation by those who called themselves democrats did immeasurable damage to the idea of democracy in Russia. By throwing the term around without resolute action to help bring about a democratic political system, Yeltsin and his advisors caused the very word "democracy" in Russia to become associated with political disorder and corruption. The rampant corruption that has plagued Russia since the beginning of this economic reform, both in the economy and among the political elite, is a direct consequence of the lack of transparency and absence of rule of law, both of which could have been addressed had political transformation been a focus from the beginning. Decisions about how to incorporate real political competition, how to foster and protect the organization of political and economic interest, and how to guarantee political and economic rights could only arise as part of a broad discussion of Russia's political institutional framework. The decision to ignore these questions in January 1992 directly led to the instability and conflict the next year.

The following chapter shows how, after that clash with the Supreme Soviet, a traumatized Yeltsin imposed on the country a constitution with minimal checks and balances to a superpowerful president, a system that set the stage for the consolidation not of democracy, but dictatorship under his successor. It created a political system in which the level of rights and freedoms for all would become dependent on the personality of the president himself. Without October 1993, Russia may instead have adopted a more balanced constitution. But the violent battle was a result of the failure to bring about rapid political transformation from the start. Ignoring that project led to the violent conflict, which derailed democracy. That unbalanced constitution would later be used to encroach on media independence and subtly rig Yeltsin's reelection. It would be used by a new rich elite to wed their own corrupt behavior to the innermost circles of power. It would be used to subvert competitive politics in the choice of Yeltsin's successor, in a hand over of power to Vladimir Putin. Putin would use the precedents to consolidate a dictatorship, closing the space for political competition and open politics.

Obviously, there is no guarantee whatsoever that had Yeltsin declared an end to the legislature and the constitution in January 1992 that a democratic system would have been created or would have stabilized. The decision to leave the communist-era institutions and constitution in place, however, put a massive barrier in the path to democracy around which Russia has been unable since to navigate.

3

Corrupting the Constitution: The Decision to Hedge Against Democracy

The decision to leave the old institutions in place produced the same sort of political crisis of contested power in Russia in 1993 that it produced in the Soviet Union in 1991. A forcible attempt to seize control of the apex of power in the Kremlin emerged from the Congress of Peoples' Deputies, the national legislature. This time, the leaders of the uprising amassed arms, gathered nationalist militants prepared to use them, and organized plans to use them. Yeltsin's response culminated in the October 1993 battle on the streets of Moscow, broadcast around the world, and highlighted most traumatically by the shelling of the legislature's "White House" building.

Widespread speculation in Moscow, in the wake of the violent fight with the Supreme Soviet, was that Yeltsin would succumb to the temptations of unchecked power and rule indefinitely like a dictator. Others hoped a liberal democratic system could finally emerge. Yeltsin, however, while consistently trumpeting democracy in his rhetoric, never fully reflected those principles in his actions. He never sought dictatorial power either. One account holds that he "understood the historical importance" of this period of unchecked power, and moved to ensure that there would be swift adoption of a new constitution and elections to a new legislature within three months.[1] Still, the trauma of the conflict was real, and affected the president and his closest advisors alike. Yeltsin proved ambivalent about the nature of political power.

The resolution of the October crisis at a minimum offered a new opportunity for Yeltsin and his administration to offer a framework for democratic politics, institutions, and processes. It was a critical period for democratic development, for now Yeltsin literally held unchecked power, he and his team had a clean slate to work with, to present to the country a new political system with which to go forward. It was, therefore, an opportunity to entrench democratic principles in a new constitution. But there was little that was clear or simple about this period. The trauma through which everyone had just emerged worked against a pro-democratic outcome. It prevented the focus from being on the opportunity to advance the cause of democracy, diverting attention to matters of security. Yeltsin and his advisors felt as if at war. The result was a constitution vulnerable to the consolidation of dictatorship rather than promising for the future of democracy.

There were options available, options that on the surface offered hope for a democratic outcome to the horrible events that had just transpired. The Constitutional Assembly had completed its work over the summer.[2] On July 12, it unveiled and widely published a compromise draft constitution that it had adopted and that had received presidential approval. Yeltsin's closest advisors, including his chief of staff, led the proceedings and were actively engaged in every step of the process. Yeltsin himself accepted the draft that the Constitutional Assembly had approved in all five of its chambers. That meant it had approval from virtually the entire political spectrum. The Constitutional Assembly's chambers included members of the now-defunct Supreme Soviet Constitutional Commission, representatives from a wide range of political parties and interest groups, business leaders, politicians from all of the country's regions, and legal experts. The Assembly had managed to take elements from many drafts, including one written over several years in the Supreme Soviet Constitutional Commission and another that Yeltsin had requested from a small group of handpicked legal advisors, to hammer out a compromise draft.[3] That compromise included a strong section on rights and freedoms, taken largely from the "Supreme Soviet draft," a strong presidential political system, as envisioned in the "Yeltsin draft," and a balance of powers between legislative, executive, and judicial branches achieved in the give-and-take of negotiations in the Assembly's working groups.[4]

With his approval of the draft, Yeltsin authorized its publication and distribution for discussion in July, on the understanding that it would serve as the basis for adoption. What remained was to decide on a process for adoption. This draft remained unamended at the time of the October confrontation with the Supreme Soviet. It was available after that crisis to be ratified in the national referendum on a new constitution that Yeltsin's decrees mandated be held in December, along with elections to a new legislative body which that constitution would establish.[5]

However, the referendum on the constitution did not ratify this draft. Instead, shortly after the violence ended, Yeltsin empowered a small working group to make substantial revisions to the draft Constitution, in light of the crisis and the removal of the Supreme Soviet from the political scene. Over the next several weeks this group worked, and the final draft published in November and voted on in December was the result of their work.

If one counts by articles amended, the vast majority of the changes consisted of innocuous linguistic revisions. Only a few of the articles underwent substantive changes. But those substantive changes undermined the core democratic principle of balance of powers between the executive and legislative branches. They did so by removing from the document legislative levers for checking the president and his government, creating an unchecked, superpowerful presidency. With these changes, the nature of politics in the country, the prospects for democracy in Russia, would depend, not so much on adherence to formal rules and laws, as on the personal predilections of the individual occupying the office of the president. A president who tolerates opposition, works to forge consensus, is guided by principles of openness, accountability, and representative government, remained a possible outcome in Russia. To his everlasting credit, Yeltsin generally did try to adhere to those principles. He always allowed criticism, opposition politics, and an open media. But that same constitution also enabled a president to ignore or work against these democratic principles, and that is what has ultimately enabled a return to dictatorship under Vladimir Putin.[6]

While the earlier draft would by no means have guaranteed a democratic future for Russia, the substantive changes made to that draft weakened the prospects for democracy by substantially weakening checks on presidential authority. They opened the door to an incumbent who so desired to assume unhindered authority, and thereby seriously reduced the hopes for a democratic outcome in Russia. Exactly what happened and why has remained a mystery. Nothing clear has been written about the circumstances surrounding these changes; indeed, the very fact that the constitution as adopted contained substantial changes to the July Constitutional Assembly draft still comes as a surprise to many among the political elite in Russia.

Although the period fills the final three volumes of the stenogram records of Constitutional Assembly sessions, a reading of those volumes makes it abundantly clear that the important discussions took place elsewhere, in private discussions, after the October crisis.[7] Something was going on behind the scenes involving the most fundamental aspects of the new constitution. Who made the critical changes that undermined democratic checks and balances in the constitution? Why did they make those changes, and by what process? This chapter offers some answers to these questions. While parts of the story remain unclear, the following pages explain who were behind the changes and why they made them, and analyze the content and significance of both the changes and the process for the prospects for democracy in Russia.

"Since I Heard Last Night on Television That the President Had Already Decided His Position on This, I Don't See Where Our Opinion Is Really Important"

While the fight with the Supreme Soviet remained a political battle, Yeltsin pursued compromise and negotiation. It was Yeltsin who convened the Constitutional Assembly and mandated that it include members of the Supreme Soviet Constitutional Commission. The Assembly considered as a basis for the new constitution both the Supreme Soviet Commission's draft and the draft produced by Yeltsin advisors in developing a consensus version. A process was in place for moving forward with inputs from regional executives and legislatures, possible amendment in the Assembly based on those comments and suggestions, and submission of the resultant draft for final adoption of the Constitution.

However, after the armed conflict, everything changed. Formal rules and the purity of the process became less important; Yeltsin and his staff still felt and acted as if they were operating under conditions of attack. "Yeltsin, having won the fight, wanted to secure the victory by strengthening presidential at the expense of legislative powers. It was a matter of seizing the victory they had won."[8] One of the architects of the constitution scoffed in retrospect at the notion they could have proceeded with the July draft that included the concessions to the Supreme Soviet. "Imagine yourself Yeltsin. Yesterday evening they almost shot you. Now in the morning you go to work and say, 'Let them all remain!' Is this possible? No!"[9]

From the perspective of Yeltsin's team, it was the other side, the Supreme Soviet, that had acted in a manner requiring action from the Kremlin. The other side destroyed the possibility for compromise, prepared to attempt an armed seizure of power, and provoked the violence. They had delegitimized their role in the constitution-writing process with those actions. There was in the Kremlin no euphoric feeling of victory. They felt attacked and responded accordingly. One can interpret the approach to the Constitution either as a rush to consolidate the victory and prevent any repeated attempt to attack the regime or as being guided by the notion that any concessions made prior to the clash were invalid and subject to revocation.

Both attitudes are evident in the comments of Yeltsin's Chief of Staff Filatov, who ran the Constitutional Assembly process and was involved in the small group that made the final changes to the draft. Filatov frequently instructed the participants to "take account of the events of October 3–4."[10] He explained, "The last draft of the Constitution was adopted in the Constitutional Assembly as the result of an earlier period, when we exerted all efforts to reach compromises, compromises with the Supreme Soviet and with the ideology which it represented." This meant that, "it is now possible to undo several of the compromises which found their way into the draft Constitution before the October situation."[11]

In short, the constitution-writing process in Russia was not one of founding fathers writing a pretty text to withstand the test of time. As one Western analyst put it, "Yeltsin and his team were hastily and haphazardly imposing a new set of political rules on the Russian Federation."[12] A polarized political environment fraught with conflict defined the process prior to October, and fear and trauma defined it after. Fear inclined Russia's political elite to make decisions that would erect enormous barriers in the way of democratization. So, too, did a form of group think to which even the intellectual elite were highly susceptible. As one writer lamented in an op-ed piece at the time, "Today the circle of Russian intelligentsia…instead of trying to form some kind of opposition to Yeltsin in order to introduce some kind of correction to the unchecked activities of [the president] and his entourage, is again applauding all the leader's undertakings and is again urging him to take resolute measures…. We have experienced all of this before."[13]

If there had been no October crisis, a more balanced institutional arrangement would still have satisfied the administration as an acceptable constitutional outcome. The Constitutional Assembly's compromise draft of July could have gone forward. In the aftermath of the armed conflict, however, Filatov, Shakhrai, and others involved in the process felt like partisans in a violent battle who had emerged in their bloody battle gear. The White House was still smouldering. Yeltsin and his advisors had escaped political destruction at best, physical destruction at worst. Under these conditions, and quite understandably, balancing powers and including all political interests in discussions on the future political system was hardly at the forefront of their minds. Their overriding priorities were to protect themselves, individually and politically, and to guarantee political security for Yeltsin, his team, and his policies. They wanted, above all else, to insure that the opposition that had just taken up arms would never again be able to take such action. In other words, they were still fighting the battle.

While the short-term consequence of not taking swift action after the April referendum was the violent conflict in October, the long-term consequence for democracy of that failure was to restrict the range of possible constitutional outcomes. It created conditions during the final drafting of the Constitution unfavorable to open politics, wide-ranging dissent, and open negotiation. Prior to the fighting, the plan was to elect an interim legislature that would make the final changes to the Constitutional Assembly's draft, considering above all proposed amendments from regional legislative and executive bodies, and then ratify the final document within six months, after which there would be new presidential elections. This plan was in accordance with Yeltsin's Decree No. 1400, which dissolved the Supreme Soviet. After the October violence, however, Yeltsin decided, in a new decree, that the constitution would be adopted simultaneously with the election of the new legislature, in a national referendum.[14] The opportunity for continued open discussion and the involvement of a variety of political forces in the country was gone. So, too, were hopes for constitutional checks and balances.

Yeltsin reformed the Constitutional Assembly, collapsing the earlier five chambers into two, a Social Chamber and a State Chamber. The former included representatives from political parties, interest groups, and business leaders while the latter included representatives of regional and local governments, legal experts allied to Yeltsin, and members of the administration. The records offered no indication as to how many participated in either chamber, and names only appeared when one spoke from the microphone, but no list appeared. Those who did participate, however, noticed a dramatically changed discussion when the body reconvened on October 15. They engaged in discussion but had no role in writing or changing the final text. They were informed of but not making decisions. Delegates no longer paid close attention to the details.

There had been a fight, and Yeltsin emerged the victor. But he and his team were traumatized victors, of a fight they had not wanted and, in the Kremlin's eyes, a fight forced on them by the Supreme Soviet.[15] In this defensive, frightened mode, Yeltsin and his advisors were using all the levers they could, and the Assembly essentially had the role to watch and approve. Less than one month before the draft had to be published in advance of the December referendum, even the Working Commission only met for two two-hour sessions daily, from 10 A.M. to noon, and from 4 to 6 P.M. The substantive work was being done somewhere else, not in these formal bodies.

The Working Commission was a smaller body containing members of the larger Assembly who wished to work on a more regular basis on the constitution. According to the Stenograms, any member of the Assembly was free to take part, though they were requested either to work full time or not at all, as latecomers or interlopers tended to disrupt work and lurch the group back to matters already decided upon when they unexpectedly dropped in. At most a few dozen took part. In addition to this, on September 8, 1993, Yeltsin formed a Working Group, of twenty-three members, to work out the final version of the draft. This group included several members of the old Supreme Soviet Constitutional Commission and several Yeltsin advisors and legal experts.[16] However, just three weeks after he formed the group, he issued Decree No. 1400 dissolving the Supreme Soviet. There is no record of this group convening after the October crisis.

What Filatov and others refer to as the "Working Group" or "Expert Group" was not this body. Rather, it was a tiny group of, at most a handful of, close Yeltsin loyalists, including Filatov himself, who made the substantial changes to the draft constitution. The real work was done in this smaller, ad hoc group. No records exist from their deliberations, and exactly who was involved remains a mystery. Filatov said he headed the group "and included the leaders of each Chamber [of the Constitutional Assembly]. We used a small group to edit proposals. Baturin also had the idea of including leading judges and academic experts."[17] But Baturin, far from having played a central role, expressed opposition to the changes, skepticism about the process, and was not included.[18] Moreover, as discussed in the next section, the head of one of the two chambers, Anatoliy Sobchak, issued such blistering attacks against the changes that it is simply not credible to suggest he played a central role in writing them. Filatov certainly was, but it remains unclear who else was involved.

That the identities of the authors of the changes remains shrouded in mystery more than a decade later in itself confirms it was a closed process, one by definition incompatible with democratic principles. It was an unfortunate precedent from the start for the new founding rules for the country. The changes made in this process undermined some of the most important democratic provisions, those aimed at limited and accountable government. No dissenting voices were allowed. Advisors such as Satarov, who would have argued for going ahead with the July draft as hammered out in the Constitutional Assembly, were not asked to take part and were isolated from the developments. Those who became aware and were troubled by the moves found a stone wall when they tried to protest, as "Yeltsin did not want to hear it."[19] The changes that removed or watered down checks on executive authority "were not discussed in a wide circle. Two or three people, no more."[20]

While the Constitutional Assembly chambers and Working Commission met, the record of their proceedings reveals that the decisions were in fact made by the small group of Yeltsin's closest advisors or by the President himself. The intent and effect of those changes was to alter the balance of power to provide maximum authority to the presidency with limited possibilities for interference from the new parliament. The working group reported directly to the President on a daily basis. Filatov, referring to the October crisis and violence with the Supreme Soviet, reports that this group "took account of the events that had just occurred," and "redid almost everything concerning state structures."[21] They made few but critical changes to Chapters 4–6, on the president, the Federal Assembly, and the government, respectively.

President Yeltsin remained actively involved. Filatov clearly referred to Yeltsin in his opening address to the Working Commission after the violent events, on October 15. After cryptically mentioning the changes written to the draft by the "working group," he said, "I think that these should be included in the final adoption of the draft constitution, all the more so as this will ensure support from those who are closely monitoring this constitutional process."[22] On critical issues, Yeltsin himself made decisions that would have lasting consequences. During the Working Commission deliberations, for example, when discussion of the hot topic of whether government ministers could simultaneously sit in the lower house of the legislature, the State Duma, one member said, "We were instructed to work on [this] question...but since I heard last night on television that the president had already decided his position on this, I don't see where our opinion is really important."[23] And, in the end, it was not. The Constitutional Assembly had little substantive impact in the weeks between the October crisis and the final publication of the draft constitution in early November. As just one example, the Societal Chamber of the Constitutional Assembly voted by a large margin to reject the change allowing members of the government to serve in the Duma, their vote proved meaningless.[24] The provision remained in the rules governing the transitional period; Yeltsin overruled the Assembly's decision. Filatov sternly rejected any voice raised against this decision, and continually referred to Yeltsin's decrees. Despite a similar vote in the full Assembly, Yeltsin himself decided.[25]

There are similar occurrences throughout the record. For example, the Assembly voted overwhelmingly to include the heads of government of each federation member as members of the federal government, a provision which, despite the vote, never found its way into Article 110 of the constitution.[26] Notwithstanding the argument that a constitutional provision making governors cabinet members would have been at best of questionable wisdom, the Constitutional Assembly deliberated, voted, and was summarily ignored. Filatov said "the decision was made *dehors* the Constitutional Assembly, in working order," meaning, in closed discussions with Yeltsin and one or two advisors.[27] Yeltsin also made changes with his own pen to what turned out to be the penultimate draft. For example, he added as the second item in the list of powers of the president the right to chair sessions of the government, and he added a provision that made the Federation Council, the upper house of the legislature, an ad hoc body during the transitional period of the first two years of the constitution.[28] But these were not the most serious changes hastily made to the draft Constitution in the few weeks before its ratification. The seismic shifts concerned control over the government.

"So We Are Going to Make It the Ratification of an Autocracy"

Although several dozen changes were made, those that affected the development of democracy concerned a handful of changes in Chapters 4–6, on the president, Federal Assembly, and government. These substantially altered the relations between the president and the legislature on the question of control over and responsibility for the government. Who names the members and head of the government, who has the power to remove them, and who controls the policies of the government, in short, the balance of powers between the executive and legislative branch, were the subject of the changes made to the draft constitution after the October crisis.

It was these issues that had caused deadlock between the Supreme Soviet and the Kremlin. They were the most important issues the Constitutional Assembly had resolved in the July draft. Then, in October, those compromises were no longer to be honored. Yeltsin authorized changes to that consensus draft of July that significantly widened the power imbalance in favor of the presidency. The greatest of these powers, those allowing the president to name the prime minister and government ministers, to chair government sessions, to head the Security Council, and to determine the state's domestic and foreign policies, all appeared after the October crisis, and undid compromise language that would have brought stronger checks and balances between the branches of government.

The sharpest debate in the two years of discussion on a new constitution had swirled around the power to appoint and dismiss the prime minister. The Constitutional Assembly had struck a compromise between the Supreme Soviet's draft, which called for a parliamentary system in which the government would spring from the legislative body, and Yeltsin's, which would have put the government entirely under presidential authority. The compromise July draft read that the president "shall submit to the State Duma a proposal on the appointment of the Chairman of the Government." However, the Duma would have jurisdiction over "appointment of the Chairman of the Government."[29] The president would submit a candidate, and the Duma would have the power to confirm appointment. The president would approve the prime minister's selections for the other ministerial appointments, in effect giving the president control over those posts.

The changes made after the October crisis undid these compromises reached earlier. Now, as the first in an extraordinary list of presidential powers in the constitution, the president "appoints the chair of the government with agreement from the State Duma."[30] The Duma's role is "to give its agreement to the president's appointment of the chair of the government."[31] Combined with other changes and existing provisions, the legislature lost the ability to check executive branch power. This change undid the most important compromise in the new constitution, a compromise reached after years of debate, a compromise to which Yeltsin had given his agreement less than three months earlier, a compromise reached with the widest possible group of representatives from all walks of life around the country. It affected the single most important issue of relations between the legislative and executive branches. The significance is understood only in the context of other provisions. Indeed, Filatov scoffed at those who wished to dwell on the appointment power, given another change the working group made to give the president exclusive power to dismiss the government. The Constitutional Assembly's compromise draft of July read, "The president has the right to raise the question of the government's resignation before the State Duma."[32] The Duma, however, again held the power of decision. The Working Group eliminated the Duma from the process, with the provision now reading, "The president may adopt a decision on the dismissal of the government."[33] The Duma would no longer have a role in the dismissal process. As a result, Yeltsin secured for the president the power to appoint and dismiss the government, relegating the Duma to observer status. The legislature would have no powers over government personnel.

In the public record, the idea for these changes first appears in an almost offhanded way during discussion of a minor issue, in the form of a question to Filatov. Filatov seized on the matter, saying, "Let's hand this over to the experts, let them work on it."[34] This quickly became the center of discussions, as the change necessarily affected provisions in several other articles relating to appointment of government ministers, dismissal of ministers and of the entire government, and of the Duma's role in confirming ministers and in holding votes of no confidence. In fact, a reading of the record of Constitutional Assembly proceedings of October 1993 makes clear that the formula of strong checks and balances was gone even before the discussion was raised in the meeting. Filatov put it bluntly, "If we trust our president, as the top official, with the formation of the government and responsible for its actions, we need to give him complete freedom in this regard—that is, to appoint [the prime minister] with approval [from the Duma], but to dismiss without the need for approval."[35] And so, in fact, it went.

Control over government policy and personnel is the defining factor for institutional balance in a system with a president, a prime minister, and a legislature. The democratic principle of separation of powers combined with checks and balances requires that the government neither spring from the legislature as in a parliamentary system, for that would leave the president with emasculated authority, nor be under the exclusive authority of the president, for this would render the legislature powerless. Balanced powers are necessary to prevent any one entity from amassing too much power. Democracy is predicated on shared, open processes of decision making. Constitutional provisions placing unchecked power in the hands of a president open the door for closed processes, rights abuses, and violations of basic democratic principles. The Constitutional Assembly had understood that shared responsibility and balanced powers would be needed in a democratic system, and achieved a compromise that would have brought shared responsibility. That compromise gave the legislature a formal power to appoint the president's nominee to head the government. It would have required negotiation, transparency, accountability, and representative input.

After October, however, the Yeltsin administration lost interest in sharing power with the legislative body. They were still fighting the last battle with the Supreme Soviet that had tried "to appropriate to itself the government's powers," and to restore communist-era personnel and policies. That intransigent position, and the Supreme Soviet's role in stalling implementation of policy, provoked Yeltsin to act to dissolve it. In the wake of the violent dispute, Yeltsin and his advisors now moved to put the powers squarely under the office of the president.[36] Having won the battle, now the president would guarantee such contestation would never happen again. That these changes directly flowed from the victory over the Supreme Soviet, and from Yeltsin's desire to remove the possibility of legislative checks on the executive branch, Filatov made explicitly clear later, in defending the changes before the full Assembly. "A government between two centers of power— the parliament and the president—does not allow for stability in the country. This was confirmed by the [recent] events," Filatov said.[37] "The lessons of October 3–4 [demonstrate], unfortunately, that when we developed the conception of the separation of powers…this would not have supported normal cooperation, normal and complete working collaboration between these branches."[38] In the wake of the trauma, "normal" understandably came to mean an executive unchallenged by another branch. It did not necessarily mean democratic. Yeltsin, operating in the traumatic environment after the October crisis, was now inclined to separation, but not balance, of powers. The president would hold the powers.

Nowhere in the Stenograms of the Constitutional Assembly is any opposition visible after October to giving the president exclusive power to dismiss the prime minister. Not even after Filatov's frequent observations on the significance of the change. "If the formula is such, that the president on his own can dismiss the government without legislative approval, then it makes no difference how the government is appointed."[39] Filatov frequently repeated this point during debate over the appointment language. If the president can dismiss government ministers at will, singly or as a whole, then the question of who formally appoints them is inconsequential. Some found debatable, or did not understand, Filatov's suggestion that the appointment process was trivial, for the issue repeatedly came up in the discussions, and in the Working Commission there was an even split on how to word the question of the appointment of the prime minister. But Filatov was right, ultimately that issue is not significant, and nowhere in the Stenograms is there evidence that anyone ever questioned Filatov's view of the importance of the dismissal power, nor can there be found any opposition to investing that power exclusively in the president.

The extraordinary nature of these changes, and the degree to which they emasculated legislative powers, becomes clear when one considers them in the context of a provision already agreed to, a concession made to Yeltsin in the Constitutional Assembly before October. That compromise allowed a president, in the event the Duma expresses no confidence in the government, to respond by dissolving the Duma and calling new elections. This, the argument went, would prevent disagreements over government policy or personnel "from turning into a crisis."[40] When the Constitutional Assembly made this concession to the president's draft, however, it did so as part of a larger set of compromises under which the Duma would have held the powers to appoint and dismiss the prime minister and the government. If the Duma proved unable in several attempts to approve a prime minister or repeatedly voted no confidence in a period of three months, it would risk being dissolved.[41]

The new changes destroyed the balanced compromise of the July draft. Now, not only could a president still react to votes of no confidence or opposition to his appointments by dissolving the legislature, he would also hold exclusive powers to appoint and dismiss the government. Indeed, Yeltsin's aides further strengthened presidential powers to dissolve the Duma. The July draft had given the president merely the option to dissolve the Duma in the event it rejected three candidates for prime minister.[42] The new, amended language changed this to automatic dissolution of the Duma and allowed the president to simply name his choice without reference to the Duma at all.[43]

Only one serious objection to this strengthening of the executive at the expense of the legislative branch appears in the Constitutional Assembly proceedings. It came from Anatoly Sobchak, the Mayor of St. Petersburg and longtime Yeltsin ally, during the final approval of the changes to the draft. Yeltsin had tapped Sobchak to chair one of the two Assembly chambers after the October crisis, and Sobchak had played a leading role in work on the constitution throughout. He referred to the long arguments on these provisions over the past two years and in the Constitutional Assembly's work in producing the July draft. He lamented the abandonment of balanced powers that had been the result of a long process of negotiation and feared the consequences of a constitutional system in which the national legislature would lack influence on and oversight over the executive branch. "The changes from Filatov's commission represent an attempt to put the government completely under the president. This would be wrong. ...It would, of course, be dangerous," he argued.[44] A short debate ensued, with several speakers urging support of "the prior formula" while others supported strengthening presidential powers. The discussion, however, did not touch on the needs of democracy in terms of checks and balances. Rather, it followed support of either parliamentary power or presidential power in isolation of those concerns. Just before calling for a vote, Sobchak, a lawyer by training and staunch advocate for democracy, made an impassioned appeal in defense of the future of democracy in Russia, and warned of the dangers of erasing a core democratic principle from the constitution:

In my view, in all of the arguments before us the recent confrontation is present, the views of Khasbulatov and Yeltsin, the spirit of battle between these two branches of power, which for long months hovered over the country. What we should be considering in the Constitution, however, are not questions of two concrete figures in power today, but rather we should be considering a real mechanism. And if we truly will formulate it as written in the final version as Filatov's working commission proposes, then this will sharply strengthen the position of the president, pushing him even higher (and this was correctly pointed out) than the figure of a constitutional monarch. Despite all of the need for strong authority, and order, despite all of the problems which come with a parliament, nevertheless it is impermissible to forget about the extraordinary dangers inherent in this sort of strengthening of presidential powers, the danger for the task of creating a democracy. Particularly in a country that has been denied democratic traditions and in which these authoritarian and dictatorial tendencies are fairly strong.

Therefore, it seems to me, that even a purely formulaic relationship to this, not that "The president names," but "The president proposes the head of the government," brings a respectful approach to the opinion of the people who have elected the parliament, brings potential for the parliament, as it were, to hold the government responsible for its actions. That is, it is a more strictly balanced political system, in which there are very strong elements of a presidential republic (we have given the president extremely great powers), but which also has clear elements underlining the role of the parliament.

Therefore, I would support our earlier proposal, that formula which we wrote in the July 12 draft, that "The president proposes to the State Duma a candidate for the chair of the government."[45]

Despite his appeal, 60 percent of the Assembly voted for the changes. "That means we are going to leave Article 83 and Article 10[3] in the form proposed by Filatov's working commission," Sobchak said. "And so we are going to make it the ratification of an autocracy."[46] Little did he know that it would be his deputy mayor and former law student, Vladimir Putin, who would use the immense and unchecked powers of the presidency to realize Sobchak's fears about a return to autocracy in Russia.

Every aspect of the relationship to the government tipped entirely toward the president. The president names the prime minister. The Duma must give its consent. If it refuses to do so, the president can simply resubmit the same candidate. If this takes place three times, then the president still gets to name his choice for prime minister, this time without Duma approval and, to top it off, he must dissolve the Duma and call for new elections.[47]

The president had already been given, prior to the October changes, the power to appoint all federal ministers. Article 112 merely states that the prime minister submits proposals to the president for these positions. The Federal Assembly has no role whatsoever. In the end, the president gained exclusive control over the government appointment process, with the Duma's only role being either to consent or be dissolved, with the president's choice becoming the head of government even in spite of rigid Duma opposition. The legislature lacks any control over government personnel.

The president also gained exclusive control over the dismissal process. As clearly spelled out in Articles 83 and 117 after the changes made in October, only the president may remove the government. While Article 117 does allow the Duma to express no confidence in the government, the president need not take any action when this occurs. Moreover, if the Duma passes a second no confidence motion within three months, the president may decide to dismiss the government, but he can also decide to preserve the government and dissolve the Duma. Similarly, the prime minister can press the issue of confidence. The Duma must act, and must do so under duress. If it fails to express confidence, the president again must choose either to support his government and dismiss the Duma, or to dismiss the government. In short, the Duma lacks any real power over the personnel or policies of the government. It approves, or faces the prospect of dissolution.

In terms of policy, the Duma has even less of a constitutional role. While Article 105 states that the Duma adopts federal laws, Article 106 only states that the Federation Council must act on Duma laws on the budget, taxation, finance, treaty ratification, and war and peace. Nowhere, however, does the constitution state that the Duma in fact has purview over these matters. While none of these provisions reflect changes from the July Constitutional Assembly draft, this all becomes significant in light of a change that was made to Article 80, in which the president was given responsibility for "the state's domestic and foreign policy." When combined with the sweeping decree powers given to the president in Article 90, the Duma becomes, formally, superfluous to the policy process.

There is, as a result, separation of legislative and executive powers under the Russian Constitution. But there are no checks and balances. Sobchak's prediction that it would become a constitutional autocracy was prescient. According to Article 10, the branches are separate and "independent," and according to the rest of the constitution, the president has overwhelming powers while the legislative branch retains few levers of its own.

Consequences

A constitution is a founding document. It defines a country's political system and sets the rules and the tone for how politics will be conducted. Not only are its provisions important, but also how it is written and adopted sets precedents for the conduct of politics. This chapter describes tinkering with provisions in Russia's draft constitution prior to its ratification that held negative consequences from the perspective of democratic political development. The substantive changes all undermined democracy, in that they created imbalance and eliminated checks and balances rather than creating them.

It is important to note that any analysis of the July Constitutional Assembly draft would have to conclude, as the members of the Assembly itself concluded, that the system it would have created was a presidential system with strong presidential powers. There is by no means any guarantee that the July draft, had it been the version ratified, would have promoted democratic development in Russia. But there is no doubt that the version that was ratified made democratic development far less likely an outcome than would have been the case with that earlier draft. Few, though, publicly predicted a danger of dictatorship from the new constitution, and those like Sobchak who did were largely ignored. One proved absolutely correct in principle if not in the person in warning, "If Yeltsin is prepared to use his overwhelming authority to promote compromise and consensus-building (as French President Charles De Gaulle did under the Fifth Republic), then this new constitution may lead to a more democratic political system. If, on the other hand, Yeltsin uses presidential authority to suppress all opposition, then a new constitutional dictatorship may emerge."[48] Yeltsin did not go so far, but his successor, Putin, has used and abused the constitution to "run roughshod over the opposition" and has brought "a return to dictatorship."[49] Yeltsin lacked the desire to do so, not the means. Putin lacks neither.

The point is worth emphasizing. Yeltsin respected opposition, respected the Duma and worked diligently with it. The Duma, while plagued internally by inefficient rules and procedures and fractured political divisions, had influence over policy on everything from budgets to privatization to criminal and other legal codes.[50] That influence, however, depended not on the Duma itself. It depended entirely on a president who had shown a commitment to negotiation and compromise, and a tolerance of dissent and criticism from politicians and press alike. The Russian Constitution does not obviate the possibility of democratic politics. It has made possible the emasculation of democratic politics by a president inclined to push the country in that direction. Putin has been so inclined.

The unbalanced constitution allowed for precedents that Yeltsin's successor could seize on in consolidating dictatorship. Yeltsin issued hundreds of decrees, and in his second term virtually ruled by decree. While the constitution allows this, it set a precedent of legislating without a legislature. On critical issues, this has a destructive effect from the point of view of democratic political development. It is important to note that Yeltsin always included the legislature, even in his decrees, and he issued decrees when the legislature failed to act. For example, when the Duma failed to pass a law on privatization of medium and large enterprises in 1995, Yeltsin created a process by decree. But he did not decree the original proposal submitted to the Duma; rather, he issued a decree creating a program including substantial amendments and compromises agreed upon with several Duma committees and representatives of all Duma political factions.[51] Nevertheless, the resulting loans-for-shares rigged auctions was one of the most corrupt programs ever conceived on such a scale, and brought corruption directly into the president's inner circles that would not only shape the next presidential election, but would also push Russia away from even democratic electoral politics.

Putin has used rule by decree to eliminate political competition and remaining vestiges of democratic politics. He has used the power to reduce regional and local government powers, and then having these decrees ratified as laws by his stacked Duma. Without institutional limits on presidential power, Putin's steps have amounted to many small steps in the direction of building dictatorship. The degree of presidential control over the Duma has been realized beyond what the worst predictions about this constitution could have held. As the concluding chapter describes, Putin has filled the Duma with fellow veterans of the KGB and other security services, who approve his proposals with minimal opposition or debate. The Duma has become a rubber stamp, what was cooperation between the Kremlin and the Duma factions has become Kremlin control over the Duma membership.[52] Indeed, the corridors of the Duma, which used to bustle with discussion and debate, are now largely empty and quiet. Little of significance takes place in the Russian legislature, because the constitution puts all of the important levers of power in the presidency.

That the Duma has failed to provide a significant balance to executive authority is hardly its own fault, though some would place the blame there. Filatov blames the Duma for failing to demand influence, for failing to legislate, and for failing to use the Audit Chamber to flex its muscle.[53] However, the Kremlin has actively used its many levers to bloc the legislature from exerting influence. Yeltsin increasingly over time realized and took advantage of the substantial powers of the Russian presidency, and the significance of the Duma in the policy process declined steadily. Government ministers and Kremlin officials have paid less attention to the deputies and their committees over time. The Duma lacks any power to compel members of the government to testify or to otherwise provide it with information on any issue, including the budget. While the first Duma, for example, managed to open up the budget to over fifty pages detailing sixty three articles, with another sixty pages of detailed appendices, budgets under Putin have returned to the closed, general documents first submitted to the Supreme Soviet, numbering only a handful of pages. Much of the budget is relegated to secret "reserve" items that the public never sees.[54] The Duma is virtually powerless before the president or government. It is not clear, even if the Duma had the ability and inclination to reject the budget—which it most certainly does not—that anything prevents the president from adopting it by decree.

Yeltsin used his constitutional powers, as the next chapter shows, to rig his reelection in 1996, to rule by decree over and around the legislature, and to do so without consequence. Putin, as Chapter 6 details, has used those powers to consolidate dictatorship, packing the Duma and government with loyalists from the secret service and other security organizations, seizing control over the media, and limiting political competition or challenges to Kremlin policies. Both used them to prosecute a wildly destructive war in Chechnya at enormous cost and with blatant human rights violations, without the threat of consequence or legislative limitation. The Duma is little more than a bystander, and under Putin an increasingly silent bystander, in the processes of governing Russia. It has no powers of oversight, no powers to compel testimony, and no powers to prevent a president from carrying out harmful or illegal policies. It cannot challenge a president. And the unchallenged presidency has paved the way to dictatorship, not democracy, in Russia.

4

Corrupting the Elections: Enter the Oligarchs

In any state hoping to create a democratic political system, competitive politics pose a challenge to the leaders. Where no recent experience with peaceful leadership change exists, or in countries like Russia where there is no such experience at all in history, the rise of organized and serious political competition as elections approach presents dilemmas for those in power. Even with a balanced constitution in place, the laws on paper guarantee nothing in terms of performance. Precedent matters, behavior matters, in short, leaders matter.

In Russia, five years after the fall of communism and two years under the new constitution, serious political questions confronted President Yeltsin and his advisors as his first term in office neared its end. For the first time, Yeltsin faced a hostile public, which gave him deeply negative ratings, at the same time that a range of new groups had appeared with strong political interests. The drop in popularity was expected as a result of the societal pain associated with the myriad economic changes taking place. The strain many segments of society felt from the economic transformation guaranteed a decline in support, as it had previously for the new leaders in every postcommunist state that implemented market reforms. In Russia, violence, corruption, and hardship all hit people hard. The streets of large cities often resembled conflict zones, as entrepreneurship merged into organized crime.[1] Price liberalization and the rapid, often disorganized privatization brought skyrocketing inflation, while the government was cutting many of the social services the public had become accustomed to under communism. Across the country, millions of people lost everything they had to pyramid schemes, bogus "mutual funds," and corrupt financial pirates who promised astronomical earnings to investors but instead deposited the money into private offshore accounts, often disappearing altogether themselves. Much of the public had come to equate "democracy," the label under which all of these reforms had taken place, with theft, impoverishment, corruption, and disorder.

As the first presidential and parliamentary elections under the new rules neared, Russia faced a crossroads. How would Russia's leaders handle the challenge presented by the rise of strong political opposition? Would free and fair, truly open and competitive elections decide who would lead Russia for the next four years? Would unfettered democratic contestation set the precedent for the future? Would the incumbent leader allow a fair contest for power in which he would potentially lose? Or would such a prospect tempt the incumbent to rig or otherwise control the outcome to prevent such a possibility? In short, would the first elections chart a democratic course under the new constitution?

Free and fair elections were not to be. The new structures could not guarantee them, and the leaders were not prepared to enforce them. Yeltsin and his team chose a course that would set the precedent of controlling electoral outcomes, with tactics that would hold long-term consequences nobody at the time seems to have considered. The 1996 Russian election cycle featured numerous violations of the basic democratic principle that national elections be free and fair, and made evident the authoritarian potential in Russia's new political system. That the conventional wisdom in much of the world is that this election was free and fair, that it was a positive step forward for democracy in Russia, defies logic and reason. The most prominent Western analysts of and major media covering Russian politics conveyed the message that Yeltsin won because he "ran the right kind of campaign."[2] In "historic" fashion this "emerging democracy" had purportedly shown its mettle, abided by its new institutions and rules and had a competitive election for the leadership of the country; this was "true progress!"[3] Elections were now supposedly "the only game in town," and the "precedent-setting election" promised a "democratic renewal in Russia."[4]

Except for the part about setting precedents, the rest was so much tripe. This sort of wishful thinking, which by extension it penetrated into Western government officials and international institutions, amounted to wilful neglect and only contributed to the "crib death of Russian democracy."[5] The flawed portrayal contributed to continued inflows in subsequent years of billions of dollars into Russia, much of which wound up lining the pockets of corrupt public officials and organized crime bosses who had engineered the outcome, and who came to understand that anything they did a fawning West would call liberal and democratic, while showering rewards into their foreign bank accounts.[6]

The 1996 elections in Russia violated many requirements of free and fair elections, and of the country's own election rules. This chapter details the decisions that produced a 1996 presidential campaign that dealt another severe blow to hopes for a democratic future.[7] Among the most consequential actions were reestablishing Kremlin control over that media and using it to savage an opposition afforded no opportunity to respond, and inviting the wealthiest and most criminal business elite into the highest circles of power where they infused billions of dollars of laundered money pilfered from the state to finance not only Yeltsin's victory but also their ascension to positions of political power and continued access to state resources. Yeltsin, as the incumbent responsible for his own campaign, was responsible for that campaign's violation of the rules and violation of democratic principles that this chapter demonstrates. Under the new constitution, how Russia's central political institutions perform and relate to each other is entirely dependent upon the occupant of the office of the presidency. How power is distributed and how decisions are made and carried out depend on the president. Yeltsin used the superpowerful presidency to dictate the outcome of his own reelection, which set precedents of intolerance to political opposition that ultimately paved the way to the return of dictatorship.

This was hardly preordained. The alternatives clearly existed to enable open political competition, with a variety of political candidates, organizations, and interests represented, in the 1996 presidential campaign. The legal framework was in place, both in electoral law and in media law, as were a range of opposition organizations with several viable presidential candidates, notably Gennady Zyuganov, leader of the Russian Communist Party, Georgiy Yavlinsky from the small but fairly well-organized social-democratic party Yabloko, and the charismatic former General Alexander Lebed. Russia could have had a freewheeling, spirited campaign to determine the leadership of the country going forward, five years after the collapse of the Soviet regime. In other countries, these elections brought the ouster of the first postcommunist leaders without a return to a communist past, even where former communists emerged victorious. Of course, those countries, such as Poland in Eastern Europe, and the Baltic States closer to home, enjoyed a more clearly identifiable consensus for democratic politics and market economics than did Russia, a consensus formed in the immediate period after the collapse. Yeltsin did not use his window to forge that consensus, as detailed in the Chapter 2. They also did not suffer the violent conflict with an opposition threatening a return to a closed system, if not a return to a Stalinist system.

Having recently endured that violent conflict, and fearing the possibility of communist restoration in Russia, Yeltsin and his advisors chose a different path that proved antidemocratic in the precedents it would set. Even those among the political elite who actively promoted democratic development in Russia consistently confused the victory of their preferred candidates who accepted and trumpeted the shorthand label "democrats" with the victory of democracy itself. There was a general failure, in Russia and the West alike, to distinguish between preferred individual candidates and the political system. Moreover, these same officials tended to categorize candidates and parties according to these preferences, actively opposing and fearing a wide spectrum rather than actively working for unity around the principles of open, democratic politics. The damage this orientation caused to democratic development is difficult to overstate.

In 1996, Yeltsin and his advisors endorsed a philosophy of "win at any cost," political or financial, regardless of what the law might say or the long-term consequences might be.[8] Fear was the motivation that generated the "win at all costs" mentality. In the face of rising competition and opposition, Russia's leaders chose a path that amounted to stealing the election with the help of the criminal, corrupt, and newly superrich business elite. They enabled Yeltsin to circumvent all financial restrictions, to close the press to the competition, and as a result to corrupt the elections by violating rules for competitive democratic politics. This attitude to the first presidential elections under the new constitution legitimized and ultimately institutionalized an assault on press freedom, official accountability, responsible government, and free and fair elections. It undermined the prospects for a democratic future rather than being a signal of democratic consolidation. This chapter explores not only why this happened but also how, for it is in the how that the real consequences for Russia's future lie.

Fear as a Motivator

As is regularly the case in authoritarian regimes, and particularly throughout much of Russia's political history, fear served in 1996 both as a motivating factor inspiring the leaders to act and as a weapon in their hands. Fear, real and imagined, guided the main figures involved in the corruption of Russia's 1996 presidential election. Different motivations drove different actors. For some it was, paradoxically, fear of Yeltsin that fueled the no-rules approach to getting him reelected. As Yeltsin's popularity dropped into the single-digits just three months before the election, the prospect loomed of an electoral defeat.[9] As no such transfer of power had ever occurred before in Russia, advisors who genuinely fought for democracy feared Yeltsin might not cede power should he lose. They even wondered how they would advise him to act in the event of a Zyuganov victory. They feared both Zyuganov's communist rhetoric in the Duma and his political allies, among whom were several who played key roles in the Supreme Soviet uprising in 1993. Reflecting the doubt among his own advisors about what Yeltsin would do in the event of electoral defeat were rumors that ran rampant throughout the media and society in early 1996 that Yeltsin would never cede power to the communists, or to anyone.[10] Such rumors both fueled and reflected the thoughts of these advisors. The possibility that Yeltsin might ignore or nullify valid election results, in particular in the first elections under the constitution, was something they naturally saw as catastrophic for democracy.

Such were their fears, and they were not necessarily unfounded. Yet these supporters of democracy were unbending in their insistence that elections were absolutely necessary. There was only one conclusion available to them: Yeltsin had to win, even if in the end the elections themselves were for the sake of appearances, to allow Yeltsin to make a claim to honestly remaining in power. This was the path they saw to defend democratic development in Russia. Yeltsin remained, for them, the only viable guarantor of democracy in Russia.

These individuals were outnumbered by the self-serving. They were Yeltsin associates who, having played a role in shaping policies, some having gotten rich off of them, feared for their own safety. It remains in political Russia a widely accepted, though never verified, truth that the leaders of the October 1993 Supreme Soviet uprising in October 1993 maintained a list of individuals to be "liquidated" in the event that their coup proved successful.[11] This rumored list consisted of present and former members of Yeltsin's government and circle of advisors, as well as liberal-minded journalists, business people, politicians, and activists. Because it was merely rumored, anyone could have placed themselves on that list in their own mind, and many did. It was also a common, though deeply-flawed shorthand to equate the Communist Party under Zyuganov in 1996 with the organizers of the violent opposition in 1993. What was relevant was not the evidence to back these presumptions, but rather the tangible fear felt by those who had themselves on such a list and who had convinced themselves of the personalities in the hypothetical future government. For one who believed that they would follow murderous policies, Yeltsin's defeat came to be synonymous with their own physical demise. The fear was real, whether or not it corresponded to reality.

Some had good reason to fear arrest under a communist return to power, or for that matter under the rule of law were this to emerge in Russia. Loss of access to a continued stream of graft would not have been the only consequence of a Yeltsin defeat. There would also have been the real possibility of punishment for deep corruption for billions of dollars swindled away, by officials in government ministries, members of the Yeltsin administration, and business magnates with whom these officials were in cahoots. The rampant corruption in government in Russia has been well documented in scholarly books with titles like *Tragedy of Russia's Reforms: Market Bolshevism Against Democracy*, *Comrade Criminal: Russia's New Mafiya*, and *Godfather of the Kremlin: The Decline of Russia in the Age of Gangster Capitalism*, and in pioneering studies by the Russian NGO INDEM.[12]

The mutual, if different, fears of those who had crafted the reforms and those who profited off them led to a marriage that would win Yeltsin's reelection while doing long-term harm to democratic development. The "oligarchs," as they came to be known, openly feared that a communist victory would spark "bloodshed and violence."[13] The business community that had grown rich off of policies such as rigged privatization auctions, that had squandered away foreign loans and the state treasury into private foreign bank accounts, was afraid for their fortunes and afraid for their lives. "No one in this [business] elite wanted to see Yeltsin lose a presidential election" because they "owed [their] existence and riches to the state."[14] The common presence of fear among the political and financial elite about the consequences of Yeltsin not remaining president propelled a direct alliance between the wealthiest and most corrupt, if not criminal, business leaders with the innermost circles of the Kremlin.

In the December 1995 Duma elections, the Communist Party emerged as the largest faction with over 22 percent of the vote, while the xenophobic nationalist Vladimir Zhirinovskiy's LDPR came second with 11 percent. The government's electoral bloc headed by the prime minister polled just 10 percent. What came to be known as "The Family" around Yeltsin was born in discussion over whether to cancel or steal the presidential elections, for by this stage a Yeltsin victory in an honest campaign had become impossible for anyone to envision. It was simply not going to happen.

The question was, what to do? Yeltsin, through three rounds of elections, had steadfastly refused to create, lead, or even directly associate with any fledgling party. Yeltsin continued to follow a simple but to that point successful political logic: to be *partiiniy,* a party member, had become a dirty word after three generations of Communist rule. In the conditions of "hyperdemocracy," it was better for each to go it alone.[15] This strategy was brilliant on a personal level and proved hugely successful. Moreover, it fit Yeltsin's picture of himself as Russia's George Washington, the first American president.[16] By remaining free of any party, Yeltsin could remain "above the fray," not hindered or tarnished in the midst of fierce policy differences among the populace in a new country charting a new course. It afforded policy flexibility and an air of political purity, not to mention superiority.

However, the consequence was the fragmentation of Democratic Russia, the movement that had helped propel him to power and topple communism, and the irreparable splintering of the political elite that constituted Yeltsin's most important power base and of the larger masses that constituted his logical popular base. In early 1996, as a result, when Yeltsin found himself with microscopic approval ratings, no political organization existed to rally behind him. His natural base of support was fragmented among other contenders, real and potential. The only hope for Yeltsin to muster a comeback was to regenerate the anticommunist fervor, the fear, and to do so in any way possible. He needed help to do that. And thus "The Family" was born.

Enter the Oligarchs

Throughout the first half of the 1990s, associates of Russia's wealthiest financial bosses had been killing each other on the streets of Moscow and Russia's other large cities. Cars, stores, restaurants, and sidewalk kiosks would suddenly blow up. People would be shot in the back entering their apartment buildings at night. Few were ever arrested.[17] Boris Berezovsky, head of a network of automobile dealerships, quasi-banks, and media outlets had openly sought the murder of Vladimir Gusinsky, head of a rival network of quasi-banks, media outlets, and other commercial properties. Though they had never met, they were in virtual war with each other and Berezovsky has not denied suspicion that he at one point had a contract out on Gusinsky's life.[18] In January 1995, many of Russia's new, rich business leaders attended the annual World Economic Forum in Davos, Switzerland. In addition to Berezovsky and Gusinsky, Vladimir Potanin, Aleksandr Smolensky, Vladimir Vinogradov, Mikhail Khodorkovsky, Rem Vyakhirev, and Roman Abramovich, the heads of all of the private banks and largest privatized industries, all attended.[19] Chubais, their closest patron in government, joined other government officials in Davos, and Communist Party leader Gennady Zyuganov.[20]

Berezovsky took a momentous step in Davos by approaching Gusinsky about the danger of the then upcoming election. They quickly agreed they had "no choice" but to set aside their differences and work together to prevent a communist victory. Common fears of what that victory would bring trumped mutual dislike. Berezovsky then approached the other financiers, who all agreed. In short order, he had brought together the wealthiest Russians, a group of heretofore mortal enemies, to work together and suspend their wars with each other.[21] They agreed they had to cooperate to prevent a communist return to power, or risk losing the spectacular wealth they had amassed, and perhaps more.

Berezovsky knew firsthand, and it was widely known, that Yeltsin's reelection effort had been managed to then by incompetent buffoons. A group of drab hardliners, including longtime Yeltsin security aide Aleksander Korzhakov, FSB Director Mikhail Barsukov, and Deputy Prime Minister Oleg Soskovets, controlled the campaign plans and coffers. Under their direction it was like a ship without a rudder, "it burned fuel, made noise, vented steam, created waves around itself, but stood still."[22] These men were in fact opposed to elections, and were already counseling the president to cancel them.[23] Berezovsky, as an acquaintance of Yeltsin's daughter and son-in-law, was part of a wider circle included in the campaign strategy sessions, and could see all of this for himself.

Zyuganov, with his seemingly insurmountable lead over Yeltsin, went to Davos to introduce himself to the West. Zyuganov played the role of Social Democrat, striking poses that rang familiar to Western business elite.

Communists-turned-social democrats had won elections across Eastern Europe, appealing with messages of increased welfare programs to a public that had been slammed by radical neoconservative market reforms. From Estonia to Poland to the Czech and Slovak Republics to Hungary, they had furthered the development of democracy and the building of market economies. To many at Davos, it appeared Zyuganov would follow suit. Indeed, one could interpret his very presence in Davos as indicative of his interest in maintaining good relations with the leaders of the capitalist business world, and perhaps of having Russia join the ranks of leading capitalist economies.

Others saw a smoke screen, convinced Zyuganov remained an unreformed communist in the Stalinist tradition. The Zyuganov at Davos was not necessarily the Zyuganov who would have been president. In the State Duma and in interviews inside Russia he presented a distinctly hard-line communist message. Such an impression was reinforced by the company he kept.

Was he simply putting on a face to calm the West? Would he in fact have wrenched Russia back to the past? In the end, we will never know what Zyuganov would have done had he become President of Russia. The oligarchs and Yeltsin made sure of that.

Berezovsky and Gusinsky agreed at Davos to work together to guarantee that Yeltsin remain in office. Together with the other financiers, including Potanin, Vinogradov, and Khodorkovsky, they agreed to use all resources available to prevent any change in power in the Kremlin. They then approached current and former members of government, including Deputy Prime Minister Yevgeniy Yasin, Moscow Mayor Yuriy Luzhkov, Chubais, and a wider group of Russian business people, all of whom agreed to take any necessary measures to prevent a Yeltsin defeat. They agreed on the need to wake Yeltsin up to the danger, in particular to the danger residing in his own campaign team. Chubais was a key figure, because without him some of these individuals would have refused to set aside their differences merely at the instigation of Berezovsky. The distrust and dislike were too fierce. Chubais had been essential to the enrichment of each of these figures. Berezovsky used Chubais as a conduit, to help unite this financial front and to make the appeal to Yeltsin. One account has the financiers promising support only the condition that Chubais be installed as head of the campaign.[24]

Berezovsky also had Yeltsin's daughter's cooperation, through their mutual direct observation of the incompetence of the campaign staff, to influence Yeltsin. It was she, Tatiana Dyachenko, who organized a meeting between the financiers and the president, to warn him of the dangers and the need to make changes.[25] There is no doubt that the financiers offered the president their full support, and that they expected benefits in return. Whether those were explicitly or implicitly spelled out remains unclear, but the benefits most certainly were realized.

Virtually simultaneous to these events, Yeltsin received a letter from some of his top staff that contained the same basic message. While Yeltsin's rating plummeted and the security triumvirate plotted a shady course to disaster, Yeltsin's analytical staff, strong advocates of democratization to this point marginalized from the reelection planning, became distraught. One took action. In response to a request for assistance from Soskovets, Satarov issued a written warning:

> It is perfectly clear that you and your staff are not interested in normal, organized campaign work, having become so accustomed to lining your pockets with money earmarked for the campaign. I am putting you on notice that it is pointless for you to count on any sort of direct cooperation with me, since you lack the capacity to create the conditions necessary to make this possible. None of this should be taken to mean that I will stand idly by and not attempt to compensate for the evil which you, consciously or not, are bringing to the Yeltsin election campaign.[26]

Satarov then set to work with Chief of Staff Viktor Ilyushin and others to urge Yeltsin to overhaul his campaign, warning him that "normal staff work had not yet even begun," and that without changes there would be disastrous consequences for him and for the country. They were stunned to learn Yeltsin, due to the falsehoods coming from Soskovets and Korzhakov, believed he remained enormously popular.

The simultaneous pressure from the financiers, his daughter, and his aides did push Yeltsin to make a change. He put Ilyushin in charge of the campaign staff and Chubais in charge of the "analytical group" planning campaign strategy. Berezovsky and the financiers, meanwhile, continued to meet and with Chubais, Dyachenko, and others to coordinate their efforts. They controlled the major electronic and print media outlets, and had virtually unlimited finances. Dyachenko played the key role as intermediary between the various interested circles—the campaign staff, the financiers, and her father. However, changes meant changes, and staff changes were far from Yeltsin's only option. Another tempting option beckoned: why hold an election at all?

The Charge to Cancel the Elections

Yeltsin was inclined to take drastic steps. The Soskovets–Korzhakov–Barsukov security triumvirate had been prodding Yeltsin to cancel the elections and to remain in power, and as the three-sided pressure to make changes mounted, perhaps Yeltsin saw such a step as the compromise path to satisfy the greatest number of advisors. It most certainly fit the general need to take action and make changes. Clearly, the forceful step was the chosen path of the hardliners. The financiers and corrupt officials worried less about elections than they did for their safety, for self-protection, for remaining in power, and for continuing the stream of state resources into their pockets. Cancelling the elections would achieve this and satisfy that group. If a way could be found to make it appear constitutional, even democratic, this could mollify the analytical staff.

Yeltsin instructed his staff on March 17, less than three months before the scheduled elections, to provide him the legal basis and a draft decree on dissolving the Duma, banning the Communist Party and suspending the elections.[27] Soskovets seized on a Duma action to push Yeltsin in this direction. Two days earlier, the Duma repealed the December 1991 resolution denouncing the Treaty on the Creation of the Soviet Union. In other words, they reversed, on paper at least, the dissolution of the USSR. In so doing, they of course dissolved their legal basis as deputies and that of the Duma itself. Yeltsin at first responded with a pronouncement that he was bound to defend the country and the constitution. But he was upset, and all the warnings about the dangers posed by the upcoming election inclined him to action. He wanted to preempt any chance of a repeat of the October 1993 crisis.

He gathered Chief of Staff Ilyushin, legal advisors Baturin and Shakhrai, political advisor Satarov, and other aides and instructed them to develop decree language and legal justification. An order from the president is an order from the president, and the advisors saw no choice but to carry it out. Their choice in *how* to carry it out demonstrates their unwavering commitment to democratic principles. Focusing on the legal aspect, they compiled a list of reasons why the idea was a bad one, in a document they called "Counter-arguments and Alternatives."[28] First, they expressed extreme doubt that any legal basis existed for doing what Yeltsin had requested. Second, they argued the proposed response was out of proportion to the significance of the Duma's actions, which could—and would—be overturned by the Constitutional Court. Since the Duma lacked authority to take such action, either the upper house, the Federation Council, in whose sphere of powers such matters lay, or the president could lodge such an appeal. Third, the Duma act was consciously planned to spur a violent response from the president and would play into the Communists' hands. Fourth, it would alienate noncommunists, who would see Yeltsin's proposed response as entirely out of proportion to the threat, particularly since the president had already proclaimed that the Duma's action carried no legal consequence, meaning there was no crisis demanding any response. Fifth, regional authorities would never accept these actions, and their negative response could spiral the country toward civil war. Yeltsin's staff indicated a number of alternative steps, including working with the Federation Council on a ruling that the Duma had created circumstances making elections impossible, and delaying them for two years.

Yeltsin was far from satisfied, and barked, "Why is there no text of a decree? In 1993 two people figured it out." He ordered them again to write the decree and sent them out of his office. He also met with his ministers to prepare them for the steps ahead. The president had been telling selective ministers about his plan to dissolve the Duma, ban the Communist Party, and cancel the elections, instructing them to prepare measures related to their spheres of activity. At each meeting he told the official in question that everyone else supported this plan. Believing this to be the case, each thought "if everyone else is in favor then I better agree with them." Only the Minister of Internal Affairs, Anatoly Kulikov, after hearing the president out asked him to wait a few hours before issuing a decree, so that he could "provide you with several proposals." Kulikov was also under the impression that everyone else was on board. But when he saw the justice minister and Chair of the Constitutional Court, and revealed that he had deep reservations, he found them similarly concerned. These three decided to develop a list of arguments in support of the radical steps Yeltsin was seeking, and a list of arguments against those steps. Together they would bring these to the president.

Each group saw the other as leading the president astray. The president had told his aides that everyone else supported his idea, and believing this they glared with disdain at Kulikov, Yuri Skuratov and Vladimir Tumanov as they crossed paths in the president's office. In reality, the latter group had just told the president exactly what those staff members had told him earlier, that "We have thought long on this and we are of the opinion not to proceed." Yeltsin was irate that Kulikov had not told him of his opposition when they first met. "I am not happy with you!" he said. When Kulikov tried to protest that it was his job to fully inform, Yeltsin interjected, "No! That is all! You will carry out my orders! You will get the decree." As Interior Minister, after all, his job was to receive and implement orders to guarantee security inside the country.

An angry Kulikov went straight to Ilyushin, who was huddled with the rest of the analytical staff, and said, "So, you are writing the decree?" The staff, in turn, glared at him again. Kulikov handed them the notes the president had so energetically rejected, and they handed theirs to him. They were practically identical, and both groups were now on to Yeltsin's game. Realizing they all opposed, rather than supported, the demand, they united their efforts. Just then, Chubais entered Ilyushin's office and started lecturing them that the author of the decree, regardless of the president's signature on the document, would bear responsibility. All that would remain for them is their resignation, as this would be the political death of the president. They merely handed Chubais their work and found another ally. Meanwhile, the president had left for his dacha, instructing Ilyushin to bring him the decree in one hour.

This was at 10 P.M. Instead, they drafted a joint note to the president, in which they wrote, "The decree could not be written, since no legal basis exists for taking such action. Moreover, the decree is an inappropriate response to the Duma resolution...and would risk a civil war." Not even 11 P.M. yet, they called the president, learned he was already asleep, and decided to wait until morning.

Yeltsin saw the note at 6 A.M., in a meeting with his security ministers and chief of staff. He asked who wrote it. Ilyushin named, among others, the president's main analytical staff (himself, Baturin, Shakhrai, and Satarov) Chubais, the interior and justice ministers and Chair of the Constitutional Court. Fifteen minutes later, Kulikov attended a meeting with Yeltsin, Prime Minister Viktor Chernomyrdin, Deputy Prime Minister Nikolai Yegorov, Barsukov, Soskovets, and Ilyushin. The president decided against using force, announcing instead that he would go ahead with the elections as planned. Military maneuvers in the Moscow region were brought to a halt the next day. Apparently, they had been preparing to move on the issuance of a decree.[29]

The decision not to use force, and to proceed with elections as called for by law and by the constitution, reflected the pro-democratic alternative chosen at this critical juncture. Clearly, other options were on the brink of being chosen, and in fact had been ordered by the president. The choice also marked the marginalization of the hard-liners and the reemergence of those in support of democracy in control of the campaign. Certainly, all of the major players saw the alternative of holding or cancelling elections as a major decision, and it was. Sadly for democracy, however, this was only one piece of the puzzle.

The democratization literature overemphasizes formal elections, and the literature on Russia since the collapse shares this flaw. The mere holding of this election meant less than how the elections were conducted. The future of democratic development and the performance of the new constitution and legal framework still hung in the balance. First precedents are important. Indeed, one can say that if cancelling scheduled elections because of fear of defeat is not merely a real but a central consideration, it is difficult to speak of democracy. The question really was whether these first presidential elections would help to put democracy back on course after the jarring effects of 1993.

The decision to bring in the financiers made sure this would not happen, as it, in effect, ensured that the elections were not free and fair. The alliance brought massive violations of virtually every important law regulating the campaign and deeply corrupted the presidential election process. While Berezovsky did not take over campaign operations, in fact he only appeared twice in the offices of the campaign staff in the Presidential Hotel, he did help to control the outcome. Chubais and Dyachenko kept the oligarchs informed on the progress of the campaign informally, but the oligarchs' most important work was behind the scenes. It is in the heavily laundered money and the direct control over a national propaganda machine where the election was truly stolen.

(Not) The Oligarchs' Money

The half-dozen or so most influential oligarchs were all highly skilled in the shadowy art of money-laundering.[30] Currency transactions brought them their spectacular wealth. Much of that wealth they siphoned off from the state coffers, depositing billions of dollars into foreign bank accounts for purported business purposes. After several transfers, each involving large siphons as kickbacks to themselves, they took out the remaining money as cash and transported it back to Russia, by then untraceable to the original source or purpose. During the campaign, they simply branched off the siphon to create a loop, putting state funds they had received directly into the president's campaign treasury. In essence, the conspirators devised a classic money-laundering scheme to disguise state budget funds as private donations into the Yeltsin campaign. The exact figures most likely will never be known, and, because the actions were so patently illegal, the true figures may not even be possible to know. While rumors that it amounted to billions of dollars are probably inflated, Chubais is on record describing the legal limit of $3 million as "an insignificant sum" compared with what was in fact spent.[31]

During the parliamentary campaign the previous December, financing worked the same though on a smaller scale. Several oligarchs financed the prime minister's electoral bloc, Our Home is Russia, on condition that they be given allowances in the budget for their own projects, monies that they would in fact divert into the campaign. Having perfected the scheme then, they repeated it on a scale increased by several factors of ten. Not only did they donate hundreds of millions of dollars to the campaign treasury, but also Berezovsky, Smolensky, and Dyachenko managed that treasury separate from the rest of the campaign team. Overall, they received several billion dollars in government subsidies in Spring 1996 for their efforts.[32] This differed little from how they had been running their empires for the last few years, with the exception of the giving large chunks of money to the president.[33] Normally, all the siphoning would go directly into their hidden bank accounts scattered around the world.

While the use of money from rich financiers in democratic elections is seldom illegal and widely practiced, this was different. In the American robber-baron period, for example, Henry Ford, J.P. Morgan, and others frequently corrupted elections and politicians at all levels with their money; however, it is impossible to argue that their wealth was entirely parasitic and extractive. They were independent actors, contributing to a growing industrial base and economic development. Their economic activity was independent of the state, and their political activity was independent of the state. They were not simultaneously members of Congress or of the president's cabinet. While corruption existed, parties changed power, incumbent lost, competitive politics continued. Moreover, they invested back into the American economy and were the engine for its growth. They bought politicians and elections, clearly antidemocratic and illegal activities. Eventually, the legal system put a halt to the effort. Antitrust legislation broke up their monopolies. Again, they were independent of the state.

All of this was different in Russia. The oligarchs' association with the Kremlin was not independent—it was semiofficial. Their assistance on the campaign came with *quid pro quos* of government positions and direct decision-making power. Their access would be direct, the line between government and business thoroughly blurred. This was institutionalized corruption in the making, corruption of government itself, and of the procedures necessary for democracy to have any hope. They were not just lending money to the campaign, they were becoming the campaign and taking over the administration, or rather, that is what it all meant.

Paradoxically, this election financing scheme meant that more of the money from the state budget made its way directly to people around the country who needed it most than might otherwise have been the case. The massive infusion of available cash enabled the campaign to present a revived and effective president to a public longing for exactly that. Laundered through the financiers to the campaign, the cash proved useful to Yeltsin on the campaign trail, where he doled it out as he traversed the country. And that he did. He took thirty-three trips in four months on the campaign trail. His staff wrote more than 400 speeches, and he issued hundreds of decrees to give the appearance of carrying out a program. But what brought him votes is that at every stop, Yeltsin promised and delivered money, sometimes right on the spot, for local projects and needs. These amounted to hundreds of millions of dollars in tax breaks, in back pay for miners and other laborers, new building programs, and even basic goods and services for individual voters.[34]

Like the Tsars and Communist Party General Secretaries of old, Yeltsin courted patron–client relationships with local officials and guaranteed support for himself by paying out huge sums of money wherever he went. The images the electorate received was not just of a popular leader, but a leader who cared and delivered with astonishing speed and effectiveness in dealing with local problems around the country. Yeltsin's ratings began rapidly to rise, and within a few weeks he had caught Zyuganov in the national polls. Little known was the mass infusion of money that came from the oligarchs, money they had received from the state budget for projects never carried out. No other candidate had anything remotely approaching the vast stores of cash. There was no way to compete. Indeed, they could not even present a message, for the oligarchs controlled the message-making industry.

Erosion of Press Freedom and Fair Access

Gusinsky's Independent Television Network (NTV) offered the highest-quality news coverage in the country, by far. Perhaps the most objective praise possible of the quality of NTV programming comes from Berezovsky. "You can say anything you want about Gusinsky, but he created a unique television station. Unique, and not only in the Russian context. Compared to the Western television I have seen, and I have seen a lot, NTV was in those years a highly-quality, professional product both in terms of news and entertainment."[35] Coming from Berezovsky, Gusinsky's fierce rival and owner of Channel 1 (ORT), this comment speaks volumes. NTV News was a fiercely independent, genuinely informative news program on which talented journalists conducted quality investigative reporting, and where informed and intelligent hosts offered insightful and enlightening programs on subjects related to politics and policy, economic and social. NTV was the network to turn to for information.

The 1996 campaign set in motion events that would ultimately destroy the network and its owner. In Spring 1996, having joined forces with the Yeltsin campaign, Gusinsky assigned NTV Director Igor Malashenko the additional task of running advertising and public relations for that campaign.[36] He similarly delegated other NTV staff to work on the campaign. In retrospect, given the Kremlin's seizure of control over electronic media and the restoration of censorship across the press, it might appear that this was Yeltsin taking direct control of the media. It was not, but it did create conditions that paved the way for Putin to restore this control. In 1996, the oligarchs who orchestrated the financing and overhaul of the campaign happened to own the major television networks and newspapers. In essence, they donated these to the campaign and, as a result, closed off competition and guaranteed a Yeltsin victory. What became an oligarch–Kremlin marriage under Yeltsin opened the door to direct control by the next president.

Yeltsin, however, was not seizing media assets. He did not close publications or networks, or censor the wide a range of viewpoints across the print media, which ranged from fascist to Trotskyite. The best journalists in the major media, and the owners of those outlets, feared a Yeltsin defeat just as the rest of the political, power, and business elite feared it. To them, Yeltsin was the guarantee that they could continue to work as journalists. Throughout Yeltsin's first term, investigative reporting on government and society flourished, and the dedication of young journalists served as one of the best hopes for a democratic future for the country. Under Yeltsin, Kremlin backlash to reports it did not like could sting, but there was no crackdown. Gusinsky, for example, tried before Spring 1996 to expand his network's access to the airwaves from a few hours to a full twenty-four hours. He shared Channel 4 with the Sport channel. Unfortunately for Gusinsky, Yeltsin and his security chief Korzhakov liked the Sport channel, and instead of more time for NTV Yeltsin issued a decree giving more time to Sport. Gusinsky was furious and had NTV unleash a torrent of attacks on Yeltsin and his staff, with angry private exchanges between Gusinsky and the staff ensuing. It is quite probable that Berezovsky, the owner of ORT Channel 1, had a hand in this sequence, working through Dyachenko and Yumashev to prevent NTV from receiving more broadcast time. But through the scandal and the critical reports there was never a crackdown. Yeltsin never tried to censor or exert direct control over press content. Journalists worried that their freedom to report and investigate would disappear should Yeltsin lose the election and communists again occupy the Kremlin offices. To prevent this, they willingly and actively promoted Yeltsin while savaging his opponent. They sacrificed objectivity hoping to preserve their freedom. The choice ultimately cost them both.

The media owners viewed themselves as independent political players, and were so viewed by public officials. They behaved not merely as observers and watchdogs, but as active participants in political battles with their own political objectives. From the very first thoughts about the 1996 campaign, Yeltsin's advisors understood that "any hope for success would depend on a close and friendly union with the mass media."[37] The 1996 presidential campaign substantially strengthened this tendency and blurred the line between the Kremlin and the media into the future. The oligarchs had their media outlets go not merely lockstep for Yeltsin, they openly campaigned for him.[38] Only Yeltsin received prime-time air coverage on television, despite the law's demand for equal air time for all major candidates. Channel 1 simply did not show Zyuganov other than to air scandals about him. Not only was there no coverage of his campaign, Zyuganov was not afforded paid commercial time during prime viewing hours. Any straight reporting of the Zyuganov campaign or running of advertising spots took place in the wee morning hours, to ensure the smallest possible viewing audience.[39]

This policy was carefully organized between the campaign staff and the media owners and directors, as indeed these entities overlapped. The media "became vehicles of the Yeltsin publicity campaign, resulting in a blurring between the line that separates political advertising from news."[40] Media executives did not limit themselves to creating that advertising campaign. They assisted in creating branches of the president's communications office across the country, to promote coverage of the president in the regional press. They used these structures to bring provincial reporters to Moscow, to meet with members of the Administration in the Kremlin on fully paid junkets.[41] There were also reports that the Kremlin spent millions of dollars bribing journalists around the country for articles and reports favorable to the president. To an individual writer for a provincial newspaper, $100 for a story was a mammoth sum.[42]

This media and advertising effort for the Yeltsin reelection campaign was made possible by the decision of the president and the oligarchs to unite their efforts. The president welcomed the financiers in, and they made possible a media monopoly for the president. Together, in close cooperation with staffs merged, they crafted a propaganda onslaught that overwhelmed the electorate and made a mockery of laws on spending or fair use. The controllers of the media violated the law and were rewarded, not punished.

For those close to Yeltsin, advocating enforcement of the law to allow Zyuganov equal time on television was counterintuitive. The law was clear: the media had to provide equal coverage and equal access to all candidates. But television time of any sort was advertising, and the Yeltsin team was not going to force the media to advertise Zyuganov, whom they saw not merely as a political opponent but as an enemy. The law was not in their interests, which they equated with the country's interests, and so they ignored it. They had convinced themselves that the imperative was to prevent a return to communism. The free press became a casualty of this mind set, though few, if any, supporters of democracy saw any such danger at the time. Their fears of the danger of a Yeltsin defeat blinded them to these other risks. One of Russia's most respected and talented young journalists, Sergei Parkhomenko, told the *Los Angeles Times,* "This is not a game of equal stakes. That is why I am willing to be unfair. That is why I am willing to stir up a wild anti-Communist psychosis among the people."[43] This reporter and others like him knew exactly what they were doing. And they did it well.

Fear as a Tool

The problem the newly overhauled campaign staff faced was how to raise a mass of people to vote for Yeltsin, given his ratings in early 1996 stood at less than 10 percent.[44] If the vote were seen as a referendum on his performance, Yeltsin faced almost certain defeat. They had to make Yeltsin seem like the safe, stable choice. The strategy they adopted was to demonize Zyuganov, who continued to poll around 30 percent. As noted above, many among Yeltsin's staff, as among the broader political and business elite, really did fear for the future were Zyuganov to win. Fearful themselves, they knew the mass populace either was in fear or could be made to fear. Relentless exaggeration was the recipe, and with the media then at their disposal the task was straightforward.

They cast Zyuganov as a demon, representing a demonic ideology. The media began to consistently portray him as wild, an uncontrolled buffoon prone to dangerous outbursts. Nightly broadcasts on every network portrayed Zyuganov as a monster. Reporters, interviewers, documentaries, and other programs fomented fear of a restoration not merely of the Soviet system, but of full-blown Stalinism should Zyuganov win. The formula was simple. Zyuganov was the Communist Party leader, the Communist Party had created the gulags and ruled by terrorizing the populace, so a

Zyuganov victory would mean the return of the gulags, the end of private enterprise and property, in short a return to the dark days of Stalin's Russia. It would mean famine and terror. These messages aired in the oligarch-controlled media and were reinforced throughout the campaign in slogans, posters, badges, letters to voters, in every conceivable format. Every format, except for one. Yeltsin never directly attacked Zyuganov; instead, he continued to issue campaign promises and dole out pork at every stop he made. He mostly ignored his opponent.

The propaganda turned the choice presented to the public as being between catastrophe and stability. This was exactly the choice the campaign wanted, knowing the electorate would always choose stability. While most voters might see it as a choice between the lesser of two evils—between the president you know though may not like, or the Communist who may bring famine, terror, and civil war—the choice would be Yeltsin. Voters, once convinced that this was indeed the choice they faced, found it a simple one to make. The barrage media and propaganda blitz effectively "made a mish-mash" of the peoples' brains.[45]

There were few public complaints from any pro-democracy or free press advocates in Russia or abroad at the time.[46] On the contrary, these constituencies enthusiastically supported what was hailed as Yeltsin's energetic revival, and rescuing the country from the danger of a communist restoration. They acted as if they bought into the campaign propaganda hook, line and sinker. Journalists demonstrated no sense of fear that the same tactics could be used against them in the future, no sense that precedents were being set that could come back to haunt them. Yeltsin would be the victor, and freedom would be protected. What haunted was the recent memory of the violence that emanated from the Supreme Soviet in 1993, the coup in 1991, and the prospect of a communist revival. They enthusiastically supported the newly invigorated Yeltsin and his aggressive campaign, which amounted to supporting the closing of the media to Yeltsin's opponent and the vigorous anticommunist explosion in media. They feared a restoration of censorship and of a closed political system, and had no problem actively hitching their wagon to Yeltsin's reelection effort if that would mean preventing a communist restoration. We will never know if those fears were founded or not, but what is certain is that the precedent set in 1996 backfired on them terribly.

The propaganda campaign was not limited to nightly news broadcasts on the campaign. Other programming aired with the goal of scaring the voters against Zyuganov. The major networks broadcast exposes of Stalin's crimes, of the famine caused by forced collectivization in the 1920s and 1930s, of the decimation of the officer corps immediately prior to the German invasion in World War II and the disaster that followed, of the gulag, of the hard labor camps, and of the purges. All served as not-so-subtle hints to the electorate of the perils of communism. When they ran movies they were often *Burnt By the Sun* and other anticommunist exposes, and interview programs featured survivors of the gulag and widows and orphans of the purges and Great Terror, all recounting their terrible experiences during Stalin's reign. Program hosts or network officials would introduce or interrupt to interject references to the current campaign and to Zyuganov, making the connection unmistakable. If you elect Zyuganov, you bring back Stalin.

Those who tried to convey the message that 1996 was not 1936, and that Zyuganov was not Stalin did not get far. Their efforts were overwhelmed by the other images and messages conveyed and fell on deaf ears. Why take the risk? It was all gross exaggeration, of course. As a former journalist for *Forbes* magazine noted, "To speak of...Zyuganov's Communist Party in the same breath as gulags, famine, and civil war was a bit like describing today's South Carolina as a land of Ku Klux Klan gatherings and lynchings."[47] But the propaganda frenzy engulfed the electorate and swept it in the desired direction.

The problem was, of course, not the negative strategy. Election campaigns in established democracies are often fiercely negative and always have been. It is the democratic requirement that all candidates have the ability to campaign, have equal access to the media, and have an ability to respond to statements made by opponents. This is all required for free and fair elections, and this is precisely what the marriage between the oligarchs and the Kremlin prevented. The requirement of equal access demands that news coverage give equal time in reports on candidates. It also requires equal access to advertising time and space, that any candidate willing and able to pay receives air time and that there be no discrimination in the offering of time slots.

The 1996 Russian campaign was not free or fair in any of these respects. When candidates lack equal access, a mishmash is indeed made of the electorate's brains. The oligarchs denied Zyuganov access throughout the onslaught. No major outlet would afford him advertising spots or provide him a chance to respond in news interviews. The only times offered and the only news coverage of his campaign were between the hours of midnight and 6 A.M. The networks closed access to Zyuganov during main viewing hours. Zyuganov simply did not have an opportunity either to present his own message or to fire back against Yeltsin. The Central Election Commission, ostensibly set up to oversee elections and ensure adherence to election laws, never stepped in, hardly a surprise as it is staffed by and answers to the Kremlin.

It was this closure of media access that set the antidemocratic precedent for the future. The decision to wed the Yeltsin campaign to the oligarchs effectively stole the campaign. It ensured that there would not be a free and fair election, the most basic and necessary element of democratic politics. The oligarchs, and thus the campaign, controlled the media, they denied Zyuganov access to that media, and they used the media to whoop up a frenzy of fear about both Zyuganov and anyone affiliated with him.

More shadowy processes may also have been at work. On June 11, five days before the election, a bomb exploded at the Tulskaya metro station in Moscow, killing four and injuring more than a dozen passengers. There were no claims of responsibility, and no arrests were ever made. At the time, rumors of official involvement seemed so wildly unfounded as to not be taken seriously. In retrospect, given similarly timed deadly blasts in each future national election, never with any claim of responsibility and never any assigned in the form of arrests, the rumors seem less wild.[48] Suggestions that the FSB (Federal Security Service, the successor to the KGB) had a role in the June 1996 bombings place among the variety of motivations the desire to create a state-of-emergency situation put the security forces back at the center of Kremlin power, and realize the earlier desire of Korzhakov and Barsukov, detailed above, to cancel the elections altogether.[49] None of that happened, of course, however Yeltsin did use the bombings both to confirm the fear the campaign had generated and to call for stability in the face of that fear. "Don't give in to provocation," he said. He condemned efforts "toward destabilizing the situation in the capital and creating an atmosphere of uncertainty and fear in Russia," and said, "The best answer to the extremists is to vote on June 16, vote for civil peace, for stability and for the future of Russia."[50] In other words, vote for Yeltsin, or there will be worse to come. Even if it was a pure terrorist attack, the results held lessons for future unsavory acts out of the Kremlin.

The strategy of generating fear to win votes worked spectacularly well. Having fomented fear of a return to communism, Yeltsin's team prevented a Zyuganov victory, by 35–32 percent in the first round, and 54% to 40% in the second. Fear won, by uniting much of the political elite, all of the major mass media, and the newly superrich business class. By polarizing the campaign and exaggerating the danger, the combination of the oligarchs, the media, and the administration ensured a second term for Yeltsin. Yeltsin fell gravely ill immediately after the election and spent much of the next four years in hospitals and rest homes.[51] He was never the same, never at full strength in his second term. However, the oligarchs were then firmly entrenched in the Kremlin, and as a result had a victory far greater than they could ever have imagined. Nobody could touch them, because anyone in a position to do so was an accomplice.

Payback and Precedent

The first presidential election under the new constitution set an "at-all-costs" precedent, one in which the incumbent in the Kremlin controlled the outcome. There was a vote, there were several candidates, but the process leading up to that vote was not free and fair. Together the staff and the oligarchs violated without consequence all media laws on fair access. They obliterated legal limits to campaign spending and transparency. A decade later, Russia has yet to have a national election that could be termed free, fair, and truly competitive. That first election could have set a different precedent. Other options were available, some of them even worse for democracy. However, the most basic necessary component of democracy—free and fair elections—has never been met under Russia's new system, and that as much as anything is responsible for the dictatorship that has emerged.

In the short term, it meant a thoroughly corrupt regime. The close association between the president and the oligarchs in the campaign brought institutionalized corruption as a consequence. After the election, the oligarchs wanted their payback. Having set aside their differences, having promised their assistance to the president to get him reelected, and having delivered, they expected substantial rewards for that support. Given the propaganda of the campaign, they could argue they saved Yeltsin, saved market reforms, and saved the country, and who in the Kremlin could refute those claims? Indeed, they saw the victory as theirs, and they expected rewards and sought to collect them. These they received in spades.

The payback was swift and extraordinary. Yeltsin immediately named Potanin and Berezovsky to major posts in the new government. Potanin became deputy prime minister in charge of overseeing the economy. Berezovsky was appointed to the National Security Council, where he eventually would become secretary. At the same time they, like all the others who joined the government, continued to hold their corporate positions, running their businesses while serving in government. They could now use their public office to further their private gain. Potanin's first task was to reform the bank system that had been so profitable to him and his Uneximbank, and to the other oligarchs. He had no interest in making the banking sector more open, competitive, or fair! Indeed, his efforts were to close rather than open the banking sector.[52] Beyond official titles and making policy in their own interests, other benefits accrued as well. Gusinsky received his expanded time on Channel 4 for NTV. The oligarchs secured state resources and freedom from tax burdens, and won new government projects.[53]

And so grew the practice of buying politicians and policy, and of placing loyal subjects in positions of power. In government, Berezovsky, Potanin, and the others pushed their own projects, their own interests, and their own people. The most lucrative project was the new loans-for-shares scheme in the next wave of privatization, which put the energy and utilities sectors in their hands at a fraction of their actual value. Corruption in government was extraordinary and complete. The oligarchs' deal with the Kremlin in 1996 brought the precedent of the purchase of cabinet posts that continues to this day.[54] It triggered also the purchase of officials throughout government, as the other oligarchs sought to counterbalance the inside influence of Potanin and Berezovsky by purchasing their own allies in other positions.[55] Almost anyone of any significance in the Russian government "belonged" to someone.

Those who did not, those loyal to the cause of creating a market democracy, did try to effect a counterattack, to attempt to limit their reach. The ill-fated Kiriyenko government, in particular, tried to isolate the oligarchs from policymaking, and Chubais made an effort to assert his political independence and future by initiating a crackdown on the oligarchs' influence. These efforts failed spectacularly. With the assistance of Dyachenko and Yumashev, the oligarchs joined the inner circle in the Kremlin that came to be known as "The Family," that close and corrupt circle of oligarchs, relatives, and two or three personal advisors that defined Yeltsin's final years as president. Anything and anyone requiring the ailing president's attention went through his daughter Dyachenko, or his son-in-law Yumashev, or his new Chief of Staff Aleksander Voloshin. They were the people with regular direct access to Yeltsin. Through their close connections and influence, the group of bankers frequently named ministers and deputy ministers, the formation of and changes in the government.

A recent major study on corruption indicates that corruption in government has reached epic proportions in Russia. Positions in government are sold for enormous sums. To become a deputy minister today costs upwards of $500,000, with a price scale ranging from several times more for cabinet level positions all the way down to rank-and-file posts.[56] In 2005, seven men from President Putin's close circle controlled nine monopolies with assets over $220 billion, or 40 percent of Russia's gross domestic product.[57] Corruption defines the Russian government.

If the institutionalization of corruption in government was the most significant short-term consequence, the loss of independence for the media held grave long-term consequences. Those consequences were not visible right away. Having succeeded in warding off a communist return, the journalists went back to their job of investigative and independent reporting. NTV went back to its role of being a watchdog. Newspaper reporters began writing about corruption and the president's fading health in a critical fashion. That the former was a direct consequence of the campaign events in which they were a part, and the latter was easily predicted, was beside the point. As journalists in a free press they reported on the problems in the government. As for the election, Yeltsin was indebted to them, not they to him, or so they saw it. There was no reason to continue to lavish praise. This was the case for many individual journalists.

But they were exposed in ways that were not immediately apparent. The media were deeply compromised, as an institution. The campaign "exposed the dangers of reinstalling state control over the media and of turning it into a vehicle of support for the President, the Government, the State."[58] The Leninist concept of the media as a weapon, as a tool in the hands of politicians, reemerged with a vengeance.[59] Despite continued Western press accounts still casting him as the best hope for democracy, in fact Chubais was behaving as if in authoritarian control. According to one account, he called leading media executives—editors and producers—to the Kremlin and blasted them for daring to critique him and his policies, and threatened them physically should they continue.[60] Direct intimidation for unflattering reports helped fuel a growing censorship. The Kremlin expected the journalists to behave, for their bosses were part of the government. They were all on the same team, right?

More generally, the media in Russia do not and never have viewed themselves as part of civil society, are not observers, and are not a conduit between government and society. There was a chance for the Russian press to move in that direction, and it was beginning to do so, but 1996 changed all that. The media were now not oriented to informing and reaching the citizens, but rather to reaching one viewer, the president. In this way, though not immediately evident, they came to work for the president. It was a precarious position to be in, to be sure. All their eggs lay in the personal predilections of the holder of that office.

Enter a KGB field officer into that position of power, and their fate was sealed. Putin has used the precedent of Kremlin control over media messages established under Yeltsin as an excuse for seizing the media assets from Gusinsky and Berezovsky, and returning the electronic press to the state. Fearing similar reprisals, the print media have largely fallen into line. If one wants news in Russia, it is hardly worth watching the television, listening to the radio, or buying a newspaper. The legacy of the 1996 election was to destroy one of Russia's best hopes for democracy—a vibrant and open media with energetic young reporters willing to use their considerable talents to take risks in the name of informing the public. These reporters are now dead, killed in mysterious, unsolved circumstances, cowered into self-censorship, or work for foreign news agencies.

When Putin began his onslaught on the press, neither the media owners nor the journalists themselves had any possible defense. Who would have sympathy for the likes of Gusinsky and Berezovsky? The public loathed the oligarchs. Enough was known about them by 2000, paradoxically thanks to the investigative reporters, about how they amassed and abused their wealth, for the public to roundly hate whichever label was used, "oligarchs" or "family." Putin's popular support in large part was based on the belief that he would clean things up. That was a far-fetched belief, to say the least, but it was nonetheless a popularly held one. What he did, in reality, was to choose sides. Any oligarch with media interests, or any discernible political interests for that matter, was on the wrong side. The media in particular, however, were doomed.

The deep affection that developed for the free press in the late 1980s and early 1990s was lost, and largely because of the conscious and cynical manipulation of the public in 1996. That the media had become a political actor was clear to anyone who looked, and it was equally clear that politics in Russia was deeply corrupt and thoroughly nondemocratic. A plague on both your houses was the reaction. Putin used the precedent of 1996, taking the close association between the Kremlin and the press and the reintroduction of the concept of the press as a weapon, to eliminate the middleman. Why pay off media owners to have their outlets report as the Kremlin wants them to, when the Kremlin can simply seize the media and run it on its own? The oligarchs were an inconvenience, an obstacle.

In short, the 1996 presidential election brought institutionalized corruption in government that paved the way to destruction of the media as an independent voice. But tragic and monumental as each of these would prove to be, neither represented the deepest blow to hopes for democracy. This was the first election under the new constitution. Under that constitution, for elections to be free and fair requires a president and an administration that wants them to be so. Yeltsin's 1996 campaign actively violated the main laws intended to make them free and fair: laws on access to media and laws on financing. It did so with impunity. Wary of competition and fearing defeat, they made a choice to take any action whatsoever to avoid the former as a means to prevent the latter. No means existed to prevent such transgressions. But alternatives did exist. Democratic elections hinged on the inclinations of the incumbent and his advisors to want them, to allow competition and embrace the possibility that the electorate would choose someone else. It required a president willing and able to put trust in the citizens as sovereign. Such a president could have chosen to allow a free-wheeling campaign for the presidency. Yeltsin did not choose that democratic path in 1996. Nor would he ever choose it. As the first president, he set the course for future attitudes toward elections. The course he set in 1996 undermined them, and in 1999 he used another election to slam the door shut. The next chapter discusses this last critical juncture, over the problem of how to handle transfer of power at the top.

5

Abandoning Democracy: Anointing a Successor

Boris Yeltsin often liked to think of himself as Russia's George Washington. He knew about Washington, admired him, and speech writers and staff were aware of his desire to be remembered in the same light.[1] He wanted to be remembered as a great political figure in Russia, one "without whom history would be very different."[2] In some respects Russia's first elected president explicitly emulated the first American president. His decision not to associate himself with any political party, as discussed in Chapter 4, may have been the most important example of this sporadic emulation. Washington made a conscious strategic decision to "stand above the fray" of daily partisan politics, crafting for himself the air of leader of the country as a whole and serving "as a symbol of national unity."[3] As one authority on Washington put it, "[What] he cared about most passionately, [was] his reputation as the 'singular figure' who embodied the meaning of the American Revolution in its most elevated and transcendent form."[4] This is who Yeltsin wanted to be for Russia. He rejected any party affiliation and never actively supported any political organization after his departure from the Communist Party, aiming to present himself as standing above politics.[5] However, Yeltsin was selective in his emulation and ignored the most important lesson. In so doing he forfeited any hope of being remembered as Russia's Washington. The last important decision Washington made as president was perhaps the most important for the development of democracy in America: to depart at the end of his second term and allow the people to choose their next president without interference from himself. Every new democracy faces the dilemma of leadership succession and how to handle the problem of leadership change. Yeltsin chose a different path, one that, combined with the earlier decisions, closed the door on democratic development.

Democracy requires an open, free, and fair contest in which the population plays a direct role in selecting its leaders. "Democratic norms require a willingness to accept political defeat: to leave office upon losing an election, to follow rules even when they work against one's interests."[6] The decision whether to allow step down, and under what terms, is one that every first leader in a democratizing country must confront. It is a particularly difficult decision to make where no tradition or precedent exists for voluntary, peaceful leadership change or democratic leadership selection. Such was the case in Russia, as it was in the early United States and in any state lacking a democratic history.

Washington made several decisions at the end of his presidency around which the future of American democracy would pivot. He rejected, and made clear he considered insulting and repulsive, pressures from a variety of circles to anoint himself King George the First. The pressure came from those who feared the potential of chaos, instability, and even war that may result from unbridled competition for the top political position in the country.[7] Cries for stability and order accompanied the suggestion that Washington remain in office indefinitely. He rejected these calls, as he rejected similar suggestions that he become "president-for-life."[8] Instead, Washington made a momentous decision to retire, quietly exiting the political scene. But equally important to this decision was his behavior in light of it. Washington refused to appoint a successor, and even refused to state a preference in the competition that ensued. He stayed out of the campaign to succeed him, despite his own vice president's candidacy. He considered it inappropriate even to comment much less take an active position on who the next President of the United States should be. It was for the people to decide. Even in his private communications he did not express a position on the raging campaign.[9] While still holding the office, he watched as a normal citizen with the rest of the country as a freewheeling campaign ensued between his vice president, John Adams, about whom he was lukewarm, and Thomas Jefferson, whom he despised. Some suggest that had Washington been inclined to appoint a successor it would have been neither Adams nor Jefferson, but one who never became president, Alexander Hamilton.[10]

Though few authors focus on the point, it is indisputable that Washington's decision as a sitting president to stay out of the campaign to determine his successor set a tremendously important precedent.[11] He was "the first head of a modern state to hand over the reins to a duly elected successor," and his momentous decision set an example that enabled future presidential elections to proceed smoothly, and made it more difficult for the defeated to contest results or for future presidents to cling to power.[12] As one authoritative history puts it, "The most weighty factor of all in 1796 was George Washington...Hardly a step in the process of nation-building nine years before at Philadelphia would have been what it was were it not for the expectation, universal in every sense, that George Washington would be the Republic's first Chief Magistrate. What, then, would happen when Washington made his departure? Scarcely a citizen in all the Republic had more than the remotest idea."[13] Had he held office until his death, or tried to direct the outcome, "subsequent presidential successions would have been more difficult" and democracy in America may not have survived. Allowing the people to decide was one of the most important steps in entrenching a democratic path for the country. His enemy King George III is reported to have said that if Washington retired and went back to his farm, "he will be the greatest man in the world."[14] The specific precedent holds to this day: Ronald Reagan was not active in the 1988 campaign that resulted in the election of his vice president, George Bush; Bill Clinton did not participate in his vice president's controversial and ultimately unsuccessful campaign in 2000. It is, in the United States, considered improper for a sitting president actively to engage in the electoral process over his succession. They stay out.

This is relevant for Russia because, according to his speech writer, this was a history about which President Yeltsin was aware and on which he was well read.[15] In the end, however, he chose not to let that history guide his own actions. Rather than stand aside and allow a competitive campaign and open democratic election to determine his successor, rather than be the first head of state in Russia to hand power to a freely elected successor, Yeltsin made the decision for the country on his own. He preempted the campaign by naming his successor, handing the presidency to a little-known former KGB officer, Vladimir Putin, on December 31, 1999. His decision was antidemocratic in both form and content, and in the important precedent it set. While Yeltsin's action may have adhered to the letter of the Russian Constitution, it did violence to the spirit, as it did to remaining prospects for democratic development.

Yeltsin's decision restricted political competition. It compelled the liberal wing of the Russian political spectrum to capitulate in support of the chosen successor, with no hope left of making its case to the country in a spirited contest for the direction of Russia's economic and political future. It compelled centrist groups to drop out altogether, lacking any hope of organizing a campaign in the shortened timetable and against a new incumbent. It was thoroughly undemocratic and set precedents that Putin has used to consolidate dictatorship.

Why and how Yeltsin decided to hand power to a former KGB spy, rather than to allow a competitive election that would revive prospects for democratic development, is the subject of this chapter.[16] The uncertainty regarding new procedures for leadership change presents a critical juncture in the development of any political regime. As democracy is predicated on particular procedures, above all on open, free, and fair competitive elections, the precedents set in the first instance of leadership change hold particular significance for the potential development of a democratic political system. This chapter discusses how and why free, fair, and competitive elections were not allowed to take place in Russia. The concluding section will discuss the immediate political consequences of this action, and the longer-term consequences for democracy. The final two chapters will explore the nature of the rising dictatorship under Putin and the prospects for the future as Putin's second term nears its end.

The Search Is On: Everyone Is a Successor

That the matter of who would follow Yeltsin was a central concern in the Kremlin was obvious from the dizzying rotation of prime ministers during his second term. Each change brought proclamations that the new incumbent was the sure presidential front-runner. The administration, the press, and the public were acutely aware of the problem attendant to leadership change, and the prolonged buzz around this issue was unlike any other since the collapse of the communist system.[17] For their part, Yeltsin's staff began considering "operation successor" immediately after the 1996 elections, and Yeltsin personally became involved in earnest after the economic default of 1998.[18] In large part, the matter stemmed from Yeltsin's earlier decision to remain unaffiliated with and not actively to promote political parties. Had he done so, one might have expected a party nomination process would have been devised to determine the candidates who would compete. But in the absence of such a system and being resolutely disassociated from parties altogether, Yeltsin was left to be an independent player in the determination of his successor. In the final months of 1999, meanwhile, The Family became intensely worried about the possible outcome of a free-wheeling campaign to decide who would be the next president of Russia. They had no intent of allowing it to occur, and made one of their tasks, indeed their primary and most important task, to select that individual themselves.

The authors of the constitution envisioned this possibility as early as 1993. While transfer of power to the prime minister and early elections were supposed to be emergency provisions on the death, incapacitation or removal of a president, some also envisioned a hand over of power and even considered it desirable. "We understood that we needed to know how to transfer power," says former Yeltsin legal advisor Sergei Shakhrai. Voluntary resignation and hand over of power was "part of the political discussion" at the inception of the constitution.[19] Open, competitive elections free from interference by those holding power is a minimal prerequisite of democratic politics. Aversion to and fear of the outcome of an open, competitive, and free political process is, at its heart, antidemocratic. However, the 1996 election had already set a precedent for circumscribing free competition, and by 1999 a commitment to open political competition was not present in the Kremlin. Indeed, Yeltsin's close advisors, which after the 1998 economic default no longer included the pro-democracy voices, opposed such a prospect altogether. Instead, they would choose.

They had a convenient and built-in mechanism for vetting possible successors. Because the constitution gave the president exclusive power over his prime minister, a president could observe and evaluate heads of government as possible successors. In his final months Yeltsin turned the prime minister post into a revolving door of potential successors, with each occupant hailed as Yeltsin's handpicked successor to assume the presidency upon his departure. From Chernomyrdin to Kiriyenko to Primakov to Stepashin, every prime minister came to the position hailed as the obvious shoe-in to be Russia's next president. In his final two years, Yeltsin made six changes in the top government post, and each time the assumption was the same.

Yeltsin's active involvement in the search for a successor became earnest after the economic default of August 1998. The short-term treasury issue (GKO) pyramid scheme, which used government loans to fund the Russian economy and privatization markets, loans that ultimately fell prey the oligarchs' capital flight streams, crashed as the government was unable to pay off its skyrocketing debt. The Russian banks that had exclusive access to the GKO emissions put nothing back into the domestic economy. Indeed, most of the emissions after 1996 simply went to pay off the debt from the GKOs used to fuel the economy in advance of those elections. Eventually, the pyramid collapsed and Russia defaulted.[20] Scandal, which already surrounded the privatization program, now engulfed the economic system which had led to bankruptcy while a handful of oligarchs became spectacularly rich.

Any who may have hoped after the 1996 election that the political elite that had mobilized around Yeltsin would transform into a political party supporting his policies were proven naive at best. Yeltsin did not recognize or make this a priority, and those politicians again splintered into myriad factions. Yeltsin himself had disappeared for dire health reasons after the election, and by the time he returned he was weakened physically and politically. His popularity again plummeted, the coalition splintered, and the oligarchs cemented their control in the Kremlin with the support, above all, of Yeltsin's daughter and son-in-law. They promoted and benefitted from the pyramid scheme that put billions of dollars into their private accounts.

The government was bankrupt, the economists who brought the policies leading to that default were discredited, Yeltsin was ill, his base of support dissolved, and those closest to him were known for corruption and greed. It was in these conditions that the revolving door to the prime minister's post began to spin. Engulfed in the general uproar over the default, The Family and the oligarchs genuinely feared for the future of economic policies that had enriched them, for the future of their own amassed wealth, and for their physical futures. They would not risk democratic politics in the form of open electoral competition to choose the next president. Secret Kremlin machinations would control the outcome.

When Yeltsin named him prime minister and declared him his presidential successor on August 8, 1999, Putin became the sixth head of government in just seventeen months. Because Russia's president names the prime minister, it is reasonable to assume that the latter enjoys the president's trust and support. Accordingly, each of Yeltsin's prime ministers in his final months in office carried for the media, the public, and Kremlin insiders alike, the presumed tag of president-in-waiting. The certainty with which the claim was made only increased each time Yeltsin made a change. Viktor Chernomyrdin (twice), Sergei Kiriyenko, Yevgeniy Primakov, and Sergei Stepashin each had his turn as the universally proclaimed favorite and Yeltsin's hand-chosen successor to become the next president of Russia. With so many faces in such a short period of time, it was as if everyone was Yeltsin's preferred successor.

The dizzying turnover makes it difficult to believe that "Operation Successor," as the hand over of power to Putin became known in Russia, was planned out in its specific contours long in advance, despite some suggestions that the FSB secretly manipulated the political situation to bring one of its own to power.[21] As late as December 1998, Putin himself did not behave like a man who believed he had any political future, much less as Yeltsin's successor. Putin, then head of the FSB, confided to a reporter that he considered his time in government to be "an interesting page in my life," that would be short-lived. Yeltsin had clearly announced he would not run for a third term, and "The future president will of course want to have a qualified person loyal to himself, it is clear I will have to go. Boris Nikolayevich knows that I am perfectly comfortable with this," he said.[22] Putin, along with the rest of the country at the time, assumed Primakov the shoe-in to become the next president. At most he hoped to earn Primakov's trust to gain appointment to head his old unit, the special operations forces within the FSB.[23]

Yeltsin turned to Primakov after the default as a compromise choice, with the support of the left and the right. Given Yeltsin's inclination to strike such compromise, Primakov seemed a logical choice to have Yeltsin's long-time support, much as centrist former Prime Minister Chernomyrdin had enjoyed for years. Later, when Yeltsin replaced Primakov with Stepashin, there was every reason to believe that the president had bigger things for his longtime political ally who had served him in multiple capacities. Stepashin was a man Yeltsin knew well and whom he could trust. Like Primakov, Stepashin had a security background, having begun his career in the Interior Ministry forces and worked his way up the latter to serving as minister. However, Yeltsin dismissed him after a mere three months in office, turning to the virtually unknown Putin, a career spy who served as deputy mayor in St. Petersburg and in secondary administrative posts in the Kremlin before Yeltsin tapped him in a surprise move to head the FSB, a position he held for barely one year.

What explains this revolving door that embodied both the prime minister post and the presumed position as presidential successor? Why did Yeltsin chew through so many so rapidly? Why, indeed, was there a notion of "successor" at all under a constitution that called for free and fair elections to the top elected office in the country? More than anything else, fear and self-interest again moved Yeltsin to snuff out an open campaign for president.

Protection

The intersection of fear and greed drove antidemocratic decisions in the Kremlin. An open political competition would have risked election of a president hostile to The Family, who might launch a campaign of recrimination against and punishment of those who worked in and profited during the Yeltsin Administration. To some, "it was clear that there would be a revenge, and then Yeltsin, The Family and everyone would die," and so "a scheme was needed for handing over power to a strong [president] who would guarantee Yeltsin his personal security."[24]

Yeltsin's daughter, Tatiana Dyachenko, was central to the final decision to hand power to Putin. She was instrumental both to the president's decision and to his emphasis on protection. As Yeltsin's health declined, Dyachenko played an ever-increasing role as advisor, gatekeeper, and confidant. She and her fiancé, Valentin Yumashev, had much at stake if their fears came to pass, for they had facilitated bringing the oligarchs into the highest circles of power, and therefore stood to be at the center of attention of any unfriendly president. It is not so much that Yeltsin sought to protect individuals such as Berezovsky, indeed there is evidence he resented the oligarchs' influence over personnel and policy in his administration and was conflicted about their presence and their role.[25] However, Yeltsin in failing health was unable to focus on combating their growing influence.[26] Rather, he was increasingly dependent upon and concerned about a smaller inner-circle that included his daughter, Yumashev, and perhaps one or two other aides. It was they who, in turn, watched out for their wealthy friends. The latter simply had nightmares about what might become of their fortunes and of themselves.[27]

Again we see how the consequences of those first decisions in 1992 rippled through Russian politics. The effort to create a market economy without putting into place democratic political and legal institutions resulted in institutionalized corruption at the apex of power in the Kremlin.

Neoliberal economic reforms without political mechanisms for accountability and legality corrupted the new system to the core. When Yeltsin's second term neared its end, fear of reprisals for that corruption moved those around the president to maneuver to install a new leader not on the basis of competence or policy, much less electoral legitimacy, but rather for the promise of protection and even the hope that they themselves might secretly control their puppet.

Yeltsin also became preoccupied with assuring his and his family's—however one wishes to interpret that word—safety. The political consequence of the 1998 default was to clean out his administration, removing those who devised his economic reform policies, such as Gaidar, Kiriyenko, and Nemtsov, as well as his political and legal staff from speech writers on down. These were replaced overwhelmingly by those with backgrounds in the various security services such as the interior ministry police, the military, and the old KGB, now the FSB. Yeltsin's search for a successor would be limited to those with military or intelligence training, who would be unquestionably loyal to Yeltsin personally. Why the security services? Because one with such a background could offer a more plausible guarantee to be able to control those with the guns, to control that sprawling security apparatus. Such control was a necessary component to being able to protect Yeltsin and his circle.

The revolving door Yeltsin created in his government reflected his search for the right person, the most trustworthy, from among those with security service backgrounds. Primakov initially seemed an obvious choice for a handpicked successor. He was in a position to protect Yeltsin and his family, as not only did he have the KGB background but also he enjoyed support from the center and left of the political spectrum, from where the greatest danger would presumably have come. Primakov was known for his independent politics, his desire to be independent of the oligarchs, and was not himself corrupt. A longtime Soviet bureaucrat, Primakov had a biography closest to Yeltsin among likely presidential hopefuls in an election, and was close in manner and of the same generation. While these attributes did not describe the oligarchs or advisors close to the president, they did describe Yeltsin himself. And this all appealed to him.

Yeltsin, however, came to doubt Primakov's loyalty.[28] In part it was his fierce independence, but more troubling to Yeltsin was that the heart of Primakov's political support was the communist left and the nationalist right. Those were Yeltsin's main enemies. Even worse for Yeltsin was that Primakov displayed obvious ambition, he openly pined for the presidency and as he assumed more control over decision making and cemented his power as prime minister, Primakov's actions increasingly appeared threatening. Putin confirmed to a reporter at the time what many already suspected, that Primakov, with Yeltsin in a weak physical and political state, had assumed most of the functions of the presidency.[29] Primakov "never hid his political ambitions," which made him appear more out for himself than committed to Yeltsin. The ambition, independence, and power base made Primakov for Yeltsin "an unloyal successor who was absolutely unacceptable." Whether the next president would be a heavyweight or not was less important than that the individual not be threatening to Yeltsin personally.[30]

Primakov fell out of favor with The Family by trying to remove the oligarchs from the Kremlin.[31] He launched investigations into their activities, part of his strategy to expand his own popularity and power. While not threatening to Yeltsin directly, who may even have approved, the oligarchs obviously wanted Primakov out. They appealed to their patrons, above all Dyachenko and Yumashev, to convince Yeltsin to make a change. The Family wanted Primakov out, and so he was out.

Primakov's strength and popularity, however, made removing him a problem. The trick would be to replace him with someone who would not be damaged by being associated with Primakov's removal.[32] As a first step, The Family convinced Yeltsin to remove his Chief of Staff, Nikolai Bordyuzha, who increasingly appeared oriented toward the presumed successor. Bordyuzha fought back, warning Yeltsin of the massive corruption in the Kremlin, and that as a military man dedicated to serving Russia he could not continue to serve as head of the Security Council, as Yeltsin had offered. He implored Yeltsin to reconsider, and instead dismiss from the Kremlin not only the oligarchs, but also Yumashev, Voloshin, and his daughter. Whether Bordyuzha's gambit was self-interested or followed genuine ideals, it presented Yeltsin with an opportunity, another choice point that would help define the process of leadership change in Russia. Had Yeltsin chosen to follow Bordyuzha's path, it could have led to an open electoral process. He appeared noncommittal at first, saying, "Ok, I will think about this." But within hours Yeltsin dismissed Bordyuzha from all of his posts.[33] An open electoral process was not to be, and two months later Primakov met a similar fate.

Yeltsin told Primakov, "You have fulfilled your role; now, it is clear, you will need to resign. Make this easy and sign your letter of resignation, indicating any reasons you choose," Primakov refused to do so. "I don't want to make anything easier for anyone," he said. "You have every constitutional power to sign such a decree if you wish, but...you will be making a huge mistake. The issue is not me but the cabinet, which has worked extremely well."[34] Indeed, it had. Russia had emerged from default and balanced its budget. Agreement was pending with the IMF, and the government was popular both in the Duma and with the public. But for Yeltsin, Primakov had in a sense performed too well, had become too strong, and now he was threatening both the oligarchs and their benefactors. Primakov was initiating investigations into their past activities and maneuvering to remove them from positions of power. Dyachenko leaned on Yeltsin to remove Primakov, which the president did, replacing him with Stepashin.

The sigh of relief from The Family was almost publicly audible.[35] Stepashin had held many positions and long served under Yeltsin. Surely, Yeltsin had decided to anoint his close, longtime ally to succeed him. In fact, Yeltsin used Stepashin, considering him more of a loyal soldier deployed to fill a role in a larger play than as a man with long-term leadership ability. Stepashin was also popular, but his tenure lasted a mere three months before Yeltsin replaced him with Putin, whom he immediately declared as his choice to be the next president.

Yeltsin had already decided on Putin as his preferred successor when he appointed Stepashin, but recognized that the dismissal of Primakov would be wildly unpopular in the Duma, among much of the political elite, and with the general public. He needed a sacrificial lamb to buffer the sting of Primakov's firing. Prior to naming Stepashin, in fact, Yeltsin asked legal experts whether the constitution permitted him to name an interim prime minister for a defined period.[36] Told it did not, the constitution nevertheless permits the president to dismiss prime ministers at will, so Yeltsin named Stepashin to be an interim prime minister without telling anyone. He never intended to leave Stepashin in the post for more than a few months, relying on his devoted political friend whom he could trust to pave the way for Putin.

Yeltsin did not reward Stepashin's loyalty by informing him of his intentions. Adding insult to injury, Yeltsin afforded Stepashin no control over his Cabinet, and Dyachenko and Berezovsky placed into the Cabinet several compromised individuals loyal to Berezovsky and The Family. Moreover, Yeltsin saddled him with the massive problem of Chechnya but did not inform him that the military was planning a second war against the troubled province. When Yeltsin told Stapashin after less than three months in office that he was being removed, Stepashin "acted uncharacteristically for a fired premier and asked the president, 'For what reason?'"[37] Yeltsin accused him of being weak and failing to counter political attacks from Primakov and Moscow Mayor Yuriy Luzhkov. It was a flimsy argument at best. Stepashin argued with the president, laying blame with Chief of Staff Aleksander Voloshin, a Berezovsky loyalist who, by attacking Gusinsky, propelled his media empire into the Primakov camp.

Stepashin gave Yeltsin pause and inclined him to investigate. Criminal investigations of Berezovsky and other oligarchs had exploded at the international level, such as the Bank of New York and the Harvard Institute for International Development scandals that featured millions of dollars of theft by individuals in or close to the Yeltsin Administration.[38] Chubais tried to the last to protect Stepashin and prevent Putin's rise, having become wary of him as secretive and hard to read even though he was responsible for Putin's initial move to the Kremlin. Yeltsin had decided, however, steadfastly avoided Chubais and three days later told Stepashin, "You are free. Clean out your office for Putin. Good bye!"[39]

Primakov and Stepashin sealed their political demise by threatening to take action against the oligarchs. The criminal investigations constituted attacks not only on the oligarchs, but by extension on their patrons. Primakov openly told the president of his intention to isolate, remove from government, and prosecute the oligarchs at the time of his dismissal. His investigations into Berezovsky and Abramovich, in particular, and his attempts to remove the oligarchs from positions of decision-making authority, proved threatening to both Dyachenko and Yumashev. It was they who ultimately convinced Yeltsin to make a change and believed Stepashin, a longtime ally, would not upset the status quo. However, Stepashin continued the investigations Primakov had launched, and confronted The Family on several occasions despite his short stint in office. It was for their stands against the oligarchs, not weakness, that both men ultimately paid.

Perhaps Primakov and Stepashin suffered also the weakness of ambition. The office of Prime Minister of Russia brought with it presumed front-runner status in the presidential election, and the presumption of Yeltsin's support for he controlled the occupant of the prime minister's office. That front-runner status naturally would make one think like a candidate, and appearing strong against the loathed oligarchs would go a long way to claiming the votes of the centrist masses in Russia. What neither seemed to grasp was that they could never sway Yeltsin to go against the wishes of his daughter and closest confidant. Yeltsin was concerned for the future safety of his family; the weakness he feared was not in the realm of decisiveness of action, but in the realm of personal loyalty. Primakov's and Stepashin's weakness was in not understanding that their actions against the oligarchs threatened Dyachenko, who would prevail upon her father to make a change. It came across as being disloyal.

Putin, however, had demonstrated that he understood the concept of unwavering loyalty toward a political patron in his protection of St. Petersburg Mayor Anatoly Sobchak.[40] This is what most impressed Yeltsin and The Family. After Sobchak lost his reelection bid, and Putin was suddenly out of the job as Deputy Mayor, friends from St. Petersburg such as Chubais and Pavel Borodin, the head of the presidential Business Office, brought him to work in the Kremlin. Putin served as Borodin's deputy for less than two years, and then for a time as the head of the Control Administration.[41] Yeltsin in early 1998 unexpectedly tapped him to head the FSB. It was a meteoric rise that seemed to come from nowhere. What made Yeltsin take such special notice of this unassuming bureaucrat were his activities shortly after arriving in Moscow, in mid-1996. Local FSB investigators in St. Petersburg had begun investigating Sobchak shortly after his election defeat. The new mayor, Vladimir Yakovlev, having defeated Sobchak was now pursuing revenge. This is just what The Family feared on a much larger scale at higher levels. During a series of interrogations Sobchak took ill, suffering a heart attack. Putin went to Yumashev, saying he was trained in special operations and wanted to protect Sobchak.[42] Yeltsin approved, and Putin organized Sobchak's escape from a St. Petersburg hospital to Paris, where he remained in exile until shortly before his death, and only after Putin was in charge of the FSB.

Yeltsin and The Family noted both the loyalty and the continuation of the peculiar Russian tendency for new leaders to take action against their predecessors. Putin later waged a scathing campaign to discredit the Prosecutor General, Skuratov, producing a videotape of him naked in a hotel room with two prostitutes. None of the identities of those in the fuzzy video could be confirmed, but the damage was done, the prosecutor's career was over. He had rid the oligarchs of a prosecutor investigating their activities, and they certainly took note. The Family, which hoped for a future president who would protect them, was most impressed that this attack against Sobchak emanated from Putin's own agency. Putin had proven himself to be loyal to those who helped him, and able to direct the forces that could protect them. It seemed clear that Putin would prioritize personal loyalty over institutional or other loyalties. As Putin arrived in Moscow a virtual political unknown, those who promoted his rise to the apex of power hoped to reap such similar rewards from their client. They believed if they promoted Putin, he would be entirely in their debt, under their control, and they would all be safe. When Yumashev asked a skeptical Igor Malashenko of NTV to support Putin as Yeltsin's successor, he assured Malashenko, "He didn't give up Sobchak. He won't give us up."[43] In the end, this could not have been more wrong, at least as it pertained to the press.

Putin is not a politician and shows little in the way of traditional political skills. Initial reports describe a man extremely uncomfortable and not particularly skilled in public political settings. Most notably, he had absolutely no competence or real interest in dealing with members of the media.[44] He conducted himself less like a politician than he did as an intelligence officer, a spy, or a bureaucrat. Unlike Primakov, Putin did not demonstrate any political ambitions because he likely had none. At the time of his appointment as prime minister, his popularity rating stood at 2 percent, largely because nobody knew who he was or for what he stood.[45] His purpose was to serve those above him. As for political views, Yeltsin knew little more about Putin than anyone else in the country did, which is to say, he did not know much at all. Yeltsin most wanted, as was the case in 1996, to prevent Zyuganov and the Communist Party, or anyone who would threaten him and his family, from coming to power. Promoting Putin did just that.

Shortly after the operation to protect Sobchak, Yeltsin began to assign Putin to other special operations tasks to organize from within the administrative staff. Among these was to identify the sources and paths of embezzlement of funds inside the military and officer corps. It was these operations won Putin the president's trust and his appointment to head the FSB.[46] Less than one year later, shortly before naming Putin prime minister in mid-1999, Yeltsin sent Berezovsky to visit him on vacation in southern France to suggest the promotion. "And in truth, when I went with Yeltsin's proposal to become prime minister, this was understood not to be a proposal to become prime minister. In reality it was a proposal to become Yeltsin's successor."[47]

If there were any doubts about Putin's control of the guns, within weeks of his taking over as prime minister several explosions rocked apartment buildings in Moscow and other cities, killing over 300 people and injuring several hundred more. As with the 1996 Moscow apartment bombings, no credible explanation exists regarding who was responsible for the explosions. But the events conveniently served to send Putin's approval rating skyrocketing upward as he presented a military face to the country and a promise of an overwhelming response. The perpetrators were never found, but the results benefitted the new leader, and claims abound that the explosions were the work not of Chechen terrorists but of Russian security officials conducting special operations on behalf of their bosses. Whether these were the work of Putin, Berezovsky, or the FSB remains unknown.[48]

What is known is that from political oblivion, Putin used the bombs as a pretense to launch a second war against Chechnya and he garnered near-universal support. Unlike the first war, the initial weeks the new campaign, while equally savage, appeared far more successful. Russian troops swarmed into Chechnya and quickly seized control of the capital, Grozny. Putin trumpeted Russia's strength, military prowess, security and order, and doing all of that in a successful war he could present as punishing terrorists, whom he famously promised to wipe out "even if we catch them in the bathroom."[49] The air of competence and the focus on restoring order and strength to the country all appealed to a public tired of disorder and malaise.

On the day of Putin's appointment as prime minister, Yeltsin openly declared him his preferred successor. When asked about Putin's chance of becoming president, the experienced political analyst Aleksey Volin found the notion laughable. The only scenario he could construct that would "enable a hopeless client, with such low ratings and no public face" to become president was, "A small winnable war."[50] Putin's ratings after the explosions and start of the war against Chechnya rose several percentage points each week.

The Decision to Hand the Presidency to Putin

Appointing Putin prime minister, indicating a preference, and supporting him in a presidential election would have been one thing. Though hardly consistent with Washington's precedent of staying out of the fray, a fair and competitive election was theoretically possible. Handing Putin the presidency was another thing altogether. This was neither necessary nor preordained. It was another conscious decision, and an extraordinary one in the face of the available alternatives. Yeltsin could have completed his term and waited out the campaign, or he could have remained in office but announced early elections. He could have overseen, even ensured, an honest campaign and vote to determine the next president, and left a lasting, pro-democratic legacy. Instead, he chose to hand the leadership of Russia to Putin, a momentous decision that left a legacy of a final blow to democracy. The people of Russia still have never selected their political leader in a free and open competition, nor experienced an open transfer of power.

The story of how Yeltsin decided to sidestep electoral competition and hand power to Putin remains murky to this day. Few details are known, and many may never be known. In some respects it bore the stamp of a typical Yeltsin decision. First, Putin was now wildly popular, with the Chechen war an apparent success with Russian troops overrunning the secessionist forces. He presented a strong and confident face, particularly next to the infirm Yeltsin. He had shown unfailing loyalty to those who had supported him in the past and could be hoped to do so for Yeltsin and his circle in the future. As prime minister he already enjoyed presidential powers with control over the military action in Chechnya. He was capable, loyal, and popular, and Yeltsin may have decided that the task was done, so why wait?

Second, Yeltsin himself was visibly weak; his speech slowed and slurred, his attention span short, he had not been able to fulfil the duties of his office for much of his second term. The aesthetics and theatrics provided by a millennium hand over of power offered the finishing touch to the decision, but not the basis. What was clear to everyone else was likely also clear to Yeltsin: his control over his administration and government was anemic at best. Because of his poor health and lack of energy, he was unable to maintain a handle on daily events. There was also a rusk that the bureaucracy would spin out of control during a lame duck period, that bureaucrats uncertain of their future would succumb to the temptation to line their own pockets in the last days of the Yeltsin presidency and possibly their last in their offices. The reality of still being president but influencing little likely became intolerable to him.[51] The rigging of the 1996 election left Russia with a president who lacked the energy needed for the job.

Third, and perhaps the most important, a powerful attraction to Yeltsin was the desire to decide for himself, and on his own terms, the moment and method of his departure. The written process in the constitution and election laws seemed arbitrary and forced. The idea of "a nice political exit" was more appealing and a hand over offered him the ability to create just such an exit. As he had no right to another term, said one of the constitution's main authors, "to sit for a year and wait, even less than a year, this would have been stupid." [52] Yeltsin "is also one who loved theatrical actions. He loved to plan things ahead. So that he was the author of the situation, so he could dictate the conditions."[53] The popularly accepted end of the millennium on December 31, 1999, provided an opportunity for a poetic end to the Yeltsin era, a chance to leave not merely on his own terms but with an unprecedented flourish, with fireworks and parties around the world the likes of which had never been seen. Yeltsin liked a party, and here was a party like no other. He would add to the bang.

Dyachenko, Yumashev, and Voloshin wrote Yeltsin's final address to the country in which he announced his decision. They were concerned both for the president's health and reputation and for their own future safety, and urged him to take the decision to step down. But it was Yeltsin himself, who made this decision.[54] It came as a surprise to virtually everyone, including those inside the Kremlin, up to the last minute. The known details of who said what to whom to convince them to make or accept the decision, and when these conversations and decisions were made, remain few.

Inflated Egos, Naivete and Economic Bolshevism: The Capitulation of the Liberal Right

Yeltsin's decision wiped out hopes for a competitive election. It shortened the time to the presidential election from six months to just three, placing insurmountable barriers before candidates who were just beginning to organize. These obstacles, combined with Putin's enormous advantage of incumbency and the status he created for himself as a wartime president, sealed the fate of his victory. Virtually all opposition dissolved.

Primakov dropped out of the presidential race, lacking time to raise funds or to build a sufficient organization to run a presidential campaign. This was in part because Berezovsky's and Gusinsky's media savaged him in the parliamentary campaign to such an extent that, with only ninety days to the presidential election, he had no hope of making a comeback. Yeltsin's resignation left the recent front-runner no time to regroup. Several other candidates made the same decision, including virtually the entire liberal wing of the political spectrum.

The SPS (Union of Right Forces) was the reincarnation of Democratic Russia and Russia's Choice, which Chubais, Nemtsov, Kiriyenko, and Gaidar formed after their collective ouster in the wake of the economic default. Opinion polls placed SPS within the margin of error in the parliamentary elections, meaning they risked having no representation in the Duma after 1999, a recipe for political oblivion, if they stood on their own. In meetings of the leaders of several liberal groups, including Chubais, Nemtsov, Khakamada, and Gaidar, the liberal right decided to capitulate and throw their support behind Putin and Unity to save their political skin.[55] Berezovsky, operating from inside the Kremlin, had firmly hitched his future to Putin's "Unity" party, a collection of military officers, internal security police, and FSB officials entirely subject to Putin's will. Through his control of Channel One and his media machine, Berezovsky relentlessly savaged all opponents while glorifying Putin and the order he would bring to Russia.[56] SPS did not want to be subject to such attacks, as it would have meant their political extinction because Gusinsky and NTV were already doing so, having cast their lot with Yavlinsky's Yabloko, the social-democratic opposition that consistently polled 7–9 percent.

Yavlinsky and the other liberal leaders for a decade stubbornly refused to form a united liberal front, allowing personal disputes to take precedence over political utility. SPS's leaders could have tried to iron out those differences, including individually stepping aside and supporting Yavlinsky, in the name of creating a united opposition from the liberal right. But they and Yavlinsky allowed personal dislike to trump political wisdom. Another option would have been to oppose Putin on their own. But had SPS decided to go that route, it would have met with savage attacks from the entirety of the media—Berezovsky's, Gusinsky's, the government's, and the left. They would have been lone wolves. So their political choice, as they saw it, was either total defeat and the certainty of political obscurity, or to throw in their lot with Putin. They decided to throw in their lot with Putin, putting up no liberal opposition in the presidential election. Yavlinsky would run on his own as always and poll his usual single-digit result.

What is surprising, however, is that the liberal elite did not merely drop out, did not merely embrace Putin, but fully capitulated before him. Only Boris Nemtsov openly opposed the strategic decision to support Putin, for emotional or intuitive reasons, as Nemtsov explained:

> I have never supported him once...because I am deeply convinced that those who come from the KGB should not lead Russia. Not because these are bad people, but because their view on life and on the world is not compatible with the needs of a head of state. These people have been trained for something completely different. They studied for a completely different path in life. And because of their qualities, particularly their extreme suspiciousness, their distrustfulness, their closed nature, right? Everything they study in the KGB school. All of this in my mind can only be harmful when you occupy the post of head of state. I think that if Putin had limited himself exclusively to humanitarian legal education, we would live now in a different country. But that which they taught him there, in my view, is an impediment to the development of a free country....He has a deep distrust and dislike for freedom, for criticism, and for opposition. He always sees them as some sort of hatred or violence against him , which seeks to destroy him, and so forth. This is like any member of the special forces in this regard.[57]

However, even Nemtsov would fall into step, unwittingly helping Putin in his crackdown against the media and stifling of political opposition, as discussed in Chapter 6. Malashenko of NTV was also wary of Putin, telling Yumashev, "I don't know much about Putin, but I know about him one fundamental thing—he's KGB and KGB can't be trusted. So I can't [support him]."[58] This triggered another war between Gusinsky and Berezovsky, the latter orchestrating a media effort to promote Putin's "Unity" party to Duma victory, and then Putin into the presidency.

In the end, the entire liberal wing publicly declared a pledge of support for Putin, offered no opposition to him, and even campaigned with him. These liberal politicians paid selective attention to just part of his background. Like those in the West who have wanted to see democracy in Russia where it does not exist while ignoring the signs of authoritarianism, they ignored Putin's long KGB career and instead focused on what they wanted to see. Putin had worked with Sobchak, in his mayoral administration made up of democratic-minded leaders, and Sobchak was a hero in the Democratic Russia Movement in the last years of the Soviet regime. Chubais had worked to bring Putin to Moscow and find him work in the Kremlin. It was his work with Sobchak and his consequent association with those St. Petersburg liberals that made some think that he must be a liberal politician himself.

The wishful thinking was fueled by the vicious dislike among the liberal politicians themselves, most of whom appeared to find it more palatable to capitulate and hope than to unite and fight. Rather than putting up a joint opposition, they actively promoted Putin's rise. Gaidar, Nemtsov, Kiriyenko, and others worked with the Center for Strategic Planning, which Putin formed to develop policy and draft legislation for his presidency, to develop a 450-page ten-year plan for Russia. Their work formed the basis for his "Strategy for Development for the Russian Federation to the Year 2010," Putin's economic strategy document which contained most of the proposals that Gaidar, Nemtsov, Chubais, and other liberal economists presented.[59] They threw in their lot with Putin and hoped he would follow their plan for economic stabilization.

It was in many ways a repeat of the mistakes of the earlier period, focusing exclusively on economics while ignoring politics. The liberal economists believed that if they wrote the economic program, that meant they controlled everything. Only their ideas could be implemented, so in fact they would still be in control. They would have to run things, and Putin would simply be a conduit for realization of their grand ideas. The political naivete had not lessened; it had grown commensurate with the considerable egos. What also had not changed was their Marxist approach to economics and politics, the belief that politics simply followed from economics. They could not have been more wrong.

Putin and his circle certainly did not accept that notion. The Center had also developed a strategic plan for state reform as well. However, this plan was never published and was kept strictly secret because Putin never intended to implement this plan. It retained the contours of a democratic society, calling simply for reform and reduction in the size of the bureaucracy, strengthening of relations between central, regional, and local governments, and combating corruption in government.[60] It is not that he came to power intending to abolish the institutions of democracy and restore dictatorship. Rather, his inclinations were toward strong centralization, control over information, and secrecy. The plan developed in the Center placated the liberal politicians and academics involved in its creation, but had nothing to do with Putin's intentions, and for that reason was kept under lock and key.

Putin's true plans were not enshrined in any documents. He had general ideas about the need to weaken the powers of regional authorities and restore central authority in the Kremlin. For example, in early 2000 Kremlin officials inquired of Satarov how he felt about eliminating election of governors, asking, "Why is that?" when Satarov responded with abhorrence that this would be unconstitutional. They needed to be shown the constitution for evidence. Putin came to the presidency convinced that he knew what needed to be done in the area of the economy, and that economic reforms needed to be implemented without having to worry about interference from the political sphere. This meant reducing democracy, of course, because it meant restricting opposition, representation, and information. The emasculation of democratic institutions happened piecemeal and gradually; while not part of a grandiose plan at the outset, attacks on freedom, representation, and openness were also not coincidental. Putin's instinct, and that of the team of *siloviki* surrounding him, is government by control, repression, fear, and violence, rather than through open debate, compromise, and transparency.

The liberal politicians were satisfied that Putin accepted their lengthy proposals for economic reform and that a political reform package had also been drafted. Given the media barrage and the popularity of the war in Chechnya, they latched on to Putin to propel their otherwise hopeless groups into some representation in the Duma. They proclaimed that Putin's program was their own, and he in return made sure that they cleared the 5 percent barrier in the parliamentary elections that swept Unity, Putin's bloc of KGB and security service officials, into control of the legislature. Whether Putin directly used his abilities in special operations to ensure these results, or whether they in fact received enough honest votes, is difficult to know with certainty given Russia's speckled experience with elections.[61]

The liberal right gained election by clinging to Putin's coattails and lost credibility in the process. Putin erased them from the political scene. They, erroneously, thought Putin was indebted to them for their allegiance and their expertise, but it was the exact opposite—it was they who owed Putin a debt. Putin had saved them from political irrelevance, but he was President of Russia regardless of what they did. The liberals paid with their support, while turning a blind eye to the troubling political changes that began immediately with Putin's inauguration. Any notion that they would control him from behind the scenes was silly. They closed their eyes to the growing authoritarianism, remaining silent while he seemed to implement their economic program. The apparent success of the macroeconomic reforms—their own proposals—that Putin implemented kept the liberals in Putin's camp even while he was eroding basic political liberties. The liberals rationalized that this was the first time liberal economic goals had been proclaimed so unequivocally by the government, much less a President of Russia. Yeltsin never went so far. They remained economic bolsheviks, trusting that economic reforms even under Putin would bring democracy. The repeat of the 1992 mistake would come back to haunt them again, this time much more painfully. The liberal right left itself with no basis or ability to become a serious opposition when the economic program proved illiberal and the reality of dictatorship began to emerge.

Elections as Window Dressing

The methods used to erode free competition in the 1996 elections concentrated overwhelming electoral resources and access squarely in the office of the president. As a result, when Yeltsin handed Putin the office, he also effectively handed him the election. Putin now enjoyed overwhelming resources and a shortened electoral time line, for the law required that the election take place within three months of Yeltsin's resignation, that is, three months earlier than would have been the case under the standard election rhythm. The hand over predetermined the outcome in favor of Yeltsin's chosen successor.

It need not have happened this way. Yeltsin, the dominant political figure in Russia for a decade, was exiting the stage. Anticipation was high for an election campaign with an equal playing field, with a number of prospective presidential candidates such as Primakov, Stepashin, Yavlinsky, Zyuganov, and others. It had the potential to be an election like none Russia had yet experienced, a truly competitive race in which the people would decide who would lead the country. The six months leading up to the June elections could have been an open and freewheeling campaign, raucous and exciting. Had Yeltsin stood on the sidelines, completed his term and allowed society to choose the next president, Russia's future may have looked entirely different. Even had Putin run as prime minister, with Yeltsin remaining on the sidelines while a campaign proceeded, it could have been an open contest.

But the hand over of power to Putin prevented that open process. Yeltsin ensured that there would be no free election. The Kremlin dictated the results from above, rather than the citizenry creating the results from below. From inside the Kremlin, with Berezovsky committed to guaranteeing his victory, Putin now controlled the media and overwhelming financial resources. Following the 1996 script, he and his loyalists trumped up scandals and systematically annihilated all potential opponents, including Primakov and Moscow Mayor Yuriy Lyuzhkov. Potential candidates immediately saw the futility of trying to oppose this onslaught. Similarly, mysterious and unsolved apartment bombings and murders in advance of the elections, again eerily similar to 1996, including murders of journalists critical of Putin, whipped up demands for order and lifted the popularity of the former-KGB agent. It all foreshadowed the most disturbing aspects of the coming authoritarian regime. And it all followed an exaggerated version of the precedent set in the 1996 election cycle. Putin left no doubt about the outcome. Russia still has not had an open, democratic election for its national political leader.

Academics and journalists in the West, however, blinded by their desire to see democracy proclaimed Russia's first free and fair democratic, constitutional leadership change. McFaul was most influential, and on television and in print he trumpeted the March 2000 coronation of Putin as the triumph of Russian democracy.[62] Not wishing to see an authoritarian hand over of power, to an obscure KGB official no less, he and others chose to see that there was a vote, that there was more than one candidate, that the votes were counted and that the one with the most votes won. Elections were now the "only game in town," the constitution had rules for elections that were followed. This was enough for those desperate to see democracy to proclaim its triumph, ignoring the effects of Yeltsin's handing the office to Putin.[63]

Elections were not even the most important game in town, much less the only one, and they were certainly not democratic. Both the campaign and the election carried clear authoritarian warnings. For example, although no proof was offered and none has since been forthcoming, Putin immediately blamed the numerous apartment bombings around the country on Chechen terrorists and used them as a pretext to launch a new war against Chechnya. Former presidential candidate, National Security Advisor, and regional governor General Aleksander Lebed is reported to have been "convinced" that the Kremlin was behind the bombings as a pretext for launching an invasion of Chechnya in advance of the election.[64] The Russian public wildly approved, propelling Putin's popularity rating skyward. As with the 1996 apartment bombings, the government never offered any proof of any individual or group responsible, and never brought anyone to justice. Evidence of FSB involvement and Kremlin complicity, however, is strong enough to demand it not be brushed aside as wild conspiracy theory, particularly in the absence of evidence to support Putin's claim. As one Putin critic put it:

> Putin was a nobody; he became president and a hero simply as a result of an enormous television crusade, using the war in Chechnya as an instrument. They

offered a simple thesis: "They are bombing us in our homes—here is a man who can defend us." And this effectively broke the spine of any possible opposition. Remember how they destroyed such mastodons as Primakov and Lyuzhkov. This was all organized and planned, this entire project of Putin's had an absolutely primitive goal from the point of view of Yeltsin's clan, to prevent the coming to power of the Primakov and Lyuzhkov clan.[65]

Berezovsky's network portrayed Primakov as senile and Lyuzhkov as stupid. The entire political elite that had been rallying behind Primakov "got scared and accepted these rules of the game, and said, 'No, we don't need this Primakov when we have Colonel Putin who is all we need.'"[66] It was essentially the same with Gusinsky, whose rival NTV network also savaged Primakov, Lyuzhkov, and their electoral alliance, though Gusinsky as always backed Yavlinsky's Yabloko.

What did "Yeltsin's clan" have to do with all of this? It was The Family that wished at a minimum to gain protection and perhaps even to remain in power. Certainly Berezovsky wished for both. The sudden creation of a hero in Putin, in the face of an emergency, created a hysteria similar to the one this same team created in 1996, one that would destroy any remnants of Primakov's popularity and cement Putin's. Whether or not they created the crisis, there can be no doubt that the crisis was beneficial politically and that the Kremlin pounced on the opportunity to make every use of it. In later years, independent investigators into Putin's role have been arrested or, as in the case of Aleksander Litvinenko, killed under suspicious circumstances, as have prominent politicians such as Sergei Yushenkov, who had detailed knowledge of the evidence and was outspokenly critical of Putin. Berezovsky, who certainly was in a position to know, went public with accusations and evidence, including supporting a documentary film produced by two French journalists after Putin moved against his media and financial holdings and forced him into exile.[67]

Berezovsky knew what he was talking about because he had helped bring about and was firmly behind Putin's promotion, and he led the effort leading up to the campaign. He came up with the idea of a party and the name "Unity," at a meeting of The Family—Yumashev, Dyachenko, Berezovsky, and others—at which Putin is reported to have remained silent. Putin built on the 1996 experience of Kremlin involvement with the media, using Berezovsky and his control over the largest television network to savage his principle opponents. Berezovsky installed Sergei Dorenko in the news anchor chair at Channel One, from where he hammered away at Putin's opponents while affording them no chance to respond. He accused them of murders, of bad health, and of corruption, all under direction from and co-ordination with the Kremlin.[68] The onslaught was so badly damaging in the parliamentary elections that Primakov and most other serious candidates opted out of the presidential elections after Yeltsin resigned. Only Zyuganov remained among the candidates who could garner significant votes, and he would meet the same fate as in 1996. Primakov and Lyuzhkov's Fatherland alliance went from favorite to a distant third place finish in the Duma elections in the wake of the personal attacks and scandals of questionable accuracy. Gusinsky, supporting as always in parliamentary elections Yavlinsky's "Yabloko" party, unwittingly aided and abetted Putin's ultimate triumph by piling on in the attacks against the two erstwhile favorites.

As if to remove any doubt that the results had been fixed, Dyachenko was oddly nonchalant about Putin's rapid turnaround from a 3 percent rating to electoral victory in a matter of a few weeks, telling a journalist, "What unexpected results are you talking about? We had this all completely figured out from the very beginning."[69] In addition to the war and the media control, Putin and his supporters apparently rigged the vote itself. On the day of the parliamentary elections, Kremlin officials fed the results of their victory to "their" media outlets. Boasting, "See how we work!" a giddy Yumashev presented a text message of the results on his pager to a correspondent, dated early morning of election day. The results, not surprisingly, proved exceedingly accurate. They had been written up before the voting had even begun. Broadcast of results before the close of all polling stations was illegal, "But there was simply nobody around to bring the victors to justice."[70] The reports early in the day quite likely had the effect of boosting Unity's victory, as those who may have voted for others stayed home, already having been told that their preferred representatives had lost. It also helped to reward SPS for its capitulation, by helping it to cross the 5 percent barrier and thereby gain a few seats in the Duma. Whether Dyachenko's claim of strategic prowess was bravado or not, there is little room to doubt they rigged the election.

By exerting control over the media, launching a war under possibly sinister circumstances, undermining election campaigns using similar tactics, and meddling with election results, Putin ensured victory in the parliamentary and presidential elections for himself and his handpicked group of KGB and security officers who would respond to his bidding. The processes introduced in 1996 had ballooned to such an extent as to make farcical any notion that what was taking place was either free or fair.

Of course, Putin also presented the population with a figure they were prepared to embrace, a leadership style they were amenable to be swayed toward. He offered a stark contrast to Yeltsin in his strict nature, decisive language, and his emphasis on discipline and order. This phenomenon was familiar across the postcommunist space. While Putin was not the candidate of the Communist Party and did not actively trumpet a return to socialist values, he was KGB, promised a strengthening of the state, and represented a familiar image that proved attractive to a large segment of the population. He exploited these sentiments to the fullest in his dizzying rise to the apex of Russian politics.

Dictatorship as a Consequence

The consequences of the hand over of power were grave both for the constitution and even for the most basic hopes of a bare minimum electoral democracy. The 2000 election cycle, by repeating the 1996 precedents of creating crises and hysteria and exerting Kremlin control over the media, institutionalized these practices. It also established that the presidency in Russia changes with a hand over, rather than an open electoral competition for the most important office in the country. Nobody is talking any more about what kind of political system Russia should have, for the rules of the game are entrenched. The Russian political elite, rather than discussing campaign strategy and candidate selection, are discussing who Putin will choose to be his successor. These are not trivial issues; they are the cornerstones of Russian authoritarianism.

As for the constitution, Article 92 spells out the procedures for when a president resigns, dies, is incapacitated, or removed from office upon impeachment. The prime minister is to become acting president, and elections must be held within ninety days. Resigning six months before the end of a term to hand power to a chosen successor violates the spirit of the provision. It violated the any pretense to democracy by choking the regular rhythm of presidential elections. Yeltsin invoked extreme, emergency provisions to effect a desired political outcome. Shakhrai suggests that he and others who had a hand in crafting the constitution intended the provision as a loophole to allow for a hand over of power, which he claims also to have advocated.[71] It is not possible to have it both ways. Either the constitution is intended as a document to foster the development of a democratic system and Yeltsin violated the spirit of the document, or democracy was never intended in the first place.

As the next chapter shows, all of the powers Putin needed to create dictatorship were in place, and he wasted no time in using them toward just that end. Within a few months, Putin's actions made it plain to see that Russia was heading not toward, but further and further away from democracy. It is an authoritarian system and the future bodes even worse.

6

Dictatorship Becomes the Only Game in Town

Political life in Russia has changed dramatically under Putin.[1] For example, the first two Dumas under Russia's current constitution were raucous and politically charged. When in session, its corridors bustled with deputies in heated discussions, staff members assisting members, and parliamentary correspondents pursuing investigative reports. Committee rooms reverberated with contentious discussion and questioning of government ministers.[2] Though far from an effective lawmaking body, the Duma influenced and attempted to provide oversight on policy, and the new institution had potential to become an active, effective legislature. It was one of the most interesting places in the world.

Those days are a distant memory. Putin has marginalized Russia's national legislature and rendered it a comparative ghost town. Public access is restricted, and one who gains entrance finds the place hauntingly silent. There is little discussion or debate, either on the floor or in committee. Government ministers, when they bother to come at all, lecture and leave; deputies do not probe them. Journalists are quarantined in a bubble on the second floor, physically separated from casual interaction with deputies who are under orders to avoid them anyway. Putin's United Russia controls nearly 75 percent of the seats and requires members to gain permission before speaking to journalists. Most talented journalists have left the Duma, because "nothing happens there. It is dead."[3] The upper chamber, the

Federation Council, was always closer to the Kremlin and is now indirectly appointed by the president.

There is no national political entity outside of the president to which society can look as autonomous or authoritative, a precarious situation for any society.[4] Silencing the legislature is only one of many elements in Putin's onslaught against open politics. As Fish puts it, "Putin is unwaveringly committed to increasing the state's control over society and his own control over the state."[5] Whether guided by ignorance, laziness, wishful thinking, or willful deception, many academics, journalists, and politicians eagerly parrot Putin's phrase "managed democracy," insisting Russia is liberal and democratic when it is so obviously neither. Some, who come across as self-serving, brand as "paranoid" anyone who dares suggest non-liberal, antidemocratic consequences of their own economic consulting efforts, insisting Russia is "normal," a "multiparty democracy."[6] Some are blinded by wishful thinking, searching for signs the glass is "half full," insisting democracy is "consolidating," and that Russian politicians all accept democracy and elections as "the only game in town."[7] Such assessments formed conventional wisdom in the West several years into Putin's reign.[8] American newspapers, for example, widely reported the Spring 2006 resignation of the State Prosecutor as indication of "infighting among Kremlin factions," of new "political parties" positioning leaders in advance of the 2008 presidential campaign. Straining to find evidence of multiparty competitive politics, they willfully ignored the significance of the glaring contradiction in the reporting in these same articles, that Putin has already announced he will "anoint" his successor.[9] There is no competition or democratic consolidation in that.

Few have acknowledged the oxymoron in the phrase "managed democracy." If it is managed, it is not a democracy. The preceding chapters explain how and why, at each critical juncture since the collapse of communism, Russia's political leaders made choices that undermined rather than promoted creation of a democratic political system. Marxist notions of the relationship between economics and politics, a power grab that gutted balance of powers in the new constitution, fear of competition and electoral politics, and rampant corruption created conditions for the consolidation of dictatorship, not democracy. The hand over of power to Putin brought the realization of that potential.

In the opening chapter, we defined dictatorship as a system in which the conduct of politics is determined by a single individual, who makes and imposes decisions on a populace that is denied the political freedom to organize, compete, and hold leaders accountable. This is Putin's Russia. The defining aspect of dictatorship is that the nature of politics, the quality of the system—benevolent or malign—depends exclusively upon the personal predilections of the leader. While Putin is neither a Caligula nor a Stalin, and Russia is not again a totalitarian state, for those committed to independent and open politics, or to holding officials accountable for their actions, Russia is becoming an increasingly dangerous and violent place to live. Dozens of political murders of high-profile opposition legislators, of liberal political activists, and of investigative journalists, all under mysterious circumstances, have gone uninvestigated and unsolved. Putin has restored one-party rule while closing avenues for other organizations to even exist to compete, much less to have influence or power. Political and economic rights are constrained, human rights abuses are widespread, and fear has returned with political domination by the security services in positions of political rule across the country. All of this has consolidated a system that makes quite real the prospect of a more malign ruler in the future, perhaps in the near future, as the concluding chapter will discuss.

What Russia has consolidated since the end of communism is a transition from dictatorship to dictatorship. This chapter details the contours of Putin's dictatorship and the elimination in Russia of checks on presidential power.[10] The first section details the rise of the *siloviki*. Putin brought with him rule by the security services, who dominate his United Russia, a bureaucracy controlled by security service personnel rather than a political party with a policy agenda. The section documents how members of the former KGB, the military, and other branches of the sprawling security services in Russia now occupy the vast majority of top political positions across the country. The second section demonstrates how Putin has hyper-centralized political power, with all significant decisions now made in the Kremlin. Decentralization, federalism, and checks on presidential power all remain in the realm of democratic dreams. The third section details the multifaceted attack on and elimination of competitive and open politics. Putin has overseen this through the financial starvation and administrative elimination of independent political organization, the harassment, imprisonment, exile and physical elimination of independent politicians, and the end of elections as meaningful events for popular choice. Elections are now managed operations rather than open contests for political power; alternative parties have been disbanded or starved of support, and elections eliminated for regional executive offices. The fourth section details the restoration of state control over the media and the return of censorship. An increasingly violent crackdown on the media has ended press freedom in Russia. Journalists critical of the regime are murdered, such as the courageous Anna Politkovskaya, who made a career investigating human rights abuses and the general failure of the Russian military campaigns in Chechnya. In October 2006, she became the most famous in a long list of investigative journalists murdered in mysterious circumstances. The final section details the institutionalization of government corruption under the guise of eliminating it, and the return of systematic human rights abuses by the government.

The Rise of the *Siloviki*—"Operation Infiltration"

Putin brought with him to the apex of Russian politics a flock of "men in uniform," and their flow into positions of power continues unabated. Putin had no political background of his own when he came to Moscow, and investigative profiles in Russia have found him to be cold and secretive, awkward in public surroundings and lacking in policy ideas.[11] His only support base was the *siloviki*. As one early account in the Russian political weekly *Itogi* put it, "Putin has no other 'kinfolk' outside of his circle of KGB staffers," who all "look like his twins. Lean, neat, with an officer's posture, utterly inexpressive faces and vacant, glassy eyes."[12] These blank-faced, secretive *siloviki* are the people who now fill the seats in the Duma, occupy the governors' offices around the country, and dominate ministerial positions.

The *siloviki* come from the KGB's successor, the FSB, the Interior Ministry police, the military, and the regular police. Putin has elevated the *siloviki* to dominate the entire government, at all levels, and the Russian president exclusively controls the entire apparatus.[13] They are more prominent today even than in the Soviet period. Olga Kryshtanovskaya, in her pioneering research, reports that by 2003 *siloviki* occupied 70 percent of senior regional posts, and that 25 percent of senior officials in Moscow were *siloviki* still on active reserve. At the end of the Soviet period, fewer than 5 percent of such positions were held by those with a security background. By 2005, 60 percent of the president's closest advisors were security men. *Siloviki* dominate the United Russia group Putin formed to win the Duma elections in December 1999. Their job is to follow instructions of their leader on which button to push on legislative votes. Over one-third of deputy ministers are *siloviki*, and even Trade Minister German Gref, a favorite in the West, has three such deputy ministers.[14] Many of these officials are hidden, in that they occupy "second echelon" positions such as deputy minister, and the data will underreport as the biographies of such individuals often make no reference to these secret backgrounds.[15] They are in their positions because they are subordinate and report to Putin himself, not because of policy expertise in the respective ministries.

These security men fill positions across the country. At least one deputy governor in most regions, Kryshtanovskaya reports, comes from the *siloviki*.[16] Of the seven administrators of his new "super districts," five come from a security service background.[17] A *Newsweek* report on these "super districts" described them as centralized bureaucratic structures each staffed by over 1000 "tough Kremlin agents" appointed by the Kremlin or by the Putin-appointed administrator. "In every region of Russia, at every level of government, former secret-police agents are grabbing power, digging in and recruiting old KGB friends."[18] This is only the tip of the iceberg, however. Thousands of former-KGB officers working for quasi-private security companies operate at the Kremlin's beck and call, "springing to life at critical moments" to serve Putin.[19] In Putin's Russia, politics is increasingly the domain of the secret services.

Reflecting the dark history of the secret services in Russia, the *Novaya Gazeta* headline "Operation Infiltration Complete!" was heavy with wariness and sarcasm.[20] These people controlling Russia today are not defenders of open politics. As Kryshtanovskaya put it, "all their lives, [they] have been learning to obey orders.... For them, pluralism of opinions means confusion."[21] They prefer authoritarian rule, abhorring openness, debate, and competition. Their organization, United Russia, is not a political party. It is tightly managed, supremely hierarchical, and functions more like a secret service organization. It has never revealed any political ideology or program of its own. It exists to support whatever Putin wants, in the government, in the legislature, and across the country. The state created United Russia just weeks prior to the election in December 1999, and seven years later it remains "amorphous and faceless," a personal clientele organization which does Putin's bidding in return for the resources he can bestow back to them.[22] It is a system of institutionalized corruption.

It is a closed organization. In the wake of a series of deadly explosions on the eve of the 2004 elections, United Russia barred its Duma members—elected members of the national legislature—from giving interviews or otherwise commenting in public. They had to await signals from their leader, and Putin remained silent for days. Internal regulations explicitly instruct United Russia members to "avoid making any public statements, including statements to the media," before clearing them with the leadership. This applies to committee chairs as well, even when the matters are technical legislative matters. They are warned, "Before making any statements to the press, think about whether your assessment of the situation is competent," strongly implying that any utterance must be cleared by Putin himself.[23]

Opposed as they are to open politics, the *siloviki* are outright hostile to political change. A number of films and publications have appeared providing chilling evidence of the horrifying apartment bombings and subway explosions within weeks of every national legislative and presidential election since 1995.[24] Not one of these crimes has been solved, nobody has been arrested, nobody has claimed responsibility, and suspicious evidence indicates FSB fingerprints in these attacks, subsequently labeled "terrorist." *Tovarish Prezident* argues these were part of a conscious plan by the *siloviki* to take power in Russia, and the late General Lebed was "convinced" they were.[25] Putin used each incident to trump up a campaign of violence against Chechnya and stir fear among the Russian populace to prevent political change, to keep himself and his comrades in power. Other reports corroborate this evidence while ascribe responsibility to Putin for other acts he has brazenly used to label Chechen terrorist attacks in an effort to boost his own legitimacy.[26]

These reports must be taken seriously in light of subsequent events. Aleksander Litvinenko, a former KGB agent who had turned critic of the Putin regime was, with funding from Berezovsky, investigating the apartment bombings and other suspected Kremlin abuses. Berezovsky, having promoted, financed, and worked closely on the election that served as Putin's coronation, was certainly in a position to know the circumstances around those explosions. Litvinenko died in November 2006 after a mysterious poisoning by the extremely rare and even more difficult to obtain and use radioactive substance Polonium-210. He was investigating the murder of Politkovskaya when he himself was murdered.[27]

Litvinenko was not the first to be killed while investigating the Kremlin's role in mysterious crimes. In 2003, when members of the Liberal Party began to investigate the apartment bombings, its two leaders, Duma Deputies Sergei Yushenkov and Vladimir Golovlev, were murdered. Yushenkov, a former Army Colonel and Chair of the Duma Committee on Defense, was a steadfast critic of the wars in Chechnya and of Putin's erosion of democratic rights. A tireless leader and organizer of pro-democratic, liberal politicians, Yushenkov was also an unusually kind, generous man with a sophisticated sense of humor. He was shot outside of his apartment building in April 2003.[28] Neither his nor the other murder cases have been solved. Similarly suspicious murders of journalists and opposition politicians are detailed at greater length in the sections below.

The security services rule Russia. They have carried out the "transition from a country ruled by fear to a country ruled by fear."[29] Putin has "based his entire political life on the idea that he is the only man who can keep Russia from disaster," by cracking down on civil liberties and political freedoms, "creating a tyranny of the bureaucracy," and silencing any who criticize him and his regime.[30]

All Power to the President

Putin has effected a return of closed politics and hypercentralized power. He has concentrated all decision-making power in the presidency, turning his office into the "single center of power controlling the media, the special services, business, the courts, the parliament, and elections—everything," as Yavlinsky put it.[31] He has achieved this through a two-prong strategy. First, he has instituted a series of policies to destroy local independence, power bases, and authority. Second, he has snuffed any capacity for opposition political organization or competition. While these are manifestations of the same phenomenon, it is useful to discuss them separately to understand the contours of the current system and the dangers for the future.

Putin was in a hurry. Just two months after his election he issued a sweeping decree to emasculate the federal system, by subordinating regional executives to Kremlin authority. The decree created and superimposed on Russia's political map seven regional districts, each headed by an administrator appointed directly by the president, to oversee the eighty-nine federation subjects.[32] Suddenly, eighty-nine elected governors were by presidential decree subordinated to a Putin appointee, five of whom hailed from the security services. Their task was to compel the governors to adhere to Kremlin instructions and orders. Results were not immediate. Some regional bosses controlled resources that enabled them to maintain their own power, were accustomed to the independence Yeltsin had explicitly encouraged them to assume, and were reluctant to give up either. Putin imposed compliance. He removed regional executives from the Federation Council, removed unwanted candidates including some incumbents from mayoral and gubernatorial races by ordering names crossed off the ballots, and had the candidates themselves placed behind bars. He launched investigations and prosecutions against officials who resisted his will.[33] The message was clear: join United Russia and hew to Putin's demands, or face ruin.

Putin knows few limits in his quest to centralize power, as evidenced by his crass use of the Beslan school massacre. On the first day of school in September 2004, Chechen terrorists seized Beslan School No. 1 and held hostage over one thousand children and adults. As the world watched, Russian security forces behaved with stunning, and ultimately deadly, predictability. As he had done in the hostage crisis at Moscow's Nord-Ost theater the year before, Putin ordered the troops to storm the building. Apparently, no special consideration was taken for the fact that, this time, it was little children who filled the building. The terrorists were well prepared, and when the troops broke down the walls everyone started shooting. Between them, Russian troops and hostage-takers killed nearly 350 people, half of them children, and wounded hundreds more.

The events have since become shrouded in suspicion. Russian officials released a tape of an interrogation of an alleged captured terrorist, who was clearly reading a prepared statement. Former hostages revealed the man interviewed was never inside the school, and it turned out he was a common criminal plucked out of prison to read the statement.[34] Anna Politkovskaya, who revealed this bizarre fact, was unable to demonstrate the reasoning behind this or confirm natural suspicions that it raised regarding the Kremlin's role. Politkovskaya, the investigative journalist who knew more about Chechnya than any other Russian reporter, was poisoned drinking a cup of tea and then detained while attempting to get to the Beslan scene, and no charges were ever made or responsibility assigned. As discussed below, Politkovskaya would later be murdered under suspicious circumstances. Another reporter on Chechnya, Andrei Babitsky of Radio

Free Europe/Radio Liberty, was beaten and detained, also unable to get to Beslan.

Putin cynically exploited the Beslan tragedy to further his political agenda. Less than one week after the massacre for which he and the Russian forces at a minimum shared responsibility, Putin announced the elimination of elections for governors; henceforth all heads of Russia's republics would be presidential appointees. Indirectly, he cast blame on the regional leaders for the Beslan hostage crisis and massacre, as if the federal structure and regional authority caused the murderous events at the grade school. This was an arbitrary use of dictatorial power in the wake of a catastrophic political failure by a president convinced of his own infallibility. Still in shock over the tragedy, few paid attention to the significance of Putin's decree.[35] The effect was to deny the people a direct voice in selecting local officials. While regional legislatures must approve those appointments, any legislature that rejects one faces its own dissolution.[36] Representation and popular sovereignty are circumscribed, and governors and mayors created a "stampede" to join United Russia, hoping to cling to their jobs.[37] To remain in office, one now had to demonstrate allegiance to Putin, and that meant joining United Russia.

Governors and even mayors of large cities, to remain in office, had to abandon any political organization of their own. Not only was federal power eroded, but independent party development suffered as well. Putin later moved to further centralize politics, by eliminating direct election of representatives to the Duma. Now, instead of half the membership being elected from single-member districts, all 450 seats will be allocated according to votes for "party" lists, controlled in Moscow. This change further emasculates the potential for politicians to create local or regional power bases, and removes local influence over policy making by consolidating all relevant decisions at the center, in the Kremlin. Citizens will have even less ability to directly influence either representatives or policy, indeed the set of changes Putin has brought seriously reduces representation altogether.

When Putin says his goal is to bring "the right people" into government, he means people loyal to him personally.[38] Local political organization, independent power bases, decentralization, and federalism have all been wiped out. Whether *siloviki* or not, all must demonstrate fealty and loyalty.[39] This is dictatorship. Putin has populated an ever-expanding bureaucracy with *siloviki* to manage and watch over society. This bureaucracy fawns on the president in ways reminiscent of Putin's Soviet-era predecessors.[40] Russia is again highly centralized. As the next section details, Putin has destroyed mechanisms for developing political organizations, for fostering political competition, and for promoting accountability and transparency, "instinctive behavior for those in power" in authoritarian regimes. "Special operations" now define politics and policy making.[41]

The Systematic Elimination of Competition

As one astute Russian political journalist described after Putin's election, Putin "wants quietness, silence, peace of mind and even a sort of stagnation. For this he needs to be able to rely on parties with a nearly army discipline."[42] The *siloviki*-dominated United Russia is exactly such an organization. Putin has eliminated political competition, destroyed independent politics in the Duma, consolidated presidential dominance over the Duma by eliminating access for political opposition, erected barriers for small political groups to the legislature by changing election rules, and controlled election outcomes. These policies have ensured a fragmented opposition which is excluded from the Duma and more generally from formal politics. His moves cemented Kremlin control not merely over the Duma, but over the existence of and membership in political organizations. This section focuses on the attacks on independent political organizations, politicians, and open elections; the next section will detail similar attacks on the independent press and journalists.

Putin has rendered the legislature toothless. His United Russia is a bureaucratic organization rather than a political party; its members are not politicians but security officers and bureaucrats, with no political base, no political agenda, and little policy interest. Most are not present at Duma sessions, rather single deputies are assigned to punch the "yes" or "no" buttons for up to several dozen members on each vote.[43] The Duma does not legislate. An independent Duma would have formed committees to investigate the causes behind, outcomes of, and government performance during such crises as the sinking of the Kursk submarine, the terrorist attack on the Moscow Nord-Ost theater, and the Beslan school massacre. It would serve as a vehicle for oversight and accountability, providing a political check on presidential and government action. It is not, however, independent. It performs the formal role of ratifying laws but does not legislate; it does not write the laws, it does not question members of government, it provides few of the meaningful aspects of a legislature.

Those authors who focus on Duma voting marvel at the impressive discipline within United Russia and proclaim the rise of party cohesion and a democratic party system. They ignore politics and entirely miss the point.[44] United Russia cedes all responsibility to its leader Putin, rubber-stamping his positions with little debate or amendment. What has developed is stable dictatorship. There are no multiparty politics; it is a one party system with strong-handed imposition of policy. Duma votes are not real votes, and voting is not the only or the most meaningful activity in a legislature. Voting is pushing a button. Legislating is politics, it is debate, negotiation, and compromise.[45] The State Duma under Putin does not legislate, because this would involve disparate opinions and the potential to disagree with and criticize the president, none of which Putin tolerates. Putin has turned the legislature into his instrument, a tool he uses to try to soften the face of his dictatorship. It is not an independent branch of government.

Opposition political parties are unable to organize or compete. Putin's actions, cloaked in a fictitious attack against corrupt oligarchs, have destroyed the ability to form independent political organizations by decimating their sources of financial support. Ending corruption in government would truly be a progressive policy, but Putin's actions have consolidated an illiberal regime. Instead of arresting oligarchs guilty of egregious violations of the law, he has selectively destroyed only those who were politically active, who had direct ties to political organizations, and who demonstrated a tendency toward thought and action independent of the new president. Putin's unambiguous message to the oligarchs is that they may continue to conduct business as usual, with the only caveat that they not be politically active.

He wasted no time sending this message. Just four days after his inauguration, Putin had armed police enter and search Gusinsky's headquarters. Gusinsky was the oligarch who, together with Berezovsky, had engineered Yeltsin's 1996 electoral triumph, in part by donating his NTV television network staff to the campaign and directing program content to actively support Yeltsin and savage his communist opponent.[46] Yet, despite the compromising position this caused, NTV remained well-respected and returned to independent reporting and quality investigative journalism, including reporting critical of the Yeltsin administration. In 1999, Gusinsky financially backed Yavlinsky and his Yabloko party in the elections, and his NTV television network offered critical coverage of and commentary on the savage war in Chechnya. That war propelled Putin's career. After his inauguration, Putin had Gusinsky arrested and held in prison without charge, and forced a deal in which Gusinsky was compelled to relinquish his media holdings to the giant state-run gas company Gazprom, and flee into exile.[47]

It was a direct attack on political financing and independent political organization. Yabloko's primary financial patron was gone. Only tattered remnants of Yabloko remain; it exists only in name. It has no seats in the Duma, and the once-prominent Yavlinsky has been rendered invisible, he has largely disappeared from the political scene. While Yabloko's political power was never great, its influence as a steadfast opposition party willing to voice strong opposition to Kremlin policies was a mark of political openness and competition. By choking off its funding and support, Putin destroyed the organization. It was a foreboding of worse to come.

The destruction of Yabloko by eliminating Gusinsky set a pattern for the destruction of political competition generally. As the assault on Gusinsky reached its crescendo, Putin convened a meeting with the richest oligarchs in Russia. Boris Nemtsov, quoted in Chapter 5 as opposing Putin's rise, had joined the rest of the liberal politicians in their capitulation, was now working with the regime, and organized this meeting between Putin and the oligarchs. The message was obvious in the invitation list alone: Gusinsky and Berezovsky were not invited. It was a powerful signal to those who were that political activity would lead to personal ruin. Berezovsky's absence was stunning, given his prominent role in orchestrating Putin's rise. Now he was a target, and soon he, too, would be exiled, his media holdings seized by the Kremlin, and his assets under attack.[48] Why? Berezovsky had become critical of Putin because the president denied him power and access. Having promoted the unknown KGB agent, Berezovsky expected to play a role in his presidency. Then, Berezovsky's Channel 1 critically reported on Putin's actions, or rather his prolonged inaction, during the August 2000 Kursk submarine crisis. While 118 sailors perished on the sunken submarine in the Berents Sea, Putin remained silent and on vacation, away from Moscow. As longtime Moscow correspondent Paul Quinn-Judge put it in *Time* magazine, for Putin "the needs of the state always come first; individual concerns come a distant second."[49] Channel 1's criticism triggered a stinging presidential outburst against Berezovsky. When the latter helped found a new Liberal Party, Putin moved to cut him off, seizing ORT under direct Kremlin control and launching criminal proceedings.[50] Berezovsky fled the country, and the Liberal Party was left with no financial patron. As described above, Yushenkov and Golovlev, the Liberal Party's two leaders, would soon be murdered under mysterious and still-unsolved circumstances.

The crackdown on corruption has been nothing of the kind. In fact, it is a crackdown on independent politics. Russia's wealthiest men all owed their fortunes to corruption, theft, bribery, and organized crime. Every one of them could be arrested for tax evasion, conspiracy, or worse.[51] Yet Putin has moved only against those who have been politically active themselves, such as Berezovsky, or who have supported independent political actors, as in the case of Gusinsky and Mikhail Khodorkovsky. Those who remain silent and refrain from supporting any political candidates or organizations are left alone.

The decisive blow against independent politics was the persecution of Khodorkovsky, the head of the oil giant Yukos and one of the richest men in the world. Timing was everything. The arrest in late 2003 prevented Khodorkovsky's involvement in the pending parliamentary and presidential elections. In a long public show trial he was tried, convicted, and sentenced to eight years in the Krasnokamensk Siberian labor camp.[52] The state seized his considerable assets, and in a mysterious auction a hitherto unknown "Baikal Finance Group," later discovered to be a subsidiary of Rosneft, a government-owned oil company created just two days before the auction, in which the group paid far below market value for the Yukos assets.[53]

During the Khodorkovsky Affair, as it came to be known, the oligarchs abandoned Khodorkovsky as they had Gusinsky and Berezovsky before him, in hopes of protecting themselves.[54] The charge against Khodorkovsky was tax evasion, a charge that certainly made it evident to the other oligarchs that there was a political message to be learned. The charge contained a bitter irony, for what made Khodorkovsky unusual among Russian billionaires were his reinvestment in the country and his commitment to paying taxes. While all of the oligarchs could have been convicted of tax evasion, Khodorkovsky had changed after the economic default in 1998. Fearing for the Russian economy's future, taking a long-term view both for his own and for his country's future, he committed to meeting current tax obligations and bringing transparency to his business operations, while also investing in the Russian economy. The turn toward clean operation is what distinguished him from the rest, not a past of corruption.[55]

It was not, in fact, the tax arrears or corruption that ran him afoul of Putin. Instead, it was the other trait that distinguished Khodorkovsky from the other oligarchs—his reinvestment in the country and his philanthropic generosity, building and assisting programs to aid Russia's poor, to support academic and cultural institutions, and to improve the lives of ordinary Russians. He created the Open Russia Foundation, inspired by Soros' Open Society Institute, to support libraries, community development and promotion of civil society organizations essential to democracy. Khodorkovsky's philanthropic activity was matched by his support for independent political organizations, particularly for pro-democratic political organizations and politicians. These activities perhaps indicated to some that he had political ambitions of his own and was seeking to build an independent political base.

In short, Khodorkovsky sought to support the creation of civil society in Russia, independent organizations at the national and grass-roots levels, to give citizens a voice and an ability to hold government accountable. This he saw as his reinvestment in Russia's future. Such entities are essential in any democracy. He also used his resources to support politicians and political organizations that shared his views. He had begun heavily contributing to pro-democratic political organizations and opposition political parties.

The imprisonment of Khodorkovsky, following the forced exile of Gusinsky and Berezovsky, effectively stopped independent political financing in Russia. Opposition political organizations simply cannot find substantial support as those left in a position to provide it have been cowered by the state, or were never interested in the first place. All who were interested and active have been removed from the scene. Khodorkovsky's commitment to a liberal future for Russia was perhaps most evident in his decision not to flee into exile when his fate became clear.[56] Khodorkovsky forced Putin's hand, and ended up in a public show trial, convicted, and sent to a Siberian labor camp, with all of his assets seized by the state.

Political parties, like political organizations of any type, die without funding, and after the Khodorkovsky show trial and Siberian sentence, who in Russia would dare support independent political organization? The Khodorkovsky Affair has made it virtually impossible to form competitive political organizations. Anyone inclined to organize or support such activity has been shown the consequence: financial ruin and exile or a hard labor sentence. The action against the "symbol of a business that strives to be law-abiding," who "set an example of transparency for his colleagues and for the state" made the political message of the attack inescapable.[57] Khodorkovsky's threat to Putin lay in his commitment to democratic political development. Putin's rules, however, ban open political activity by anyone but the president.

Not only do Putin's actions make talk of democracy nonsense, they thoroughly discredit those who insist Putin supports a liberal economy. Aslund, Shleifer, Triesman, and others who trumpet Putin's supposed liberal economics ignore his illiberal essence. Liberalism is based on principles of decentralization, of strengthening individuals independent of the state, and protecting the sanctity of private property. Putin's agenda is the opposite of this. He is not and never has been an economic liberal, nor are the *siloviki* who surround him.[58] Khodorkovsky saw his assets as his property, and his use of that property as his right and a private matter, and he behaved in accordance with these principles. Putin, however, views entrepreneurs as those who manage assets "at the state's pleasure."[59] When the state becomes displeased with how they use those assets, entrepreneurs lose their rights. In the end, they have no property rights at all, for if one may not use one's property to promote one's own interests or ideals, the property is not his in the first place. A regime that bans such use is fundamentally illiberal, and Putin has institutionalized just such a system in which the Kremlin decides how entrepreneurs may and may not use earned assets. The rule is simple. Use them to support Putin and his policies, and one may continue to do business. But those who support independent political activity or promote a political agenda risk arrest, seizure of assets, and prison or exile.[60]

The effect has been to strangle the development of political organizations of all types, above all those that would compete for office. Political parties simply do not exist, and they have no hope of developing in the current environment. But the attack on competitive politics goes further. Putin has used more direct means to control or altogether end elections, that most critical and basic element of democratic politics.

Elections in Russia are now "operations," in the military sense of the term. The phrase "operation successor" in the previous chapter indicates that leadership change is something controlled from above rather than decided from below. They are missions to bring about a predetermined outcome. Putin's machine has perfected the political technology of election engineering. The only resemblance to democracy is that people put pieces of paper into a box. "Russians cannot change their government democratically," the international organization Freedom House concluded in 2004, reporting "significant evidence that there had been an undercount in the vote for liberal opposition parties that kept them from attaining the 5 percent threshold" for Duma representation.[61]

Elections are "virtual politics," controlled by dirty tricks and overwhelming administrative pressure on officials to carry out the Kremlin's will and effect its desired outcome.[62] In the 1999–2000 and 2003–2004 elections, smear campaigns, media censorship, apartment bombings and subway explosions, banning, eliminating or controlling opposition candidates, and outright vote fraud kept opposition voices out and secured United Russia's uncontested control in the Duma and Putin the presidency. As Wilson details, the Kremlin manages Russia's elections through administrative resources, such as control over rules and procedures to ban unwanted candidates and organizations from participating. It uses its control over the media to propagate "black PR" to destroy those Putin wishes to keep out. It deploys "active measures" to divide, distract, or otherwise dissolve opposition, including creating fictitious opposition "Kremlin Parties." The latter provide a facade of competition by entities created, funded, and supported by the Kremlin. They are not a loyal opposition, but part of the Kremlin machine. The Kremlin even employs outright vote fraud to secure required electoral outcomes.[63] Vote fraud is so widespread, some now question the integrity of observers who, without justification, endorse Russia's elections even while reporting gross transgressions.[64]

The "operation election" phenomenon, the Kremlin's administering of elections to guarantee a preferred outcome, is a direct legacy of 1996. Elections in Russia no longer resemble events in which candidates are free to organize and compete for office. The 2004 election cycle did more than "fail to meet a number of commitments for democratic elections," to quote from the OSCE report; rather, it made a mockery of democratic electoral politics.[65] While formal elements of contestation exist, there is no real competition. Putin changed media law to ban media outlets from taking positions on policies or candidates, which, combined with the Kremlin takeover of all electronic media, discussed below, has effectively silenced potential opposition.[66] There are virtual politics, but no real challengers exist. Elections are a farce because everyone knows in advance that the incumbents will win, and they do.

This is "normal" politics only for a dictatorship. Citizens have no protection from Kremlin abuse of power. Putin has restored many elements of Soviet-style elections in which people vote for whom they are told to vote. Democratic elections are events in which incumbent may lose, in which real turnover of power may take place. Russian elections under Putin offer no such prospect. There is no opportunity for democratic political change.

Putin has stifled representative institutions, terminated direct elections of local officials and local representation in the Duma, eliminated electoral accountability, annihilated independent political organizations and open competition, established Kremlin control over who may participate in elections, and rigged votes. This is Russia's electoral regime, and compelled Freedom House in 2005 to rate Russia "not free."[67] As Human Rights Watch has said, while Mr. Putin "continues to present himself as a believer in democracy and human rights, by his re-election in 2004 both the political opposition and independent television had been obliterated".[68] Open political competition in Russia may remain a dream, but it is one that is far from reality. As the next section shows, Putin has also cut off independent sources of information necessary for opposition politics.

It Turns Out Glasnost *Was* Reversible

In the late 1980s, Soviet leader Mikhail Gorbachev introduced *glasnost,* or political openness, as a spark to generate public critique of inefficient economic practices. His initiative to jump-start the economy by exposing the inefficiencies of the stagnant Stalinist economic system rapidly spiraled out of control, as intellectuals seized on the thawing of censorship to examine everything.[69] When the Soviet Union collapsed in 1991, it appeared that press censorship would be a thing of the past in Russia, as young, talented, and energetic journalists dominated a thriving print and electronic media. During Yeltsin's presidency, the media were often a raucous and fiercely critical watchdog on policy and politics.[70]

Under Putin, those seeking news need not turn on the television, and the print media are not much better. Putin has destroyed media independence in Russia to such a degree that he has earned the label "enemy" and "predator" from global organizations committed to a free press.[71] The 2006 Annual Report of Reporters sans Frontieres (RSF) paints a damning picture:

> Working conditions for journalists continued to worsen alarmingly in 2005, with violence the most serious threat to press freedom. The independent press is shrinking because of crippling fines and politically-inspired distribution of government advertising. The authorities' refusal to accredit foreign journalists showed the government's intent to gain total control of news, especially about the war in Chechnya....The lack of broadcasting diversity and closure of several independent newspapers crushed by huge fines is alarming. The government tightly controls distribution of state advertising, which amounts to blackmailing independent papers that dare to discuss the war in Chechnya. TV stations, now all controlled by the Kremlin or government associates, are also subject to very strict censorship.[72]

Even this may be an understatement. Putin has overseen the destruction of media independence, termination of private ownership of electronic media, persecution of media owners, harassment and murder of journalists, and reinstatement of censorship and self-censorship across the Russian press. In a democratic society, a free press serves as the peoples' watchdog over the activities of public officials. Free and competitive elections are intermittent events offering ultimate accountability—removal from office. A free press is a continuous check on government, a tool for transparency and a source of information and ideas independent of the authorities. As such, a free press serves as a fourth branch in democratic states.

Putin behaves as if a free press were a fifth column. RSF consistently ranks Russia in the bottom third in the world, next to Singapore, Yemen, and Colombia.[73] Freedom House has been slightly more forgiving of Russia's transgressions of press freedom, recording it as having a "partly free" press until 2003 when it fell into the "not free" category, where it has remained.[74]

Most troubling are the violent attacks against journalists. Consider just one case, that of Anna Politkovskaya. By all accounts she was a controversial figure, but her courage and persistence are indisputable. Her most important investigative reporting was on Russia's two wars in Chechnya. Not only did she question the wisdom and motivations for the military campaigns, but also she critiqued the strategies and tactics. She exposed the devastation to Chechen civilians, the savage targeting of those civilians and human rights abuses on both sides, in often gruesome detail. The extent of knowledge of human rights abuse in Chechnya owes much to her work.[75] As an unrelenting critic of War in Chechnya and of the Putin regime generally, she made an enemy of the president. Her poisoning and arrest trying to cover the Beslan school tragedy in 2004 was just one of many incidents in which authorities physically harassed her. They must have tired of her tenacity. On October 7, 2006 she was shot four times in the head after entering her apartment building elevator, and the killer left the weapon at her side. It was a professional job, carefully planned, and the killer escaped without a trace. Less than six weeks later, Litvinenko, who was conducting an independent investigation of the murder, was killed in signature FSB style, poisoning by polonium-210, an obscure and devastating radioactive substance.[76] These are typically called contract murders, but there is no evidence that they, or the other political figures mentioned in this chapter who have been murdered, had contracts on them.[77] The phrase "contract killing" suggests the sort of violence that engulfed major cities in Russia in the 1990s, as organized crime coincided with the growth of private business activity.[78] For Russian journalists killed while investigating the actions of those in government, there is less reason to suspect mob-like contracts and more reason to suspect orders from political authorities.

While the data vary, all reports on violence against Russian journalists are horrifying. Investigative journalists are routinely murdered, and no justice is ever served. It is one thing to have a closed media, quite another for the murder of a journalist to become routine. The CPJ (Committee to Protect Journalists) reports twelve of journalists in Putin's first five years as president. RSF's annual reports, meanwhile, indicate twenty-five such murders from 2001 through 2005. However, the reality facing Russian journalists is even worse.[79] According to the FZG (Glasnost Defense

Foundation), eighty-seven investigative journalists were murdered between 2000 and October 2006.[80] The variation stems from differing criteria for classifying a murder as being "in the line of work." RSF and CPJ data only count victims whom the Russian State Prosecutor qualifies as having died as a result of their work as a journalist.[81] FZG, however, counts in its statistics any investigative journalist murdered, unless the Prosecutor certifies otherwise.[82]

Since Putin took office, an average of one journalist a month has been killed in a politically motivated murder. Given the suspicious circumstances surrounding these killings, and the fact that none of the killers of these eighty-seven has ever been identified, the onus is properly placed on the state to investigate and solve these crimes. When prosecutors make no effort or turn up nothing, the murder is quite reasonably classified as political. As FZG's founder and director Aleksei Smirnov argues, given the authorities themselves are the ones under suspicion for responsibility for these murders, to rely on those self-same authorities to certify the nature of the murders makes no sense.[83] In the case of a random killing, during a robbery for example, FZG does not include that death in its statistics.[84] The organization does still consider context in its research, and probably is itself underreporting.

The timing, style, and nature of Politkovskaya's execution, and the fact that none of the other journalists' murderers has every been caught, all point to security service involvement. That Putin, after international public outcry, declared he would personally take charge of the investigation does little to reduce suspicion. Other investigative journalists have been shot in the back of the head, hacked with axes, bludgeoned with hammers, or poisoned; most of the murders have taken place in the victims' own apartment buildings, and not one of the killers has been caught or punished.[85] There is absolutely no reason to believe Politkovskaya's murderer will be sought, much less caught.

When it is journalists conducting investigations into corruption, ineffectiveness, or other wrongdoing who are murdered, this raises suspicion the murders are the work of authorities supposedly entrusted to protect civilians and constitutional guarantees of press freedom. That the increase in murders coincides with the ascension of the secret services into every branch of government only raises suspicion further. Even the lower figure, that two investigative journalists are murdered annually without anyone being punished, makes Russia the deadliest country in the world for journalists outside of Iraq.[86] One per month puts Russia beyond the pale.

Journalists covering corruption or problems in government are threatened, harassed, attacked, and killed. The state launches criminal proceedings against journalists to quiet their probes into public officials. Yuri Shchekochikhin, a Duma deputy and editor at *Novaya Gazeta*, a publication critical of the Putin and the war in Chechnya, was killed under mysterious circumstances that remain unclear but had the typical KGB signature of poisoning with a rare substance, radioactive Thallium, bearing resemblance to the dioxin poisoning one year later of Ukrainian presidential candidate Viktor Yushchenko.[87] Somewhat ominously, Shchekochikhin, like Yushenkov and Litvinenko, whose murders were detailed above, had also been investigating the series of apartment bombings surrounding elections, as detailed in Chapters 4 and 5 above. Another investigator of these events, Mikhail Trepashkin, has been arrested, jailed, reportedly tortured, and arrested again.[88] Elena Tregubova, an enterprising young Kremlin reporter and author of the first investigative account of Putin's rise to and first years in power, was forced into seclusion after an explosion outside of her apartment building nearly took her life, just days after her editor succumbed to Kremlin pressure and fired her. Her book *Tales of a Kremlin Digger,* which triggered these attacks, tells of the system of censorship enforced by Putin's press office, which uses threats both professional and physical to prevent critical reporting.[89] Shortly before the 2004 presidential election, Aleksei Venediktov, editor of the radio station Ekho Moskvy, received call on a private cell phone number known only to his immediate family. The caller told him "to think about my son, to think about what I was doing."[90] Countless direct threats and acts of violence, more than three per day each of the last three years according to FZG, mark Putin's relentless onslaught to end press freedom.

Data on other forms of violence against journalists are staggering. Between 2001 and 2004, RSF reports that eight journalists were kidnaped or disappeared. From 2001 through 2003, 38 journalists were arrested and jailed, 48 were physically attacked, and there were 124 reported instances of physical obstruction or pressure on media outlets. By 2005, there were too many instances for RSF to list individually. Their report simply stated, "Once again, a large number of journalists were physically attacked throughout the country during the year, without anyone responsible being punished."[91] Again, the FZG reports more numerous attacks, including ninety-six cases of physical attack in 2003, and more than sixty each year since. More disturbing, FZG reports over one thousand "conflicts" between journalists and officials each year since 2003, including violent physical attacks, arrests and imprisonment, threats, censorship direct and indirect, removal from employment, and other forms of pressure.[92]

Putin's crackdown on the independent media began with his inauguration. His arrest of Gusinsky, four days after the inauguration, culminated with the most successful media mogul in the country fleeing into exile and NTV, his Independent Television Network, placed under Kremlin control as ownership was handed to Gazprom, the gigantic state gas producer. Putin did not have the prosecutor deal with Gusinsky in prison, but the press minister, who informed Gusinsky that the price of his freedom would be to relinquish his company to the state. Anticipating further action against him he obliged, and fled to Israel.[93] Most of NTV's most dedicated and respected journalists left for TV6. Putin promptly seized that network too, with trumped-up legal charges and rigged court procedures. Then, when Berezovsky-owned Channel One offered critical reporting on the handling of the Kursk submarine crisis, Putin seized that network for the Kremlin as well.[94] Within months of taking office, Putin had seized all national television networks under his control.

Putin abolished independence of the electronic media in less than two years. After the 1996 campaign, and the marriage of the Kremlin with the oligarchs, the Kremlin viewed the media as its weapon, just as Lenin had viewed it during the Bolshevik Revolution.[95] Putin simply dispensed with the inconvenience of dealing with the oligarchs as an intermediary, restoring direct Kremlin control over the networks, their employees, and content. Soon this reality befell electronic media across the country, the only exceptions being small radio outlets, as long as they remained nonpolitical.

Putin has restored state control over information, with harassment and violent crackdowns awaiting any who cross the Kremlin. Less than two decades after open political reporting began under Gorbachev in the late 1980s, Putin had restored censorship to Russia's mass media. Already in early 2001, it was the case that "the media, already overwhelmingly state-controlled, have consolidated around the Kremlin. If there are no fewer newspapers, television networks, and Internet web sites than a year ago, the range of views that could be aired has certainly narrowed." They have since narrowed considerably further.[96]

That censorship has returned is not surprising given the physical risks involved. Direct censorship is evident during crises, such as the Beslan hostage tragedy. Russia's security services certainly carried out a "special operation" in Beslan, an operation against journalists.[97] Almost immediately after the terrorists entered the school, the Kremlin instructed television and newspaper editors how to word their reports. Putin was not to be mentioned, to prevent any potential for the public to associate him with the events and to limit any affect on his popularity. No information was allowed on troop deployment, names of witnesses, relatives, or the hostages themselves. The Kremlin even banned them from using such phrases as "suicide bomber" and "War in Chechnya."[98] Officials arrived in Beslan to control rather than share information, establishing no press center, confiscating tapes, preventing access to information, and instructing police to detain journalists. Politkovskaya and Babitsky were poisoned, beaten and detained, preventing them from covering the crisis. An *Izvestia* reporter was fired for his report and photographs. Two months after Beslan, when demonstrations broke out in several regions protesting Putin's elimination of election of governors, the Kremlin warned the media not to report on those protests. Editors and publishers got the message. Local media remained silent, and the protests fizzled.[99] Under intense government pressure, when murders of investigative journalists are left unsolved, self-censorship has returned.

Journalists, editors, and publishers are now "worried about what the Kremlin may think about [their stories]: if the story may affect their career in the media or if they are going to lose their job."[100] Journalists, such as *Izvestia*'s Editor-in-Chief who was fired for his reporting on the Beslan massacre, are routinely fired for their reporting.[101] Leonid Parfyonov, a prominent broadcaster and one of the only journalists to stay with NTV after the Kremlin takeover, was sacked for protesting censorship by the security services, who banned his interview with the widow of a Chechen rebel leader. That the Kremlin would move against a popular journalist who stuck with NTV, enabling the Kremlin to claim the legitimacy of its takeover, indicates the extent to which it is determined to exert control.[102]

In 2004, five of six national and 20 percent of local newspapers were still privately owned. However, they were all dependent upon state-owned printing and distribution facilities.[103] Privatization never reached these media intermediaries, and officials are able to exert pressure direct and indirect. When content appears in newspapers critical of the Kremlin, the reaction is swift and final. Censorship is again widespread, and the most oppressive form is self-censorship. Recently, a poetry web site informed authors of a list of taboo subjects reminiscent of the old KGBs *Glavlit* list of items not to be published. The list included criticism of Putin, the government, members of United Russia, or the pro-Putin youth movement, anything about the war in Chechnya or specific government policies. Explained the web site's director, "it is easier to limit publications of such works than to try and guess what the president may or may not like." Content filtering on the web and in print is extensive.[104]

The once-thriving Russian journalism profession has suffered immensely. As one Moscow journalism professor explains, Russian journalists now have to please two masters: the Kremlin and their owners. They "have lost the freedom to examine society, government, politics and business issues." As a result, "it is impossible to understand what is really going on in this country." Chechnya, corruption, and crises do not make the news, or, if they do, only the "official" Kremlin line gets reported without question or investigation, "to avoid trouble."[105] With no objective or investigative analysis possible, the Russian people lack information about the government and rumor again substitutes where reliable information is absent.

For ending press freedom, for systematically restoring state control over the electronic media and censorship in all media, and for persistent harassment of and violence against reporters, RSF placed Putin on its list of "predators," political leaders most violently hostile to journalists. He joined leaders of Burma, China, Iran, Libya, and Uzbekistan on the "most wanted list," RSF wrote, for "using his training as a former KGB official to continue bringing all the country's media to heel. The government controls the written press and radio and TV stations....Putin appears more and more on TV these days and even lectures his ministers there. Those who ordered the 2004 murder of Paul Klebnikov, editor of the Russian edition of the US magazine Forbes, have still not been identified and punished."[106] CPJ placed Putin in 2001 on its list of ten "enemies of press freedom" that includes Ayatollah Khamenei of Iran, Jiang Zemin of China, and Charles Taylor, Liberia's former henchman now facing trial for crimes against humanity in The Hague.[107] One can only agree, in the face of the evidence, with Politkovskaya's assessment that Putin "has failed to transcend his origins and stop behaving like a lieutenant-colonel in the KGB....he persists in crushing liberty just as he did earlier in his career."[108]

Corruption and Human Rights Abuses

The absence of transparency virtually guarantees corruption, and dictatorship abhors transparency. Dictatorship and corruption go hand in hand. Although Putin promised to clear out the oligarchs and end corruption, he has done neither and corruption has blossomed. Business owners serve as government ministers and Duma members, using public office for private gain. Putin embraces the marriage, publicly declaring, "it is very difficult here to see clearly where business ends and where the state begins and where the state ends and where business begins." He denies there should be a distinction, for he sees none; everything serves the state, so "protection for business is protection for the state."[109] Putin is no economic liberal.

Corruption is everywhere. Transparency International rates Russia 126th, among the world's most corrupt states, with Albania, Niger, and Sierra Leone.[110] The legislature has fallen into decay, seats are sold, voting is a meaningless charade, and legislators do not legislate. "When members of parliament wield no real influence yet retain very real privileges," corruption becomes the institutional norm. "Lobbying for business is the only sensible thing to do" for a member of the Duma.[111] It is worse among those in uniform, who steal for private enrichment and corrupt others in the process. Through *telefonnoye pravo* (telephone orders), officials call checkpoints near Chechnya ordering security people to let select few to pass without being checked, enabling personnel to transport stolen materials to build luxury homes, for example. Russian corruption is deadly. Corruption and bribery of security officials allow suicide bombers and terrorists to pass checkpoints, to buy tickets, and transport explosives onto airplanes. Similar bribery enabled the free movement of the terrorists to the Beslan school. Russian military officials are said to sell weapons to Chechen terrorists, among others.[112]

The most egregious corruption is the market for government positions, where high ministerial positions cost hundreds of thousands of dollars.[113] To get on the list of those considered for a ministerial position someone needs to place your name there. That costs money, though the individuals "on the take" are not necessarily those at the top. As one United Russia member and former government official under Putin phrased it, "it would be wrong to deny that civil service positions are like a lucrative business undertaking...[there is] pervasive bribery at absolutely all levels throughout the country."[114] The office is worth the high cost when one can use it to turn the state treasury into a stream of revenue directed to overseas offshore accounts.[115] Westerners turn a blind eye, largely because "it would be an appalling loss of face to admit that billions of dollars of assistance have largely achieved nothing."[116]

One has to wonder whether the time and effort they have spent leads former advisors to spout nonsense calling this deadly and corrupt mess "a splendid market economy"[117] and a "normal" country in the liberal, democratic sense.[118] It is neither splendid nor normal when seven senior government officials control, through the companies they head, over 40 percent of the country's GDP. The companies include gas giant Gazprom, the state oil company Rosneft, Aeroflot, the main air defense contractor, the diamond monopoly, the second largest bank in the country, the electric power monopoly, and the oil transport monopoly.[119] INDEM's massive study failed "to discover anywhere anything that matches the Russian habit of appointing officials to boards of directors," or appointing those directors to official positions.[120] The process by which officials are named remains secret and securely outside public control or oversight.

Corruption often is accompanied by widespread rights violations. Human rights protections are eroding under Putin. Rights cannot be upheld without courts, without an independent judicial system to guarantee that the rules of the game are being observed. But Russia's judiciary also "suffers from corruption, inadequate funding, and a lack of qualified personnel." It is also firmly controlled by the president. Putin controls hiring and removal of judges. As a result, from abuse of prisoners to show trials to massacres in Chechnya, human rights are again routinely violated in Russia. Authorities use methods of torture and other forms of mistreatment of prisoners with impunity.[121] In Chechnya, "all the murders of children since 1999 in bombardments and purges remain unsolved, uninvestigated by the institutions of law and order. The infanticides have never had to stand where they belong, in the dock; Putin, that great 'friend of all children,' has never demanded that they should....Not one television station broadcast images of the five little Chechens who had been slaughtered. The Minister of Defense did not resign....The head of the air force was not sacked. The commander-in-chief himself made no speech of condolence."[122]

Human rights violations in 2005 alone include some of the most chilling practices by Russian authorities.[123] Government involvement is alleged in numerous politically motivated abductions. Suspicious circumstances surround disappearances and killings in Chechnya and the North Caucasus.

Deadly hazing of young recruits in the armed forces is on the rise and goes unpunished. Most crass is government harassment and even abduction of individuals who have lodged appeals to the European Court of Human Rights, reportedly to convince them to drop their cases. In prisons, torture, violence, and other brutal or humiliating treatment is common and frequently life-threatening. Russian law enforcement is one of the most corrupt sets of institutions in the world, with officers carrying out arbitrary arrest and detention for personal gain, with the executive branch directly influencing investigations, trials and judicial decisions, as in the Khodorkovsky show trial. The government exerts extreme pressure and direct censorship of the media. Officials limit freedom of assembly and arbitrarily place restrictions on some religious groups. Discrimination, harassment, and violence against members of religious and ethnic minorities is the norm. Restrictions on freedom of movement and migration are severe. Putin has endorsed a campaign of harassment of NGOs, particularly international organizations dedicated to human rights monitoring. Endemic violence against women and children, including human trafficking and forced labor, continues to go ignored. The list is long, and the above is just a sample of rampant official abuse of human rights in Russia.

As if to verify increasing their criticism of him as intolerant and abusive of human rights, in 2006 Putin signed a law severely curtailing foreign NGO activity. This, in the wake of the persecution and prosecution of Khodorkovsky and liquidation of his assets which stifled support for Russia-based interest groups, fairly well doomed civil society. One of the first targets of the law was the Committee of Soldiers' Mothers, one of the most respected and renowned human rights groups in the world. Authorities brought a lawsuit against the organization that would have crippled it and threatened its very existence. The authorities ultimately backed down after intense international outcry.[124] To Putin, NGOs should "lobby" for Russia's interests abroad, and activity that does not "proactively" support his policies is treasonous.[125] Days after the anti-NGO took effect, authorities accused several of being riddled with "spies" and ransacked their offices.[126] Putin, in a silent nod to the harsh authoritarian nature of the law, delayed announcement of its signing during a visit from the German Chancellor, despite the legal requirement of immediate publication. It was even kept off a Kremlin web site, on the pretense that site is "reserved for laws that the public needs to know about," a curious notion, to say the least. Putin's administration has "developed a practice of being secretive about controversial legislation," as it has about virtually everything.[127]

This attack on NGOs follows a 2004 law severely restricting the right of people to assemble and protest in public areas. That legislation gave the government the power to ban groups it determines to be "extremist." Now, any organization promoting human rights, or media freedom, can be branded extremist and banned. These include the Moscow Helsinki Group and Committee of Soldiers' Mothers.[128]

Really Existing Dictatorship

Putin has consolidated dictatorship in Russia by systematically eliminating political competition, emasculating opposition organizations by cutting off their sources of funding. He has concentrated immeasurable power into his hands at the apex of the executive branch, which he has stuffed with officers of the security services hostile to the very notion of open politics. He has made a farce of elections, rigging outcomes through means direct and indirect, procedural and violent. He has forcibly subordinated regional and local politicians to himself while denying them any means to form or foster independent political bases. He has arrested, imprisoned, exiled, or eliminated those who attempt to organize against or otherwise oppose him. He has restored censorship and state control over a once-thriving, free media, having those who dare to conduct investigative or critical reports fired, physically harassed, or worse. The Russian people have no representation, no means for holding officials accountable, no ability to change their government through peaceful means, and no reliable sources of information about government activities. The Kremlin controls the legislature, it controls the media, and it controls the judicial system, putting the regime beyond the means for peaceful democratic change.

One government official was quoted outside the Duma after Beslan as saying, in a hushed voice, fearful someone might be listening, "Democracy is finished in this country...Many have already been given very severe and hard instructions not to comment. Not to criticize. And real threats. All of us are in a state of shock. We are in the middle of 1937."[129] While Putin has not brought a reign of terror, he has effectively closed political space by restoring a regime based on fear to a population that knows all about fear.

In Spring 2004, Gordon Hahn presented eight features of what he termed "stealth authoritarianism" under Putin, invoking the adjective "stealth" because each feature, he argued, was limited in scope.[130] The adjective is not appropriate. First, the tightening of the political noose in Russia has been part of Putin's conscious strategy from the beginning. As described in Chapter 5, Putin shared his strategy for economic policy with many, but closely guarded his strategy for reforming the political system, in particular keeping it secret from liberal politicians he sought to coopt. As this chapter shows, he is not concerned about the "veneer of legality" and no such concerns limit his actions. Second, his rule can no longer be described as "hegemonic" rather than "monopolistic." He does not tolerate challenges to his power at any level, seeking instead to dominate at every level. Third, the recentralization of power is complete in that one cannot speak of political autonomy or influence outside of the Kremlin. Fourth, violent attacks on autonomous organizations and opposition politicians, up to and including unsolved and uninvestigated murder, demonstrate unequivocal intolerance of open political opposition. Fifth, use of state administrative resources against such opposition is in no way subtle, it is brutal. Any political activity independent of United Russia and its leader brings personal ruin. Sixth, elections are brazenly rigged, a farce retaining nothing of what democratic elections must include to hold any real meaning. Seventh, the attacks on the media have destroyed press freedom, and these actions at the federal level have given regional bosses free reign to clamp down even harder. Finally, the security services dominate all levels of government, and their methods of control are increasingly imposed across the country.

It makes no sense to speak about prospects for democracy. Rather, what form will the dictatorship take in the future? This is the fundamental question. What future will Russia have given the system Putin has consolidated. What will Putin allow? What will Putin do? The entire question of the quality of political life in Russia and the quality of the political system depends on the answers to these questions, on what Vladimir Vladimirovich Putin will do as his tenure as President of Russia nears its constitutional term limit. The following chapter presents several scenarios for this dictatorship, analyzing their likelihood and their consequences should they be realized. The most likely future is not a happy one.

7

Looking Back and Looking Forward

Calling a state a democracy does not make it so. Politicians labeling themselves pro-democratic or dedicated to building democracy does not make them so. Observers wishing a country were democratic do not make it so. Since the collapse of the Soviet Union, Russia's leaders have called their country a democracy. Myriad Russian politicians have proclaimed themselves pro-democratic. Journalists and academics have hailed Russia's transition to democracy, and continue to cling to that framework. But Russia's leaders have consistently made decisions that have prevented rather than promoted democratic political development, and the political system they have produced is not democracy but dictatorship.

In the preceding chapters, we have tried to identify the most crucial of those decisions from the perspective of the development of Russia's postcommunist political system, and explained how and why the decisions taken came about. Our purpose has been to outline the various options that were available, to explain why the decisions made were the ones selected, and to demonstrate the consequences of those decisions for future political developments and for the nature and performance of Russia's political system. We have also described the realities of dictatorship in Russia today, in an effort to clear the misconception and deception involved in describing Russia today as democratic.

In this concluding chapter, we briefly recount the essential points of our analysis of the decisions Russia's leaders have made at each of the critical junctures since the collapse of the USSR, including the alternatives that existed at each of these junctures. In other postcommunist states, where the types of alternatives suggested here were adopted, the outcomes led to the creation of democratic norms, values, and institutions. More important, they increased the tendency to pro-democratic outcomes at future decision or crisis points. Because these decisions led to democratizing outcomes in other postcommunist states, these same alternatives may well have improved the potential for a more democratic reality in Russia's postcommunist political development.

But Russia followed a different path at each of the critical junctures it has faced. Under Vladimir Putin, Russia has consolidated dictatorship rather than democracy. Given this reality, and the fact that as this book goes to press Putin's presidency nears its constitutional end late in his second term, we offer a final section that attempts to peek into the future. In it, we outline several of the most likely possible scenarios for Russia's future political development.

Critical Decisions at Critical Junctures

Chapters two through five each focused on pivotal moments in Russia's postcommunist political development. Of course, these were not the only important decision points Russia has faced—far from it. Among the countless challenging political moments in the fifteen years since the end of communism, each requiring difficult and sometimes wrenching decisions, Russia's leaders have decided to launch two wars in Chechnya, to join the G8 group of advanced industrialized countries, to make difficult choices in response to national economic collapse and default, to participate or not participate in NATO peacekeeping operations, and many others. The critical junctures examined in this book are not the only important decisions Russia has made, are not the only important decisions any state would make. But they are particularly important moments for democratic political development in any state, and we focus on them because they are common decision points. Any postcommunist state, and perhaps any state attempting to create a democratic political system, eventually must confront each of the challenges that these critical junctures pose.

These common challenges obviously take different shapes in different places. Different options may be available in the different contexts. Yet one way or another, leaders in any new democratizing state must, at some point, decide what to do with the institutions of the *ancien* regime. They must decide how to write a constitution. They must decide how to respond to challengers in a new, competitive political environment. They must create a mechanism for leadership change. Each of these decisions is critical to the prospects for democracy. Those old institutions hold rules, procedures, powers, and behaviors incompatible with the rules, procedures, powers, and behaviors required in a democratic system. The old constitution, if indeed there was a constitution, instituted a framework for a different kind of political system and a different kind of society. Not only does a new constitution need to create the scaffolding for a democratic system, but the processes involved in writing that document need to be democratic if those values are to find their place and take hold. Society must buy into a new democratic framework if it is to have a chance to succeed, it must own it. Where political competition, opposition, and contestation are new phenomena, leaders are used to eliminating or banning their appearance. Those leaders must resist the temptation to do so and follow new rules, which need to be enforced, to ensure that those new forms of politics are allowed to proceed. Where leaders traditionally held office until they died or were forcibly removed, they must be willing in a democratic system to allow the people to choose their successors, without interference, and to abide by those decisions with grace. These all reflect changes in institutions, values, norms, and behaviors. Any state will have to meet these challenges in particular ways for democracy to emerge.

The decisions the new leaders make at each juncture will help to define the nature of the system in the short term. Perhaps even more significant, and what makes these particular decisions so important, decisions at one juncture help to shape and constrain options available at future junctures. Each decision sets precedents for future behavior and creates expectations regarding the norms of behavior in the new political system. As such, actions that leaders take shape not only short-term realities but also help to define the long-range prospects for consolidation of a democratic political system.

After the collapse of the Soviet Union, at each of the critical junctures we identify as common to all states that would pursue democratization, Russia's leaders consistently made decisions that undermined rather than promoted the creation of a democratic political system. Immediately after the collapse, as Chapter 2 details, President Yeltsin retained the existing political institutions, and the occupants of many of the offices therein, from the communist period. The communist-era institutions would remain, he decided. So, too, would the communist-era constitution, riddled with internal contradictions resulting from multiple revisions over the years, in particular, contradictions over the locus of power that had fueled the final breakdown in the USSR. But despite the attempted hard-line coup and the ultimate dissolution of the Soviet state, neither Yeltsin nor his closest advisors saw any urgency in political change in Russia. They thought they had won, a victory that they had never envisioned, and saw unity despite the indications of division from the start. Instead of seizing on the enormous authority and legitimacy they enjoyed, the new leaders focused exclusively on economic transformation. This choice left in place contradictory and competing political institutions in the short term, enabled a standoff that turned violent in less than two years, and made it more difficult to make pro-democratic decisions in the long term.

Clearly, other options were available. Russia was hardly unique in facing an urgent need for economic transformation after communism. Every post-communist state faced that urgency. Where the new leaders also dissolved existing communist-era political institutions, and set in place processes for changing those institutions. The options were numerous and included such steps as electing a temporary constitutional assembly, declaring short-term executive rule for economic reform, and convening a group including all political interests in a roundtable negotiation on new institutional arrangements. The options were not mutually exclusive; several could have been and in many countries were employed simultaneously or successively. Across Eastern Europe, wherever democracy was an outcome, in one fashion or another roundtable negotiations on institutional arrangements settled those questions. Yeltsin and his advisors had the opportunity to follow in those footsteps. Had they done so, they may very well have been able to use their authority and legitimacy, and the good will that existed from the successful defeat of the hard-line communist coup, to forge a consensus on political institutions that would have avoided the bloodshed in October 1993. Remnick reports that Yeltsin later "would castigate himself" and admit that he wished he had taken such decisive action.[1] They could have done that while still carrying out economic reform, and completed the political restructuring before the pain of economic liberalization undermined what consensus and good will did exist. A normal constitutional process could have ensued to produce a founding document favorable to democratic consolidation.

By not heeding those internal and external lessons, however, Russia's leaders set a course to conflict and suspicion, rather than to internalization of such democratic values as consensus-building and negotiation. Institutional deadlock and confrontation over fundamental issues of political authority led to violent conflict on the streets of the capital. In the aftermath of the trauma of those events, or rather, as Chapter 3 describes, still living the trauma, Yeltsin scrapped what compromise language had made its way into the new draft constitution, and by doing so consolidated uncontested authority in the office of the president. The option for a more balanced founding document existed not only in theory but also on paper and could have been presented to the people for ratification. But the violent clash between the executive and legislative branches, and the polarization of politics that consumed all political groups, made true roundtable negotiations about the future impossible, and negated the concessions that had earlier been made to opposing groups. After the violent confrontation, the temptation to undo compromise language that had been made to the now defeated and discredited groups proved overwhelming. The decision at the outset to leave the old institutions in place, in the end precluded adoption of a consensus constitution and instead led to a power grab by an executive branch in a state of fear and trauma in the wake of a violent conflict.

One can understand and even sympathize with the actions Russia's political leaders took after the traumatic confrontation, while lamenting the long-term negative consequences for democratic political development. An enlightened, forward-thinking, and trusting approach to the adoption of the new constitution would have required, under the circumstances, a truly heroic act of fortitude from Yeltsin and his closest advisors. It was not to be. From the Baltic States to the Visegrad Triangle, where leaders allowed themselves to be guided by the outcomes of roundtable constitutional processes, democracy has steadily strengthened. In Russia, where the leaders at best halfheartedly allowed such compromise processes in the first place, and then undid the compromise language that did emerge, democracy had little hope.

Suspicion, fear, and a constitution without checks on presidential power paved the way to obstruction rather than open competition in the first truly competitive round of elections. In contrast to virtually every state across Eastern Europe, where the first wave of postcommunist leaders lost their bids for reelection in open, competitive contests, Russia's leaders used the levers of power to rig victory in the presidential election. Those elections set a precedent for opposition and competitive politics, and most important set precedents for leadership change via the ballot box in fair and fairly counted votes. Chapter 4 details the Kremlin's marriage with the oligarchs in 1996, through which Russia's leaders would control the media and violate rules for free and open competition.

It was an election characterized by fear and fraud; it was certainly neither free nor fair. This was a distinctly undemocratic precedent, which has only solidified and been exaggerated in each round of elections. Russia has yet to have open, democratic elections. Competition is viewed with suspicion and abhorrence by the elite, the media, and large segments of the population. Censorship, administrative rules to ban candidates and parties, Kremlin control over fictitious opposition parties designed to create an air of competition, and other more nefarious, suspicious activities all create an atmosphere of fear, control, and restriction around the idea of political competition, rather than the democratic norms of freedom, openness, and equality. Russia lacks open, competitive politics, and the elections of 1996 set the precedents that would prevent their rise.

Not surprisingly, by 2000 openness and competition would not guide the process of leadership change in Russia. While the option for allowing a free, competitive campaign for the country's leadership existed in theory, it required a gigantic leap of faith to think that it would take place, and gross deception to argue that it did. It would also have required at that point an enormous leap for Russia's leaders in terms of commitment to democratic procedures and principles. It was not a leap that they were prepared to take or were even thinking about taking. They controlled the outcome of succession, deciding for the people who would lead them, rather than allowing the people to decide who would lead Russia. The short-term consequence was the rise of the *siloviki* to power. Led by Vladimir Putin, Russia's new leaders reinstituted one-party rule, restored censorship and control over the mass media, eliminated competitive politics, and silenced political opposition. All of these were exaggerations of but based on precedent set during the critical junctures identified here.

Putin has restored dictatorship. But it is the long-term consequence that may be more significant, namely, the precedent Yeltsin set both in the reasons for and the act of handing over power to a chosen successor. Nobody in Russia is talking in about a free and competitive election as Putin's second term draws to a close. The question is whether Putin will cling to power or anoint a successor, and whether he will abolish elections for president as he has abolished them for other positions of executive power in the country.

Authoritarian Reality and Possible Futures for Russia

Under the circumstances of the restoration of dictatorship under Putin, it is possible to identify various possible scenarios as most likely paths for Russia's near-term political development. The remainder of the chapter examines these scenarios. Possibilities other than those elaborated below could, of course, be imagined. But we dismiss them for being so fanciful as to not require much discussion, given the political realities today. For example, an open, competitive campaign and election to determine the next Russian president is a possibility of greater than zero. One can imagine Putin in 2008 proclaiming that he had succeeded in his mission (whatever that was), and announcing that Russia is now a democracy, and overseeing a free, open election for his successor to proceed. The likelihood of such a sequence of events, or of another similar to it, is so close to nil as to be dismissed without further discussion. Similarly, it is difficult to imagine Putin simply declaring himself president-for-life and remaining in power. One can, of course, imagine a scenario in which the Kremlin would concoct a crisis severe enough to provide a pretext for suspending elections and other constitutional provisions, and retaining Putin in office for an extended period of time, but this strikes the authors as extremely remote compared with the scenarios identified below.

The authors recognize that prediction in the realm of politics is an iffy proposition at best, yet scenarios such as those above seem infinitesimally remote. At the same time, the ones we elaborate below appear to form the universe of most likely paths. Judgements about the relative likelihood among these can be made based on precedent, past trends, and current political realities. We focus on three in particular, which are most likely to hold Russia's future. These three scenarios are, in increasing order of likelihood, "velvet revolution," "soft successor," and "strong dictator." We examine each in turn.

Velvet revolution, sometimes called "color" revolution after the events in Georgia, Ukraine, and Kyrgyzstan in 2003–2005, strikes the authors as the least likely of these scenarios for Russia's future political development. It is the one for which Russian society appears least organized and least prepared. The fundamental element of velvet revolution is mass popular movement for democratic political change. Mass, organized protests engulf the country and paralyze the capital, as the people adopt tactics of nonviolent resistance to protest against abuses and transgressions committed by repressive, closed regimes. The population, through these demonstrations, demands and eventually achieves the dismissal of the political leaders and their replacement with pro-democracy political leaders who promise greater openness, true political competition, and a general liberalization of politics. Velvet revolutions have tended to feature creative tactics and imagery, in part a feature of the typically substantial student participation, as in Ukraine's 2004 "Orange Revolution," Georgia's 2003 "Rose Revolution," and Kyrgyzstan's 2005 "Tulip Revolution."

There is evidence that some of the necessary components for such popular democratic uprising in Russia do exist. It is this fact that provides sufficient cause not to summarily dismiss the possibility of such a scenario from playing out, despite the admittedly remote likelihood in Russia. There is certainly a segment of the political elite who are disaffected by the current regime and the general direction of Russia's political system. There are in high-profile leaders available who could conceivably organize such a movement, without which this scenario would necessarily be dismissed as fanciful. These include, in addition to the coauthors of this work, such figures as Boris Nemtsov, Gary Kasparov, Grigory Yavlinsky, and others. There is also a segment of mid-level military and government officials, regional political leaders, and business leaders who feel disenfranchised by or disillusioned with the present state of Russian politics. The disaffection ranges across policies, from the quagmire in Chechnya to the closing of the mass media to attacks against independent business to the general level of corruption in government and society. At the same time, there is a substantial segment of the population that has not seen standards of living improve significantly.

These positive factors, however, are overwhelmed by the contraindications. The nearly-universal corruption of governing elites at all levels and the repressive nature of the regime extends to the legal system and the courts, which serve to protect those in power rather than to protect the people from transgressions committed by the powerful. Together, these realities militate against any organized opposition from forming among the authorities, and undermine any hopes that a popular movement might gain footing in those circles. Without prospects from support from a significant strata of the authorities, the people are unlikely to take to the streets. Moreover, while the reality of a closed and controlled media propaganda machine makes it difficult to judge opinion polls, nevertheless Putin enjoys stable popularity ratings by presenting an image of "order." While some organizations have been created to provide a foundation for democratic political change in anticipation of the end of Putin's reign, groups such as the 2008 Committee are not active, lack membership and resources, and show no evidence of gaining a mass following. There are simply no rumblings of widespread dissent or disaffection with the regime or its leader, making velvet revolution highly unlikely.

Perhaps the one thing that could conceivably trigger such revolutionary movement would be egregious and obvious election fraud, perhaps including violence, that could trigger a coalescence of the factors that are present. It was election fraud that sparked the color revolutions in other states. This book has documented Russia's experience with election fraud over the last fifteen years, so the condition certainly exists. One cannot discount the potential for a mass reaction in the future. However, in Russia the expectation around elections includes an understanding of lack of real competition and rigged outcomes. Velvet revolution just does not seem likely to be a part of Russia's near-term future.

The second scenario, the soft successor, would represent the maintenance of the status quo, and is likely the outcome that Putin hopes to guarantee. Soft, here, does not mean liberalizing or opening up, and does not necessarily mean weak. It signifies merely that it represents the smoothest, least wrenching sequence of events. Putin, in this scenario, will hand over power to a chosen successor, much as Yeltsin handed power to Putin. That successor would then govern, and we can identify three versions of the soft successor. In the first, or strong form, the new leader fashions himself after Chile's Pinochet, in other words a strong handed dictator executing more overt and more frequent attacks on opposition, while continuing a state-capitalist approach to the economy. The hallmarks would be less tolerance of dissent and open politics even than under Putin. In the second version, the weak form, the new leader would seek to imitate Putin, consciously and even studiously trying to preserve the status quo in every way. In the third version, the leader may follow the status quo while proliferating rhetoric about building democracy, moving toward democracy in a consistent, state-led effort.

Under all three versions of the soft successor scenario, the defining feature of the system is the preservation of uncertainty. Under all three, elections are held but they are irrelevant. They are not where decisions are made about political leaders. The real decisions, about personnel and about policy, are made through opaque, mysterious processes. There is a legislature but it does not legislate; there is a press but it does not inform. Uncertainty is everywhere. There is no transparency in government, no checks on authority, and little in the way of reliable public information.

So in the soft successor version of the future, elections may be held as a formality, or they may not be held. But real decisions about power will be made by Putin himself, in handpicking a successor. The precedent that Yeltsin set is the one that will be far and away the easiest for Putin to follow, namely, resigning the office, appointing his successor, and allowing for a shortened election that creates a facade of legitimacy on the transfer. But he could choose another means to the same end, serving out his term and using the levers of power to rig elections for his chosen successor. Either version amounts to the same thing—a continuation of the uncertainty of existence of Putinism with an ever-corrupt and sprawling bureaucracy dominated by the *siloviki*.

The third scenario, the rise of a strong dictator is the most dangerous of the likely futures and in some forms even takes on an almost apocalyptic feel. Unfortunately, the authors consider that this scenario may ultimately be the most likely for Russia's political future. In the strong dictator scenario, power will fall to a xenophobic nationalist, perhaps from the *siloviki*, who imposes the harshest form of dictatorship on the country. It is not a great stretch to identify a catalyst such an outcome, as it could easily mirror the events of each previous presidential election cycle, in exaggerated form. A wave of explosions and attacks in the heart of Russia, in major cities in various regions of the country, would spark fear and terror provoking a stronger form of Putinism—rule by those in uniform lacking hesitation to openly use violence against the population as a method of rule. Perhaps out of a struggle between various individuals or groupings seeking dominance in the post-Putin era, the more hard line among these elite would instigate such a crisis as a means of gaining the upper hand in a succession struggle.

Another, possibly more likely version of the strong dictator scenario, involves a more gradual process. For example, it is not difficult to envision strong dictatorship as the medium-term consequence resulting initially from the soft scenario. If Putin strictly follows Yeltsin's precedent, and aim consciously for preservation of the status quo, he would hand over power to an unknown, shadowy figure much as Putin was when Yeltsin anointed him. Unknown figures have unknown capabilities. He could, for example, prove to be more like Pinochet, or even worse, than his predecessor, particularly given the likely *siloviki* background. Or, he could prove simply incompetent to rule or incapable of governing, failing to maintain the status quo. A severe economic, security or social crisis, or a combination of these, were it to provoke chaos or collapse within the deeply corrupt government or other explosive events, could induce that leader eitherto shift to strongarm tactics or to propel others to overthrow him in an overt coup and bring to power a hard-line nationalist leader. Whether the strong dictator who consolidates power emerges from the communist, nationalist, military or secret service background, or holds some combination of these affiliations, is less relevant than what he stands for and how he rules, which would be disastrous for the people and potentially dangerous for the world.

Other specific chains of events can be crafted under each of the three scenarios, though as indicated we find the prospects for velvet revolution to be extremely remote. As the last version indicates, the soft successor and strong dictator scenarios are not necessarily exclusive—the one can degenerate into the other and, indeed, may even likely do so.

One thing seems clear, however. Russia has no short-term or medium-term prospects for democracy. The word has no place in describing Russian politics. The most likely scenarios as Putin prepares to exist the stage, if he indeed does exit the stage, will take the country ever-further, rather than nearer, to free and open politics that are the bedrock of any democratic political system.

Notes

Preface

1. See BBC Monitoring, "Russian Journalist Sacked for Covering St. Petersburg Dissenters' March," Text of report by Russian Ekho Moskvy radio on March 7, 2007, in *JRL #2005-55*, March 7, 2007; and *Los Angeles Times*, "Political activists, police spar in Moscow Hundreds are detained, including organizer Garry Kasparov, after defying authorities to hold a protest march," April 15, 2005, in *JRL #2007-88*, April 16, 2007.

Chapter 1

1. This book does not cover the Soviet period from 1917 through 1991. It begins with the collapse. There is a voluminous literature on the Soviet Union and the collapse of communist rule. For a concise introduction to the Soviet Union and the political history of communism, see McAuley (1992).

2. Among many examples, see McFaul (2001) and his numerous articles and newspaper commentaries from 1993 through 2004; Remington (2001); and Bunce (2003).

3. See, for example, Robinson (2003); and Triesman (2005). Many, many authors throw around the phrase "partial democracy" in connection with Russia.

4. Since Putin began trumpeting "managed democracy," media and expert analysts in Russia and abroad have parroted his language. See, Colton and McFaul (2004); and Rutland (2004).

5. For an enlightening analysis of the proliferation of adjectives, see Collier and Levitsky (1997). A Harvard report in 1999 had the audacity to outright state the assumption. See Lantz (1998).

6. For one recent example, see Hahn (2004a, 2004b, 2004c).

7. These themes dominated his most important speeches: upon his inauguration as President of Russia, July 10, 1991, before the Russian Congress of People's Deputies on October 28, 1991, and before the first session of the Russian Supreme

Soviet after the dissolution of the U.S.S.R., on January 16, 1992. See Gorshkov, et al (1994, 85–88, 96–98, 115–118). On Gorbachev's half-measures and the Soviet Union's demise, see Ostrow (2007).

8. Now called the Federal Security Service or FSB, in many ways it is more accurate to describe the officials who dominate Russia's government today as KGB, as they are drawn from all of the former agency's units: internal security, foreign intelligence, and defense intelligence. Olga Kryshtanovskaya of the Russian organization Center for the Study of Elites has the most respected data on the rise of *siloviki* to power. See *The Economist* May 22, 2004, for one account.

9. He has had a stream of journalists removed, from Yevgeniy Kisilev to Leonid Parfyenov to Savik Shuster, and had popular programs such as *Svoboda Slova* and *Namedni* removed from the air.

10. Information from Committee to Protect Journalists, www.cpj.org. See also Serge Schmemann, "Journalists' Deaths Make It Harder to Excuse Putin's Excesses," *New York Times,* July 13, 2004.

11. See, for example, Hahn (2004a, 2004b, 2004c).

12. Ibid.

13. See Shirov (2004).

14. The case against Yukos and its founder Mikhail Khodorkovsky was simultaneously an attack on economic and on political freedom. If an entrepreneur is not able to use his capital to support charitable foundations, to support interest groups, to support political activists and parties, is not able to use his resources freely, if the state arrests him for such activities, then he is not politically free. If in reaction to such activities the state shuts down businesses and seizes their capital and holdings, there is no economic freedom either, for this is a restriction on private property.

15. See RIA Novosti, "Will Russia Avoid a Party Oligarchy," in *JRL #9150,* May 16, 2005.

16. Marina Ozerova, "The Duma Special Service: What Duma Members Are Keeping Silent About," *Moskovskii Komsomolets,* February 20, 2004, in *JRL #8076,* February 20, 2004.

17. Olga Kryshtanovskaya, "Anatomy of the Russian Elite (Moscow)," as cited in Ostrovsky (2003).

18. See Medetsky (2004).

19. See, for example, Rutland (2005).

20. See Schumpeter (1950); Dahl (1971); and Huntington (1991).

21. See Fish (2005, Chapter 1). Fish's review is superb, analyzing the long and rich theoretical literature on democracy with a compelling synthesis into the definition which we embrace.

22. See, for example, Dale R. Herspring, "Conclusion," in Herspring (2005).

23. Fish (2005, 18–20), anachronistically insists on the ideal type, then invents the awkward term "monocracy" where it is not needed. Autocracy or dictatorship serves better.

24. From Bealey (1999).

25. For a chilling and realistic portrayal of Putin the man, his background, intentions and transgressions, see the film *Tovarish Prezident*. Shirov (2004).

26. Collier and Collier (1991).

27. Ibid., 27; David (1986, 30).

28. Collier and Collier (1991, 27, 30–32).

Chapter 2

1. Dallin and Lapidus (1991, 698–700).

2. Kotz and Weir (1997, 152).

3. For an inside analysis of those final months, compiled by many advisors to Yeltsin and Gorbachev at the time, see Baturin, et al (2001, 154–159, 162–180). Also see McFaul (2001, 129–140).

4. There are many accounts of these months. See Baturin, et al (2001, 160–201) for an authoritative Russian language account; see also McFaul (2001, 121–206); and Remnik (1998, 37–50), . On the impact of Gorbachev's indecisiveness, see also Ostrow (2007).

5. Satarov in early 1992 was a member of Yeltsin's President's Council, and shortly thereafter became a close political advisor and part of Yeltsin's inner circle.

6. See Ostrow (2007).

7. Beginning New Year's Day 1992, Supreme Soviet Chairman Ruslan Khasbula-tov fought to establish his power as equal to or greater than Yeltsin's. See Gorshkov (1994, 111–121). See also Ostrow (2000, esp. Chapter 3).

8. See Ostrow (2007); and Gorshkov (1994, 108–111).

9. With the creation of and his election on June 12, 1991, to the new post of President of Russia, he vacated his position as Chairman of the Supreme Soviet, thus necessitating a replacement.

10. Gleisner, et al (1996).

11. JO interview with Sergei Shakhrai. Shakhrai, Yeltsin's senior legal advisor in 1992, has held numerous positions in government and is currently Deputy Chair of the Audit Chamber.

12. JO interview with Lyudmilla Pikhoya. Pikhoya was Yeltsin's principal speech writer from roughly 1990 to 1998.

13. While Pikhoya's memory is plausible, Satarov does not recall and nobody has confirmed that Yeltsin carried such a speech or that this was seriously discussed prior to the April 1993 referendum.

14. Gorshkov (1994, Chapter 6); and Baturin, et al (2001, 162–168) give perhaps the most complete analysis available of the Novo-Ogarevo process both before and after the coup.

15. JO interview with Shakhrai.

16. Ibid.

17. Bunce (1998) makes a compelling argument regarding the connection between violent disintegration and the collapse of federal, as opposed to unitary communist states.

18. For analyses of various states in East-Central Europe, see Jacques Rupnik, "The Postcommunist Divide;" Richard Rose, "Europe Transformed;" Bronislaw Geremek, "The Transformation of Central Europe;" Richard Rose, "A Diverging Europe;" and Aleksander Smolar, "History and Memory: The Revolutions of

1989–1991" in Diamond and Plattner (2002). Also see Elster, et al (1998); and Dawisha and Parrott (1997).

19. JO interview with Yuri Baturin.

20. Yeltsin personally went to the Ministry of Defense headquarters late in the night on October 3, 1993, in the middle of armed chaos on the streets of Moscow, to demand and then ask the military leadership to carry out his orders to disband the legislature. He received a cold reception and ambiguous response. For further elaboration of these events, see Baturin, et al (2001, 366–370); and Taylor (1997).

21. JO interview with Sergei Filatov.

22. Yeltsin's alcohol problem attained legendary status after embarrassing incidents on trips to the United States and Germany. Accounts abound. For one highly readable presentation, David Remnick opens his account of Russia's early postcommunist years with an anecdote of a drunken Yeltsin. Remnick (1997, 3–4, 250, and 277).

23. On this, his personal advisor and speech writer Lyudmilla Pikhoya was most emphatic, confirming the observations of Satarov and other close Yeltsin advisors. JO interview with Pikhoya.

24. JO interview with Shakhrai.

25. Baturin, et al (2001, 173).

26. Data from Goskomstat (1996); International Monetary Fund (1998); and Baturin, et al (2001, 189–192).

27. See, for example, Gorshkov, et al. (1994, 94–98, 110–111).

28. See Ostrow (2007).

29. For a background on this economic reform plan and its evolution, see Baturin, et al (2001, 170–175).

30. This is not merely hindsight. From the time the 500 Days plan appeared in 1990, its claims often drew derisive laughter, and not only in the expatriate community.

31. See for the most important example the account of Yeltsin's first Prime Minster, Yegor Gaidar (2003). Most of Gaidar's publications since leaving office deliver the same message.

32. Wedel (1998), gives a brief account of the creation of these policies and involvement of advisors such as Sachs, Lawrence Summers, and Andrei Shleifer. For a longer account of his role and the development of the policies during these years, see Janine R. Wedel, "Rigging the US–Russian Relationship: Harvard, Chubais, and the Transidentity Game," *Democratizatsiya* 7, no. 4 (Fall 1999): 469–500.

33. The official Kremlin tally of 146 is disputed by many as not credible. The most compelling account of the Ocober 3–4, 1993, events in Moscow is Kutsyllo (1993).

34. The full text of the decree is available in Baturin, et al (2001, 358–359).

35. Ostrow (2000).

36. For a detailed study of the Supreme Soviet and its Chair, see Ostrow (2000, esp. Chapter 3).

37. See Baturin, et al (2001, 277, 291). The primary authors of the draft were Sergei Shakhrai and Sergei Alekseyev, the former a Cabinet-level advisor to the president.

38. JO interviews with Shakhrai, Filatov, and Pikhoya confirmed Satarov's memory on this score.

39. Fur further elaboration, see Ostrow (2000, esp. Chapter 3); and Baturin, et al (2001, esp. Part II, *Novoye dvoyevlastiya.*)

40. See, for further background, Baturin, et al (2001, Chapters 6 and 7, esp. 311–320).

41. Ibid., 324.

42. JO interview with Pikhoya.

43. JO interview with Shakhrai.

44. Baturin, et al. (2001, 326). Yeltsin continued to worry that reductions in their budgets and in their standing in society would make questionable the officers' support if it were needed.

45. Ibid.

46. Yeltsin (1994, 314).

47. JO interview with Pikhoya.

48. Baturin, et al. (2001, 327).

49. Ibid., 327–328.

50. On these developments, see Ostrow (2000, 85–92); and Baturin, et al. (2001, 352–376).

51. For a full discussion of how a legislature's institutional design affects the incentive structure of its members, see Ostrow (2000).

52. One certainly must consider a coup to be a form of political violence.

Chapter 3

1. Baturin, et al. (2001, 379).

2. Khakamada, as a prominent entrepreneur, was a member of the Constitutional Assembly's Business Chamber. She continued to participate in the sessions after the October crisis. Satarov was a close political advisor to Yeltsin.

3. Tolz (1993a) offers a brief account of this process.

4. There are many versions of the draft constitutions discussed in this chapter, and each version differs from the others. The authors have used several versions in Russian and English for this analysis, in an effort to provide as accurate an analysis as possible of what transpired. The most authoritative versions and the ones the authors rely on most heavily are published in Filatov, ed (1996), the stenographic record of the meetings of the Constitutional Assembly (hereafter referred to as *Stenograms*). These Stenograms contain the complete record of the debate in that body from June through November, 1993, and copies of the drafts it produced. Other versions differ from those published in the *Stenograms*, however, and the story of how the final, adopted version was arrived at could not be made without access to these various drafts. CRCR (1995) offers a valuable collated analysis between two drafts, though the title's reference to the "Yeltsin draft" of April 1993 is erroneous, for the collation in the document is, in fact, with the Constitutional Assembly's July 12, 1993, draft. See also Council of Europe CDL (1993a, 1993b); *Proyekt Constitutsiya Rossiyskoy Federatsii: Na referendum 12 Dekabrya 1993;* and Belyakov and Raymond, eds. (1994). In the following pages, "July draft constitution" refers to the

July 12, 1993, draft, published in Volume 17 of the *Stenograms*. References to the constitution as adopted are from the final draft published at the end of Volume 20 of the *Stenograms* and adopted by referendum on December 12, 1993. These other documents served as reference material to provide verification of information provided elsewhere, from interviews with participants, or from the authors' own memories.

5. Technically, Yeltsin's decree established the body so that elections could be held. There was little or no discussion about what would happen should the new legislature be elected but the constitution rejected, but the evidence of fraud in the vote ratifying the constitution suggests that steps may have been taken precisely to ensure this could not happen. See Sobyanin (1994).

6. These observations and predictions were first and most clearly laid out, though widely ignored, in Thorson (1993).

7. Discussion of the amendments does appear, but the changes themselves and, the record makes abundantly clear, the decisions on them were made outside of that body.

8. JO interview with Baturin.

9. JO interview with Shakhrai.

10. The first such reference appears in *Stenograms,* Vol. 18, 70, at the first session after the battle.

11. *Stenograms,* Vol. 18, 77–78; and Vol. 20, 45–46. Also see Vol. 19, 139–141. There are too many—more than three dozen separate instances—to list in which this theme is repeated throughout Vols 18–20.

12. McFaul (2001, 210). He nevertheless continued to describe Russia as a democracy.

13. Andrei Sinyavsky quoted in Tolz (1993b).

14. See *Stenograms,* Vol. 18, 14. Decree 1400 is on pp. 6–10; the decree on the referendum is on pp. 58–67.

15. The coauthors' description of Yeltsin and his advisors comes from their own memories and is echoed by each of the individuals interviewed for this volume, all of whom worked in or closely with the Kremlin at the time.

16. See *Stenograms,* Vol. 18, 3–4. No sessions of this "Working Group" appear in the Stenograms. It is quite possible, given subsequent events, that it never convened.

17. JO interview with Filatov.

18. JO interview with Baturin.

19. Ibid.

20. JO interview with Pikhoya.

21. JO interview with Filatov. In the Stenograms, references to this work almost always came from Filatov, who seemed to alternate between "working group" and "expert group" when mentioning it. He never mentioned names, though he was clearly one of the two or three who took part.

22. *Stenograms,* Vol. 18, 77.

23. Ibid., 370.

24. *Stenograms,* Vol. 19, 153.

25. Filatov's continuing insistence made it clear the decision already had been made to allow ministers to sit in the Duma. See *Stenograms,* Vol. 19, 252–254. On the president's unilateral decisions, see *Stenograms,* Vol. 20, 155.

26. See *Stenograms,* Vol. 20, 360–361 for the vote. Not a word about this provision appears in print after the vote, yet the Draft Constitution that went before the country in the referendum retains the amended version of Art. 110 that excludes the regional executives.

27. JO interview with Filatov.

28. See *Stenograms,* Vol. 20, 475 ff for the draft in which Yeltsin wrote his own amendments. Filatov suggests in private communication that Yeltsin made these changes in a meeting with Ilyushin and Baturin.

29. Art. 83 and Art. 102, July draft.

30. Art. 83.

31. Art. 103. See also Art. 111.

32. *Stenograms,* Art. 116, July draft.

33. Art. 83 and Art. 117.

34. *Stenograms,* Vol. 18, 123–124.

35. Ibid., 207.

36. *Stenograms,* Vol. 19, 140–141.

37. Ibid., 140.

38. Ibid., 144–145.

39. He repeated this point several times. See, for example, *Stenograms,* Vol. 19, 84–85.

40. *Stenograms,* Vol. 19, 260. On the complicated provisions surrounding votes of confidence and no confidence, see Art. 111 and Art. 117.

41. Art. 111 and Art. 116 of the July draft.

42. Art. 111 of the July draft.

43. Ibid.

44. *Stenograms,* Vol. 20, 349–350.

45. Ibid., 354–355.

46. *Ibid.*

47. Art. 83 and Art. 111.

48. Thorson (1993).

49. Ibid., 13.

50. See Ostrow (2000).

51. Ibid., 174–177.

52. On the early spirit of debate and cooperation, see Ostrow (2000, Chapter 6).

53. JO interview with Filatov.

54. See Rodin (2005).

Chapter 4

1. See Handelman (1997).

2. McFaul (2001, 304–306).

3. McFaul (1997a).

4. One wonders when the democracy supposedly being "renewed" had existed. McFaul (1997a). Also see McFaul (1997b). McFaul was by no means alone, but he was the most visible commentator in the major media in the United States. The same

messages were trumpeted in all of the major media coverage, including *The New York Times, The Washington Post, The Los Angeles Times, The Economist,* and *The Times* (London) from June 1996.

5. The phrase, with a slightly different interpretation, is from Bivens and Bernstein (1998).

6. For general overviews of corruption in Russia and the rise of the oligarchs, see Handelman (1997); and Klebnikov (2000).

7. Satarov, as Yeltsin's chief political advisor, responsible for relations with the Duma, political parties, and other political organizations, was a central member of the campaign strategy team. Khakamada was a People's Deputy in the Russian State Duma, had been a leader of a legislative faction, and as both a legislator and a proponent of small business development in Russia attended the 1996 World Economic Summit in Davos, which proved critical to the presidential campaign. Both had firsthand knowledge of the key events described and decisions analyzed in this chapter.

8. For a brief account, see Remnick (1998, 335).

9. Poll results as reported in Baturin, et al. (2001, 553).

10. For a nice review of this, see Lantz (1998). See also Remnick (1996, 49–51); and RFE/RL Daily Reports on the election in April 1996. Lantz's analysis of the election, it must be cautioned, ignores or discounts the significance of the serious transgressions detailed here, by way of defending his initial "presumption" of democracy.

11. Yegor Gaidar, the former Prime Minister, wrote "Only later did I learn of 'Rutskoi's list' of people to be immediately arrested and tried," referring to the vice president who was one of the leaders of the uprising. Gaidar describes it vaguely as an "extremely general" list that included "many well-known figures, but did not include the President's, the Defense Minister's, or my name. Evidently, the three of us were not intended to be dealt with for long." Gaidar (1996, 287–288). Many thanks to Brian Taylor for assistance in locating this source, and for confirming our skepticism that Gaidar in fact laid eyes on any such list. His account is more accurately seen as evidence of the pervasiveness of the rumor, of how seriously Yeltsin and his advisors took those rumors, and of the legendary status that for many has transformed them from rumor into fact. If ever there were a definition of political fear, this would be it.

12. See Reddaway and Glinski (2001); Handelman (1997); Klebkikov (2000); and the series of in-depth INDEM reports at www.anti-corr.ru.

13. Klebkikov (2000, 212–214).

14. Bivens and Bernstein (1998).

15. The wonderful term is from Fish (1995).

16. See Chapter 6, of this book, for a more complete discussion of Yeltsin's admiration and selective emulation of Washington.

17. See Handelman (1997); and Klebkikov (2000) for graphic and detailed analysis of the organized crime warfare in Moscow.

18. Berezovsky interview in Shirov (2004).

19. The word "bank" is used loosely. These were less banks than clearinghouses for capital flight "controlled by organized crime schemes to launder money obtained

illegally" Waller (1998). Also, in addition to the sources listed in note 10, see the reports of the American Russian Law Institute, such as Emanuel E. Zeltser's congressional testimony, at http://russianlaw.org/022.htm; and Tikhomirov (1997).

20. Conflicting reports exist on those oligarchs present at Davos, but all agree that most were, and that Berezovsky brought together them and others who did not attend. At the time of the 1995 Davos conference, Chubais was out of government. He moved in and out several times in the 1990s.

21. See Klebnikov (2000, 212–215); and Remnick (1998, 329–330) on the violent grudges between Berezovsky and Gusinsky, and for their accounts of the Davos meeting.

22. Baturin, et al. (2001, 554).

23. Ibid., 553–558.

24. McFaul (2001, 293). This version may come from Chubais himself, and is not repeated in any other account we are aware of.

25. Baturin, et al. (2001, 556).

26. Ibid., 553–558.

27. Klebnikov (2000, 216–219), has the president considering suspending the elections after a group of thirteen financiers published a letter stressing the need to avoid hostilities and bloodshed, for the various parties to work together. The account here is drawn from the coauthors' experiences, interviews, and Baturin, et al. (2001, 557–563). Remnick's abbreviated account is consistent with the more detailed version here. See Remnick (1998), pp. 331–333.

28. Baturin, et al. (2001, 559) provides the complete contents of the document. All subsequent quotes in this section come from pp. 557–563 of *Epokha Yeltsin*.

29. Baturin, et al. (2001, 563). Kulikov may have told Yeltsin that he could not guarantee the loyalty of the troops. See Remnick (1998), pp. 332–333.

30. Klebnikov (2000, 220–223, 238–240). While Klebnikov's is the most detailed published account of the campaign financing, one must also be wary as it is almost exclusively drawn from Korzhakov and his associates. The general contours, however, are accurate and square with the authors' independent knowledge and with other reports. See also Waller (1998); Goldman (2003); and Handelman (2001).

31. Klebnikov (2000, 220–223).

32. Ibid.

33. The story of how Berezovsky schemed his way to billions of dollars could be told with minor revision of any of the oligarchs. Klebnikov (2000, esp. Chapters 3, 4, 6, and 7).

34. According to Remnick, Yeltsin paid for a woman to have a telephone installed in her home! Remnick (1998), pp. 335. Baturin, et al. (2001, 568) report that he pardoned a monastery official who was under criminal investigation.

35. Berezovsky interview in Shirov (2004).

36. That is, on March 19, when Yeltsin shook up the campaign staff and the financiers began to play a more direct role. See Baturin, et al. (2001, 556–557) for the full staff listing.

37. See Baturin, et al. (2001, 546).

38. The print media did continue to span the entire ideological spectrum, but under conditions of economic collapse only a minuscule percentage of the public consumed newspapers that covered politics, and few individual papers had circulation levels of any significance.

39. For a short report on the electronic media in Russia's elections, see Oates (2000). Also Mickiewicz (1999, esp. Chapter 8).

40. Zassoursky (1996).

41. Ibid.

42. Klebnikov (2000, 226).

43. Sergei Parkhomenko, *Los Angeles Times*, June 25, 1996.

44. JO interview with Filatov.

45. Klebnikov (2000, 224–228).

46. Aside from the few newspaper reports cited above, we are not aware of substantial published concern outside of Russia either. There was much discussion among Western academics but no widespread published outcry at the time.

47. See Klebnikov (2000, 235).

48. See Felshtinsky and Litvinenko (2001). As Chapter 6 details, many, including Litvinenko, who have tried to investigate the explosions in 1996, 1999, 2000, and 2004, all election years, have been murdered under suspicious circumstances.

49. See Shirov (2004).

50. See Cable News Network (1996).

51. Yeltsin's doctors only permitted him to celebrate his inauguration for some thirty minutes. His staff immediately knew his health would be a central concern for Russian politics. Baturin, et al. (2001, 575).

52. Bivens and Bernstein (1998).

53. The payback began immediately. See Remnick (1997, 352–358).

54. See the series of INDEM reports on corruption. INDEM (2001, 2004a, 2005a, 2005b) and others at www.anti-corr.ru.

55. See Baturin, et al. (2001, 720–722).

56. See INDEM (2004a, 2004b). The specific figures were published in a report in *Nezavisimaya Gazeta,* August 15, 2003.

57. Pyotr Orekhin and Yevlalia Samedova, "Kremlin Inc. Has Performed Well," *Nezavisimaya Gazeta ,* July 26, 2005, in *JRL #9210,* July 27, 2005.

58. Zassoursky (1996).

59. Lenin (1984, 163–164).

60. See Bivens and Bernstein (1998).

Chapter 5

1. JO interview with Pikhoya. See also Remnick (1997, 37).

2. Lipset (1998, 26).

3. Ibid., 31–32.

4. Ellis (2004, 230); also Elkins and McKitrick (1993, 294).

5. See McFaul (2001, 155). Remnick (1997) offers a nice journalistic account of Yeltsin's self-imposed isolation from party politics; and Breslauer (2002) offers a thorough study of Yeltsin as a leader.

6. Lipset (1998, 26).

7. See Ellis (2004, 184, 189–190); and Lipseet (1998, 34).

8. Lipset (1998, 34–35).

9. Ellis (2004, 238–239). Also McDonald (1974, 178–182).

10. See McDonald (1974, 178) for a published account of this common knowledge.

11. Virtually all accounts of the 1796 election focus on the development of early political parties with only perfunctory mention of Washington's silence. Lipset's (1998) short article includes several paragraphs, far more than most lengthy biographies of America's first president.

12. Lipset (1998, 35).

13. Elkins and McKitrick (1993, 516). It is worth pointing out that Washington was disgusted by and disappointed in the appearance of partisan politics, by the emergence of party politics, and this was an important reason for his remaining on the sidelines. Paradoxically, his silence probably helped them to develop more rapidly, as divergent interested coalesced freely into different camps. More than 200 years later, it is a firmly established principle that modern democracy requires parties and a party system. Yeltsin, by rejecting them all, played an important role in preventing their development.

14. Lipset (1998, 24).

15. JO interview with Pikhoya.

16. After the economic default of 1998, Satarov and most of the rest of the pro-reform team left the Yeltsin Administration. Satarov had no direct participation in the events surrounding the hand over of power, though he was involved in the initial discussions about the succession problem prior to his dismissal. Khakamada was one of the coleaders of the SPS (Union of Right Forces), a conglomeration of those who had engineered the economic reforms and pro-democracy advocates. SPS played an important role in Putin's rise, as described below.

17. See Baturin, et al (2001, esp. *"Proshchaniye"* (Farewell), 778–791); and Baker and Glasser (2005, Chapter Two).

18. See Baturin, et al (2001, 778–791 passim); also Dunlop (2004).

19. JO interviews with Shakhrai, and Filatov.

20. For a concise and compelling analysis of the pyramid scheme and the default, in a normally entirely unreliable Russian tabloid, see Avrora Potemkina, "Fraud of the Century: IMF Loan Money Could not Have Vanished Without Mikhail Kasyanov's Knowledge," *Sovershenno Sekretno*, May 6, 2003, in *JRL* #7178, May 12, 2003. Also Klebnikov (2000, 279–281) .

21. See Shirov's (2004) film *"Tovarish Prezident"* for a presentation of the argument that the KGB/FSB maneuvered over a period of several years to consolidate control over Russia.

22. Tregubova (2003, 154).

23. Ibid., 155–156.

24. JO interview with Shakhrai.

25. See, for example, Tregubova (2003, 150–151).

26. Baturin, et al (2001, 781–782). The last chapter of the book describes nicely the impact of Yeltsin's health on the role of the oligarchs, and his inability to affect the situation.

27. Berezovsky interview with Shirov (2004).

28. Nemtsov interview with Shirov (2004).

29. Tregubova (2003, 155–56).

30. Nemtsov interview with Shirov (2004).

31. See Primakov (2002).

32. Baturin, et al (2001, 782–784).

33. See Primakov (2002, 204–205).

34. Ibid.

35. See Klebnikov (2000, 290–293), on the oligarchs' role.

36. Baturin, et al (2001, 783).

37. Tregubova (2003, 200–201).

38. Wedel (2000). These scandals also implicated some advisors and consultants in the West for money-laundering and other corrupt and illegal activities.

39. Fragmentary and contradictory information exists surrounding Chubais's position relative to Putin and Stepashin. The most plausible is Tregubova (2003, 199–202).

40. There are several accounts of this history. Baker and Glasser (2005, 45–52) offer a thorough treatment of these events.

41. Glavnogo Kontrolnogo Upravleniya Administratsii Prezidenta, sometimes called the Monitoring Administration. That office is responsible for inspections and control over budget and personnel matters at the regional level, a position from which Putin would develop his impressions of regional affairs and the contours of his plans for recentralization of federal relations. See Huskey (1999) for additional information on these details.

42. See Baker and Glasser (2005, 45–52).

43. Ibid., 51.

44. See Tregubova (2003, Chapter 8).

45. Ibid., 202–203.

46. See Ibid., 146–151.

47. Berezovsky interview with Shirov (2004).

48. See below for further discussion. Also Shirov (2004) and Klebnikov (2000, 302–306); and Felshtinsky and Litvinenko (2001).

49. Baker and Glasser (2005, 54).

50. Tregubova (2003, 201–204).

51. JO interviews with Pikhoya, and Shakhrai.

52. JO interview with Shakhrai.

53. JO interview with Pikhoya.

54. Baturin, et al (2001, 789–791). The story is reported also in Yeltsin (2000, 6) and Putin (2000, 185–186, 204–205).

55. Khakamada, as one of the leaders of SPS, was integral in discussions of the group's political strategy. See also Nemtsov interview with Shirov (2004).

56. Klebnikov (2000, 311–314) details Channel One's treatment of Putin's new "party."

57. Nemtsov interview with Shirov (2004). Nemtsov, as discussed in Chapter 6, served Putin in various capacities, including organizing the meeting at which Putin warned the business elite to stay out of politics.

58. See Baker and Glasser (2005, 52).

59. Center for Strategic Planning (2000).

60. Satarov became aware of the plan later, when some who worked on it became disenchanted that no effort to implement it was being made.

61. See Tregubova (2003, 201–204) for concrete evidence of vote-rigging in the 1999 parliamentary election. See also the discussion below.

62. McFaul was everywhere, from Public Television (PBS Newshour, January 3, 2000), http://www.pbs.org/newshour/bb/europe/jan-june00/russia_01-03.html) to Congressional testimony, (Senate Foreign Relations Committee, 2000). Journalists, commentators, and academics continued to repeat this notion for at least the next two years, though some like McFaul did begin to backtrack and put less complimentary adjectives in front of "democracy," such as "partial" or "limited."

63. See McFaul (2004), and his "Russian Electoral Trends," in Barany and Moser (2001).

64. Klebnikov (2000, 302–305). See also Feltishinsky and Litvinenko (2001).

65. Piontkovsky interview with Shirov (2004).

66. Ibid.

67. See *Los Angeles Times*, May 20, 2004. The film by Deniau and Gazelle (2000) drew much attention. See the written account in *JRL #6118*, March 6, 2002. Shirov's *Tovarish Prezident* (2004) presents additional, more recent, and compelling evidence. See also Felshtinsky and Litvinenko (2001). Yushenkov's murder in broad daylight as he entered his apartment was never solved.

68. See Baker and Glasser (2005, 54–57).

69. Tregubova (2003, 216).

70. Ibid., 214–216, 225–226.

71. JO interview with Shakhrai.

Chapter 6

1. While Khakamada was a Duma member during Putin's first term and opposed him in the presidential election, neither she nor Satarov was actively involved in or close to his decision-making process. As such, this chapter is almost entirely reliant upon secondary sources. Moreover, because of Putin's destruction of media independence, described in this chapter, we rely wherever possible on confirmation from outside sources.

2. On the work of those early Dumas, see Ostrow (2000, 2002).

3. Several parliamentary correspondents independently repeated this phrase; most left the Duma for other assignments, and abandoned domestic press outlets for reasons discussed below.

4. See "Georgy Satarov: No Opposition, But Discontent is Strong," *Nezavisimaya Gazeta*, August 25, 2004, in *JRL #8342*, August 25, 2004.

5. Fish (2005, 262).

6. See Shleifer and Triesman (2004); and Aslund (2000, 2002). These consultants to Russia consistently tout Russia as a liberal, capitalist democratic "success story."

7. Michael McFaul, "Russia's Glass Is Half Full and Leaking," *RFE/RL The Russian Federation Votes: 2003–2004*; Carnegie Endowment for International Peace meeting, "Future of Democracy in Russia," February 28, 2002, Carnegie Endowment for International Peace, in *JRL #6116*, March 6, 2002; and McFaul (2004).

8. Shleifer and Triesman continued to insist on their position until an investigation into Anatoliy Chubais began in late 2005; McFaul until the collapse of Yukos and the murder of *Forbes Russia* editor Paul Klebnikov. Russia's purported democratic credentials was a favorite subject of these and such analysts as Thomas Graham, Anders Aslund, Richard Sakwa, and many others. See Fish (2005, Chapter 2) for a thorough review of this disappointing literature.

9. See *Chicago Tribune*, June 4, 2006; and *The Washington Post*, June 3, 2006.

10. For other assessments, see Baker and Glasser (2005) for the account of two reporters; and Fish (2005) for a more quantitative approach to detailing politics under Putin. Most other recent works still place Russia in the category of a democracy, albeit with adjectives.

11. By far the most insightful profiles of Putin are Shirov's (2004) film, *Tovarish Pezident*; and Tregubova (2003).

12. "Putin: A Man Without Guarantees: The West Is Satisfied But the Acting President Has few Policies," *Itogi*, March 8, 2000, in *JRL #4156*, March 9, 2000. This analysis was written by Aleksandr Golts and Dmitry Pinsker, two highly respected political reporters in Russia at the time.

13. "Operation Infiltration Complete!" *Novaya Gazeta*, no. 63, August 30–September 1, 2004, in *JRL #8349*, September 1, 2004.

14. Mara Bellaby, "Putin's Government Packed with Former Security and Military Officers," *Associated Press*, March 5, 2005, in *JRL #8103*, March 6, 2005; and "Operation Infiltration Complete!" *Novaya Gazeta*, no. 63, August 30–September 1, 2004, in *JRL #8349*, September 1, 2004.

15. "Operation Infiltration Complete!" *Novaya Gazeta*, no. 63, August 30–September 1, 2004, in *JRL #8349*, September 1, 2004.

16. Olga Kryshtanovskaya, "Dangerous People in Civilian Clothing," *Yezhenedelnyi Zhurnal*, no. 10, March 15, 2004, in *JRL #8130*, March 22, 2004.

17. This was widely noted at the time of the appointments. See "Putin tightens his grip on Russia," *The Globe and Mail*, July 28, 2000; and Orth (2000).

18. "Return of the KGB," *Newsweek International*, November 24, 2003, in *JRL #7421*, November 17, 2003.

19. Ibid.

20. "Operation Infiltration Complete!" *Novaya Gazeta*, no. 63, August 30–September 1, 2004, in *JRL #8349*, September 1, 2004.

21. Olga Kryshtanovskaya, "Dangerous People in Civilian Clothing," *Yezhenedelnyi Zhurnal*, no. 10, March 15, 2004, in *JRL #8130*, March 22, 2004.

22. The label comes from Andrei Piontkovsky, quoted in "Presidential Address: At a Loss for Words," *Profil*, no. 18, May 12, 2003, in *JRL #7180*, May 13, 2003.

23. See "The Duma Special Service: What Duma Members Are Keeping Silent About" *Moskovskii Komsomolets*, February 20, 2004, in *JRL #8076* , February 20, 2004.

24. Shirov (2004); Deniau and Gazelle (2000); Felshtinsky and Litvinenko (2001); and Nekrasov (2004).

25. Shirov (2004); and Klebnikov (2000, 303–304).

26. See *Los Angeles Times*, May 20, 2004.

27. An exhaustive account in the German *Der Spiegel* places strong suspicion on the Kremlin for Litvinenko's murder by Polonium-210 poisoning. See "Following the Litvinenko Trail: Death by Poison, Direct from Moscow," *Der Spiegel*, December 5, 2006, in *JRL #276*, December 6, 2006.

28. On Yushenkov's murder, see *JRL #7147* April 19, 2003, and *JRL #7148*, April 20, 2003, for reports from Agence France Press, *The Independent*, and others. Ostrow's reflection on Yushenkov is in *#7148*.

29. "Fear Returns to Russia," *San Francisco Chronicle*, June 27, 2004.

30. Gessen (2004).

31. "Yavlinsky: Russia is Slipping Away, And There's Nothing to be Done About It," *Moskovskiy Komsomolets*, January 30, 2004, in *JRL #8041*, January 30, 2004.

32. He issued the decree May 13, 2000. See *RFE/RL*, Vol. 4, No. 93, Part I, May 15, 2000.

33. See "Putin Strengthens Power Vertical," *Gazeta*, September 14, 2004, in *JRL #8367*, September 15, 2004.

34. Politkovskaya (2004). Politkovskaya suggests doubts that Chechen terrorists were even behind the events.

35. Few of the accounts at the time focused on the significance of his brazen actions. See, for one example that attempted to, "Whispered in Russia: Democracy is Finished," *Los Angeles Times*, September 19, 2004.

36. Similarly, the Duma may reject or vote no-confidence in the federal government only under the duress of dissolution.

37. See *The Times* (London), September 25, 2004.

38. "Putin's Cure Could Be Russia's Poison," *Financial Times*, September 16, 2004.

39. See Hahn (2004a, 2004b, 2004c). Also see the comments of Alexei Kara-Murza in "Putin" Preliminary Results. "The Liberal View," *Nezavisimaya Gazeta - Stsenari*, no. 1, 2001, in *JRL #5058*, January 30, 2001.

40. See "Russia Election Said Not to be Democratic," *Associated Press*, March 15, 2004, in *JRL #8119*, March 16, 2004. The OSCE and COE report on the elections described the lavishing and exaggerated coverage of Putin.

41. See "Irina Khakamada: We Were Shown An Episode of Life in the Soviet Union," *Ruskii Kurier*, May 11, 2004, in *JRL #8203*, May 11, 2004.

42. Dmitry Pinsker, "Kremlin Returns to Once-Malfunctioned Idea of Bipartisanship to Put an End to Political Turmoil," *Itogi*, no. 15, April 13, 2000, in *JRL #4246*, April 13, 2000. Grammatical errors in the translation corrected here.

43. See Ostrow (2002).

44. The most prominent of the vote-analyzers is Thomas F. Remington. See Remington (2006); and Remington, "Putin, the Duma, and Political Parties," in Herspring, ed. (2005).

45. See Ostrow (2000, 2002) for analysis of the politics of legislating and the work of the pre-Putin Duma. The most prominent of the vote-analyzers is Thomas F. Remington. See Remington (2006); and Remington, "Putin, the Duma, and Political Parties," in Herspring, ed. (2005). The fraudulent behavior that takes place on every Duma vote renders meaningless and misleading analyses of those votes.

46. See Chapter 4, above.

47. The story of the relentless attacks against Gusinsky has been well documented in mass media accounts and elsewhere. Baker and Glasser (2005, 78–83) offer a nice synopsis of this in the context of Putin's coordinated attacks against an open press.

48. Ibid., 88–91. Baker and Glasser's account of Berezovsky's demise is founded in interviews with the latter. See also Jamestown Foundation Monitor (2000).

49. See "The Needs of the Many," *Time*, September 4, 2000.

50. In fact, ORT only began critical reporting after Putin ignored Berezovsky's advice that the new president return to Moscow from vacation to manage the crisis, in which over 100 submariners died at the bottom of the Berents Sea. See Baker and Glasser (2005, 88–90).

51. See Handelman (1997); Reddaway and Glinski (2001); Klebnikov (2000); INDEM (2004a, 2004b); and INDEM's "Corruption Project" at http://www.anti-corr.ru/projects.htm#15.

52. For an exhaustive chronicle of reports on the affair in Johnson's Russia List, see http://www.cdi.org/russia/johnson/jrl-2005-yukos.cfm.

53. See "The Money Trail Leading to Yugansk," *Moscow Times*, June 6, 2005, in *JRL #9170*, June 6, 2005.

54. An insightful point made in passing by Baker and Glasser (2005, 292).

55. Ibid. Also see Marshall Goldman (2004), "Putin and the Oligarchs," *Foreign Affairs*, 83, no. 6 (November/December).

56. See *JRL #7385*, October 27, 2003, for example, for early reaction to the arrest and multiple biographies of the oil tycoon.

57. See "Business Community Faces a Choice," *Vedemosti* October 27, 2003, in *JRL #7385*, October 27, 2003.

58. Fish (2005, 261–263) alludes to this, but rarely is this truth seen in print.

59. Hill (2003).

60. Johnson (2004).

61. Freedom House (2005a).

62. Wilson (2005) offers a masterful study on the fraudulent nature of Russia's elections.

63. Ibid.

64. See Fish (2005, Chapter 3 and esp. 45–52).

65. See Organization for Security and Cooperation in Europe (2004). The Parliamentary Assembly of the Council of Europe pronounced them "free but not fair," a

gross understatement. *Novaya Gazeta,* No. 6, January 29, 2004 offers an assessment of the report.

66. See "Putin's Victory All down to PR," says former Yeltsin aide, *BBC Monitoring,* in *JRL #8119,* March 16, 2004.

67. Freedom House (2005a).

68. "Asylum Decision Suggests that US Patience with Putin Is Wearing Thin," *The Guardian* (UK), February 2, 2005.

69. Ostrow (2007). See also Stephen F. Cohen and Katrina vanden Heuvel, *Voices of Glasnost: Interviews with Gorbachev's Reformers* (WW Norton, 2000).

70. See, for example, Mickiewicz (1999). Also Ostrow (1995).

71. See Reporters Without Borders, "Predators of Press Freedom."

72. Reporters sans Frontieres (2006), "Russia—2006 Annual report."

73. See Reporters sans Frontieres, Annual Worldwide Press Freedom indices.

74. See Freedom House "Freedom of the Press" in their Annual Reports.

75. Anna Politkovskaya, *Putin's Russia: Life in a Failing Democracy* (Metropolitan Books, 2005); Politkovskaya, *The Dirty War* (Harvill Press, 2004); and (2002).

76. "Following the Litvinenko Trail: Death by Poison, Direct from Moscow," *Der Spiegel,* December 5, 2006, in *JRL #276,* December 6, 2006.

77. See, for example, "Russia: Contract Killings Once Again On The Rise," *RFE/RL Newsline,* Vol. 10, No. 188, Part I, October 12, 2006.

78. See Handelman (1997).

79. Committee to Protect Journalists (2001); Mereu, "Russia: Putin Presidency at Two-Year Mark," (Part 2)," *RFE/RL Reports,* Moscow, April 19, 2002; and "Russia: Pressuring Journalists Becomes More Frequent," Interfax, Moscow, January 11, 2006, in *JRL #12* January 12, 2006.

80. Fond Zashchity Glasnosti (Glasnost Defense Foundation) information from their "Monitoring" data at www.gdf.ru.

81. Oddly, and going against their methodology, CPJ and RSF reported Politkovskaya's murder as the thirteenth of a journalist in the line of work. But the prosecutor certainly has not certified anything to that effect. See "Russia: *thirteen* murders, no justice" Committee to Protect Journalists, http://www.cpj.org/Briefings/2005/russia_murders/russia_murders.html.

82. The authors thank FZG President Aleksei K. Smirnov for clarification on their methods.

83. Details on the FZG "Monitor" methods and data are on the organization's web site.

84. For example, Dmitry Pinsker, the extremely talented *Itogi* journalist, died in a tragic horseback riding accident in 2003. While sad, tragic, and a blow to Russian journalism, it obviously was not a political murder. Similarly, the murder of Paul Klebnikov, the American editor of Moscow's *Forbes* magazine, cannot be positively linked to the Kremlin as the work he was conducting at the time of his July 2004 murder centered on corruption in the business world, not directly in high political circles.

85. The gruesome details on each case are available in FZG's "Monitoring," at www.gdf.ru.

86. Matthew Hansen (2006). "Deadly News," Committee to Protect Journalists, at http://cpj.org/Briefings/2006/deadly_news/deadly_news.html.

87. See "Russian Radio Accuses Kremlin of Resorting to Autocracy," Ekho Moskvy radio report 1600 gmt, January 4, 2005, in *JRL* #9006, January 5, 2005; and "Asylum Decision Suggests that US Patience with Putin Is Wearing Thin," February 2, 2005.

88. "Asylum Decision Suggests that US Patience with Putin Is Wearing Thin," February 2, 2005.

89. Tregubova (2003, esp. Chapter 12).

90. See report in *The Times* (London), March 10, 2004.

91. Reporters sans Frontieres, "Russia—2005 Annual Report."

92. Fond Zashchity Glasnosti (2005).

93. See Baker and Glasser (2005, 80–83).

94. Ibid.

95. See "Dekret o Pechati" (Decree on the Press), November 10, 1917, in *V. I. Lenin o pechati* (Lenin on the Press), (Moscow: Gospolitizdat, 1984).

96. "NTV Takeover Homogenizes Russia," *Associated Press*, April 15, 2001 in *JRL #5205* April 16, 2001.

97. "Special Operation in Beslan a Success: Operation Against Journalists," *Novaya Gazeta,* No. 69, September 20, 2004.

98. *Christian Science Monitor,* September 21, 2004.

99. See *Russky Kuryer* November 2, 2004, in *JRL #8437,* November 2, 2004.

100. For a report on this, see Robert Coalson, "A War on Terrorists or a War on Journalists?" *RFE/RL Newsline,* September 7, 2004.

101. Ibid.

102. For a nice report on these events, see "Russian TV Network Sacks Rebel Anchorman," *Reuters,* June 2, 2004, in *JRL #8235,* June 3, 2004.

103. See United States Department of State (2004).

104. See Julie Corwin, "From Censorship to Content Filtering," *RFE/RL Media Matters,* Vol. 5, No. 4, February 9, 2005.

105. Andrei Raskin, quoted in Mereu, "Russia:," (Part 2)," April 19, 2002;

106. See Reporters Without Borders, ND, "Predators of Press Freedom."

107. Committee to Protect Journalists (2001).

108. "Anna Politkovskaya: Putin, Poison and My Struggle for Freedom," *The Independent* (UK), October 15, 2004, in *JRL #8411* October 15, 2004.

109. "President Putin: Introductory Words at the Congress of the Russian Union of Industrialists and Entrepreneurs," *Kremlin.ru* November 14, 2003, in *JRL #7420,* November 15, 2003.

110. Transparency International (2005).

111. Kagarlitsky (2003).

112. Anonymous, "Putin, Authoritarianism and Corruption," *JRL #8445,* November 9, 2004.

113. INDEM (2002).

114. See "A Bombshell on Late-Night Television," *Nezavisimaya Gazeta,* August 15, 2003, in *JRL #7290,* August 15, 2003.

115. *Ibid* offers a startling account of bribery and nepotism.

116. *Ibid.*

117. Anders Aslund, "What Has Putin's Russia Become," Carnegie Endowment for International Peace, September 23, 2004, in *JRL #8455*, November 16, 2004.

118. Shleifer and Triesman (2004).

119. See "Putin's Advisers Control Over $200 Billion in Key Industries," *RFE/RL Newsline*, Vol. 9, No. 140, Part I, July 27, 2005.

120. "Russia" New INDEM Study Questions Sincerity of Government Anticorruption Program," *Nezavisimaya Gazeta*, May 19, 2004, in *JRL #8219*, May 19, 2004.

121. See Freedom House (2005a).

122. "Anna Politkovskaya," 2004; and Politkovskaya (2002).

123. See United States Department of State (2006).

124. "Soldiers' Mothers in the Crosshairs," *Moscow Times*, April 20, 2006.

125. "Yakovenko Speaks Against Foreign Funding of Russian NGOs," *RIA Novosti*, December 1, 2005, in *JRL #9309*, December 1, 2005.

126. "Spies Use NGOs as Cover in Russia: Official," *Agence France Press*, December 7, 2005, in *JRL #9315*, December 7, 2005.

127. "Putin Quietly Signed NGO Bill Last Week," *Moscow Times*, January 18, 2006.

128. See *RFE/RL Newsline*, Vol. 10, No. 17, Part I, January 30, 2006; and *Financial Times*, January 28, 2006.

129. *Los Angeles Times*, September 19, 2004.

130. Hahn (2004a, 2004b, 2004c).

Chapter 7

1. Remnick (1997, 38–39).

Select Bibliography

Aslund, Anders. "Economic and Political State of Russia." Carnegie Endowment for International Peace, January 20, 2000.

———. "Russia's Detractors Ignore Success Story." *St. Petersburg Times,* February 12, 2002.

Baker, Peter, and Susan Glasser. *Kremlin Rising: Vladimir Putin's Russia and the End of Revolution.* New York: Scribner, 2005.

Barany, Zoltan, and Robert G. Moser, eds. *Russian Politics: Challenges of Democratization.* Cambridge: Cambridge University Press, 2001.

Baturin, Yu. M., et al. *Epokha Yeltsin: Ocherki Politicheskoy Istorii* [The Yeltsin Epoch: Essays on Political History]. Moscow: Vagrius, 2001.

Bealey, Frank ed. *The Blackwell Dictionary of Political Science.* Oxford: Blackwell, 1999.

Belyakov, Vladimir V., and Walter J. Raymond, eds . *Constitution of the Russian Federation: With Commentaries and Interpretation by American and Russian Scholars.* Brunswick Publishing Co and Russia's Information Agency—Novosti, 1994.

Bivens, Matt, and Jonas Bernstein. "The Russia You Never Met." *Demokratizatsiya* 6, no. 4 (Fall 1998): 613–47.

Breslauer, George W. *Gorbachev and Yeltsin as Leaders.* Cambridge: Cambridge University Press, 2002.

Bunce, Valerie . "Subversive Institutions: The End of the Soviet State in Comparative Perspective." *Post-Soviet Affairs* 14, no. 4 (1998): 323–54.

———. "Rethinking Recent Democratization: Lessons from the Postcommunist Experience." *World Politics* 55, no. 2 (January 2003).

Cable News Network, "Yeltsin Blames Political Extremists for Subway Blasts," June 12, 1996. At http://www.cnn.com/WORLD/9606/12/russia.blast/.

Center for Strategic Planning. "Strategiya Razvitiya Rossiyskoy Federatsii do 2010 goda." Moscow: Center for Strategic Planning, 2000.

Collier, David, and Steven Levitsky. "Democracy with Adjectives: Conceptual Innovation in Comparative Research," *World Politics* 49 (1997):3.

Collier, Ruth Berins, and David Collier. *Shaping the Political Arena.* Terre Haute, IN: University Of Notre Dame Press, 1991.

Colton, Timothy, and Michael McFaul. *Popular Choice and Managed Democracy.* Washington, DC: The Brookings Institution, 2004.

Committee to Protect Journalists. "CPJ Names 10 Enemies of the Press on World Press Freedom Day," May 3, 2001. Accessible online at http://www.cpj.org/enemies/enemies_01.html.

———. "CPJ News Alert 2006: Russia: U.S. House Condemns Impunity in Journalist Murders," 2006. Available online at http://www.cpj.org/news/2006/europe/russia17may06na.html.

Council of Europe CDL. *Draft Constitution of the Russian Federation Approved By The Constitutional Assembly on 12 July 1993, Translation Provided by the Rusisan Authorities* Vienna: Council of Europe, 1993a, 43.

Council of Europe CDL. *Revised Draft Constitution of the Russian Federation.* Vienna: Council of Europe, 1993b, 43 Revised.

CRCR Bibliographic Guide/Documents Series.*The Constitution of the Russian Federation with Introduction, and Collation with First 'Yeltsin' Constitution.* Ottawa: Center for Research on Canada–Russian Relations, September 1995, No. 6.

Dahl, Robert A. *Polyarchy.* New Haven, CT: Yale University Press, 1971.

Dallin, Alexander, and Gail Lapidus, eds. *The Soviet System in Crisis.* Boulder, CO: Westview Press, 1991.

David, Paul A. "Understanding the Economics of QWERTY." In *Economic History and the Modern Economist,* edited by William N. Parker. Oxford: Blackwell, 1986.

Dawisha, Karen, and Bruce Parrott. *The Consolidation of Democracy in East-Central Europe.* Cambridge: Cambridge University Press, 1997.

Deniau, Jean-Charles, and Charles Gazelle, directors. *Assassination of Russia.* Transparences Productions, 2000.

Diamond, Larry, and Mark F. Plattner, eds. *Democracy After Communism.* Baltimore, MD: Johns Hopkins University Press, 2002.

Dunlop, John B. "'Storm in Moscow': A Plan of the Yeltsin 'Family' to Destabilize Russia," Project on Systemic Change and International Security in Russia and the New States of Eurasia, Johns Hopkins School of Advanced International Studies, 2004.

Elkins, Stanley, and Eric McKitrick. *The Age of Federalism: The Early American Republic, 1788–1800.* Oxford: Oxford University Press, 1993.

Ellis, Joseph J. *His Excellency George Washington.* New York: Alfred A. Knopf, 2004.

Elster, Jon, et al. *Institutional Design in Post-Communist Societies.* Cambridge: Cambridge University Press, 1998.

Felshtinsky, Yuri, and Alexander Litvinenko. *Blowing Up Russia: Terror from Within.* New York: Liberty Press, 2001.

Filatov, S.A. ed. *Konstitutsiyonnoye Soveshaniye: Stenogrammy, materiyaly, doku-menty* [Constitutional Assembly: Stenograms, Materials, Documents]. Moscow: Yuridicheskaya Literatura, 1996, 20 volumes. Cited in the notes as "Stenograms, Vol. #, pp. #".

Fish, M. Stephen. *Democracy Derailed in Russia: The Failure of Open Politics.* Cambridge: Cambridge University Press, 2005.

———. *Democracy from Scratch: Opposition and Regime in the New Russian Revolution.* Princeton, NJ: Princeton University Press, 1995.

Fond Zashchity Glasnosti. 2005 Monitor, "Konflikty zafiksirovannyye FZG v teche-niya 2004 goda na territorii RF" [Conflicts Documented by FZG in 2004 on the Territory of the RF (Russian Federation)], 2005. Accessible online at http://www.gdf.ru/monitor/2005/2005.shtml.

Freedom House. "Freedom in the World." Freedom House Annual Reports, 2005a. Reports may be accessed at http://www.freedomhouse.org/template.cfm?page=15&year=2005.

Freedom House. "Freedom of the Press." Freedom House Annual Reports, 2005b. Reports may be accessed at http://www.freedomhouse.org/template.cfm?page=16&year=2005***.

Gaidar, Yegor. *Dni porazhenii i pobed* [Days of Defeats and Victories]. Moscow: Vagrius, 1996.

———. *State and Evolution: Russia's Search for a Free Market.* Seattle, WA: University of Washington Press, 2003.

Gessen, Masha. "Red to Brown." *New Republic*, September 27, 2004.

Gleisner, Jeffrey, et al. "The Parliament and the Cabinet: Parties, Factions and Parliamentary Control in Russia (1990–93)," *Journal of Contemporary History* 31, no. 3 (1996): 427–61.

Goldman, Marshall I. *The Piratization of Russia: Russian Reform Gone Awry.* New York: Routledge, 2003.

Gorshkov, M.K., V.V. Zhuravlev, and L.N. Dobrokhotov, eds. *Yeltsin–Khasbula-tov: Edinstvo, Kompromiss, Bor'ba* [Yeltsin–Khasbulatov: Unity, Compromise, Battle]. Moscow: Terra Press, 1994.

Goskomstat. *Metodologicheskie polozheniya po statistike* [Methodological Regulations on Statistics]. Moscow: Goskomstat, 1996.

Hahn, Gordon . "Putin's Stealth Authoritarianism." *RFE/RL Political Weekly* 4, no. 16 (2004a).

———. "Putin's Stealth Authoritarianism." *RFE/RL Political Weekly* 4, no. 17 (2004b).

———. "Putin's Stealth Authoritarianism." *RFE/RL Political Weekly* 4, no. 18 (2004c).

Handelman, Stephen. *Comrade Criminal: Russia's New Mafiya.* New Haven, CT: Yale University Press, 1997.

———. "Thieves in Power: The New Challenge of Corruption." In *Nations in Transit*. Freedom House, 2001.

Herspring, Dale R. ed. *Putin's Russia.* New York: Rowman and Littlefield, 2005.

Hill, Fiona. "More than a Moscow Morality Play," *Los Angeles Times*, November 5, 2003.

Huntington, Samuel P. *The Third Wave: Democratization in the Late Twentieth Century*. Norman, OK: University of Oklahoma Press, 1991.

INDEM. "Diagnostica rossiiskoi korruptsii: Sotsiologicheskii analiz" [Diagnoses of Corruption in Russia: Sociological Analysis], 2001. This and all reports of INDEM research on corruption in Russia may be accessed online at INDEM's "Corruption Project" at http://www.anti-corr.ru/projects.htm#15.

INDEM. "Zarabotnaya plata i korruptsiya: kak platit' rossiyskim rabotnikam" [Salaries and Corruption: How to Pay], 2002. www.anti-corr.ru/projects.htm #15.

INDEM. "Diagnostika korruptsiyogennosti zakonodatel'stva" [Diagnoses of Corrupt Legislation], 2004a. http://www.anti-corr.ru/projects.htm#15.

INDEM. "Stimuly, effektivnost', korruptsiya" [Stimulus, Effectiveness, Corruption], 2004b. http://www.anti-corr.ru/projects.htm#15.

INDEM. "Corruption Process in Russia: Level, Structure, Trends," 2005a. http://www.anti-corr.ru/projects.htm#15.

INDEM. "Business and Corruption: How to Combat Business Participation in Corruption," 2005b. http://www.anti-corr.ru/projects.htm#15.

International Monetary Fund. *International Financial Statistics Yearbook*. Washington, DC: International Monetary Fund, 1998.

Jamestown Foundation Monitor, an electronic news archive service on Russian politics, may be accessed at http://www.jamestown.org/edm/.

———. "Authorities Suddenly Interested in Berezovsky and Abramovich Entities," *Jamestown Foundation Monitor,* July 28, 2000.

Johnson, Juliet. "Putin's Power Politics." *The Globe and Mail,* October 28, 2004.

Johnson's Russia List, an electronic news archive service providing comprehensive news and analyses of Russian politics and society from Russian and non-Russian language sources, may be accessed at http://www.cdi.org/russia/johnson/. Notes will refer to items followed by *JRL ##,* Date.

Kagarlitsky, Boris. "Parliamentary Decadence." *Moscow Times,* November 20, 2003.

Klebnikov, Paul. *Godfather of the Kremlin: The Decline of Russia in the Age of Gangster Capitalism*. New York: Harcourt, 2000.

Kotz, David, and Fred Weir. *Revolution from Above*. New York: Routledge, 1997.

Kutsyllo, Veronika. *Zapiski iz Belogo Doma: 21 sentryabrya - 4 oktyabrya*. Moscow: Izdatel'skiy Dom "b", 1993.

Lantz, Matthew. *"The Democratic Presumption: An Assessment of Democratization in Russia 1994–1998*. Belfer Center for Science and International Affairs, Harvard University, 1998.

Lenin, Vladimir I. *What Is To Be Done?* New York: International Publishers, 1984.

Lipset, Seymour Martin. "George Washington and the Founding of Democracy." *Journal of Democracy* 9, no. 4 (October 1998): 24–38.

McAuley, Mary. *Soviet Politics: 1917–1991*. Oxford: Oxford University Press, 1992.

McDonald, Forrest. *The Presidency of George Washington.* New York: WW Norton, 1975.

McFaul, Michael. "The Election of '96." *Hoover Digest,* no. 4, 1997a.

———. *Russia's 1996 Presidential Election: The End of Polarized Politics.* Stanford, CA: Hoover Press, 1997b.

———. *Russia's Unfinished Revolution.* Ithaca, NY: Cornell University Press, 2001.

———. "What the Elections Tell Us. " *Journal of Democracy* 15, no. 3 (July 2004).

Medetsky, Anatoly. "Siloviki's Pyramid of Power Revealed." *St. Petersburg Times,* no. 936, January 20, 2004.

Mickiewicz, Ellen. *Changing Channels: Television and the Struggle for Power in Russia.* Durham, NC: Duke University Press, 1999.

Nekrasov, Andrei, director. *Disbelief* . Dreamscanner Productions, 2004. See www.disbelief-film.com.

Oates, Sarah. "Russian Elections and TV News: Comparison of Campaign News on State-Controlled and Commercial Television Channels." *The Harvard International Journal of Press/Politics* 5, no. 2 (Spring 2000): 30–51.

Organization for Security and Cooperation in Europe. "Office for Democratic Institutions and Human Rights: Russian Federation Elections to the State Duma," OSCE/ODIHR Election Observation Mission Final Report. January 27, 2004.

Orth, Maureen. "Russia's Dark Master." *Vanity Fair,* October 2000.

Ostrovsky, Arkady. "Putin Oversees Big Rise in Influence of Security Apparatus," *Financial Times* (London), November 1–2, 2003.

Ostrow, Joel M. *Comparing Post-Soviet Legislatures: A Theory of Institutional Design and Political Conflict.* Columbus, OH: Ohio State University Press, 2000.

———. "Conflict-Management in Russia's Federal Institutions." *Post-Soviet Affairs* 18, no. 1 (2002).

———. "Political Liberalization and the Collapse of the USSR." *Journal of Cold War Studies,* 2007.

Politkovskaya, Anna. *Vtoraya chechenskaya* [The Second Chechen Campaign]. Moscow: Zakharov, 2002.

———. "Anna Politkovskaya: Putin, Poison and My Struggle for Freedom." *Independent* (UK), October 15, 2004.

Primakov, Yevgeniy. *Vosem mesyatev plyus* [Eight Months Plus]. Moscow: Mysl, 2002.

Proyekt Constitutsiya Rossiyskoy Federatsii: Na refreendum 12 Dekabrya 1993 (Vsenarodnoye golosovaniye) [Draft Constitution of the Russian Federation: For the Nationwide Referendum]. Moscow: Yuridicheskaya Literatura, 1993.

Putin, Vladimir. *Ot Pervogo Litsa: Razgovory S Vladimirom Putinym* [In the First Person: Conversations with Vladimir Putin]. Moscow: Vagrius, 2000.

Radio Free Europe/Radio Liberty, RFE/RL NEWSLINE, may be accessed online at www.rferl.org/newsline. Notes will refer to items followed by *RFE/RL Newsline,* Vol., No. and Date.

Reddaway, Peter, and Dmitri Glinski. *The Tragedy of Russia's Reforms: Market Bolshevism Against Democracy* Washington, DC: United States Institute of Peace Press, 2001.

Remington, Thomas F. *The Russian Parliament: Institutional Evolution in a Transitional Regime, 19891999.* New Haven, CT: Yale University Press, 2001.

———. "Presidential Support in the Russian State Duma." *Legislative Studies Quarterly* XXXI, no. 1 (February 2006).

Remnick, David. *Resurrection: The Struggle for a New Russia.* New York: Vintage Books, 1998.

Reporters sans Frontieres. "Annual Report," 2006. Annual reports available online at http://www.rsf.org/article.php3?id_article=17476.

Reporters sans Frontieres. "Annual Worldwide Press Freedom Index." Annual indices available online at http://www.rsf.org/rubrique.php3?id_rubrique=554.

Reporters Without Borders. "Predators of Press Freedom." Available online at http://www.rsf.org/article.php3?id_article=13580.

Robinson, Neil. "The Politics of Russia's Partial Democracy." *Political Studies Review* 1, 2003.

Rodin, Ivan. "Byudzhet—2006 bolshe smakhyvayet predvybornuyu reklamu: dokument budyet utverzhden vopreki rezkoy kritike oppozitsii" [The 2006 Budget More Resembles an Election Campaign Advertisement: The Document Will Be Adopted Despite Sharp Criticism by the Opposition], *Nezavisimaya gazeta*, September 20, 2005.

Rutland, Peter. "Russia: Democracy Dismantled." *Eurasia Daily Monitor* 2, no. 6 (January 2005).

———. "Russian Politics: Routine Maintenance for Managed Democracy." *Eurasia Daily Monitor* I, no. 24 (June 24, 2004).

Satarov, A. Georgiy. *Demokratura - 3: Pora Predlagat Strane Novuyu Povestku Dnya*[Democratorship III: The Country Needs a New Political Agenda] *Novaya Gazeta* no. 82, November 4, 2004.

Schumpeter, Joseph A. *Capitalism, Socialism, and Democracy.* New York: Harper, 1950.

Shirov, Pavel, director. *Tovarish Prezident.* Moscow, independent film, 2004. The authors have obtained the complete, unedited transcripts of the interviews conducted for the film and of the film itself. Quotations from the film are from these complete manuscripts.

Shleifer, Andrei, and Daniel Triesman. "A Normal Country." *Foreign Affairs,* March/April 2004.

Sobyanin, Alexandr. "Byli ili ne byli falsifikatsii na vyborakh 12 dekabrya?" *Nezavisimaya gazeta,* July 07, 1994.

Taylor, Brian. "The Russian Military Outside Politics: A Historical Perspective," PONARS Policy Memo 2. Cambridge, MA: Belfer Center for Science and International Affairs, Kennedy School of Government, Harvard University, 1997.

Thorson, Carla. "Russia's Draft Constitution." *RFE/RL Research Report* 2, no. 48 (December 3, 1993).

Tikhomirov, Vladimir. "Capital Flight from Post-Soviet Russia." *Europe-Asia Studies* 49, no. 4 (June, 1997): 591–615.

Tolz, Vera. "Drafting the New Russian Constitution." *RFE/RL Research Report* 2, no. 29 (July 16, 1993a).

———. "The Moscow Crisis and the Future of Democracy in Russia." *RFE/RL Research Report* 2, no. 42 (October 22, 1993b).

Transparency International. *Corruption Perceptions Index 2005*, 2005. Available online at http://transparency.org/policy_research/surveys_indices/cpi/2005.

Tregubova, Yelena. *Bayki kremlevskogo diggera* [Notes of a Kremlin Digger]. Moscow: Ad Marginem, 2003.

Triesman, Daniel. "Russia Renewed?" *Foreign Affairs* 81, no. 6 (November/December, 2005).

United States Department of State. "Country Reports on Human Rights Practices—2003. Russia," February 25, 2004. Available online at www.state.gov/g/drl/rls/hrrpt/2003/27861.htm.

United States Department of State. "Country Reports on Human Rights Practices—2005. Russia," March 8, 2006. Available online at http://www.state.gov/g/drl/rls/hrrpt/2005/61671.htm.

Waller, J. Michael. "FBI Says Organized Crime Dominates Russian Economy." *Russia Reform Monitor* no. 543, November 6, 1998.

Wedel, Janine R. "The Harvard Boys Do Russia." *The Nation*, June 1, 1998.

———. "Tainted Transactions: Harvard, Russia, and the Chubais Clan." *The National Interest*, Spring 2000.

Wilson, Andrew. *Virtual Politics: Faking Democracy in the Post-Soviet World.* New Haven, CT: Yale University Press, 2005.

Yeltsin, Boris. *Zapiski Prezidenta.* Moscow: Ogonek, 1994.

———. *Midnight Diaries.* New York: PublicAffairs, 2000.

Zassoursky, Dean Yassen. "Freedom and Responsibility in the Russian Media," *Post-Soviet Media Law and Policy Newsletter*, Benjamin N. Cardozo School of Law, Issue 32, September, 1996.

Joel M. Ostrow conducted formal interviews with several sources in Moscow in 2004 on particular issues related to this book that required information to confirm or fill in gaps in the coauthors' independent knowledge. Interviews ranged in length from one hour to four hours. In several instances, these were supplemented later with private communications. They are cited in the notes as "JO Interviews with (name)." The interviewees were as follows:

Yuriy Baturin, June 22, 2004.

Sergei Filatov, June 29, 2004.

Ivan Rodin, June 23, 2004.

Sergei Shakhrai, June 28, 2004.

Pavel Shirov, June 27, 2004.

Ivan Trefilov, June 28, 2004.

Lyudmilla Pikhoya, June 23, 2004.

Index

About the Authors

JOEL M. OSTROW is Chair of the Political Science Department at Benedictine University in Lisle, Illinois. He is a tenured Associate Professor of Political Science specializing in Russian politics, democracy and democratization, nationalism and terrorism, war, political violence, global affairs, and international organizations. He is the author of *Comparing Post-Soviet Legislatures: A Theory of Institutional Design and Political Conflict* (Ohio State University Press, 2000).

GEORGIY A. SATAROV is cofounder and President of the INDEM (Information for Democracy Foundation), a Moscow think tank. From 1991 to 1993 he served on Russian President Boris Yeltsin's President's Council, which served as an advisory board to the president, and from 1993 to 1998 he was senior Political Advisor (including duties as President's Liaison to the Russian State Duma). He heads a large project grant on the study of corruption in government (see www.anti-corr.ru) and is copresident of the All Russian Civic Congress. He is widely published on Russian political affairs.

IRINA M. KHAKAMADA served three terms as a People's Deputy to the Russian State Duma from 1993 to 2003. In the Duma she served on the Committee on the Economy, the Budget Committee, and as a member of the Russian delegation to the Parliamentary Assembly of the Council of Europe. She served in numerous leadership positions in the Duma, including as Deputy Speaker from 2000 to 2003. In 1997, she served as the Director of the State Committee for the Development of Small Enterprise, and as a member of the Government Committee on Economic Reform. In 1999, she headed the State Committee on Entrepreneurship. Prior to her political career, she founded several business, and served on the Board of Directors of the RTSB, the largest Russian stock exchange.